The Essential Guide for Experienced Teaching Assistants

Second Edition

This indispensabl︠ ︡xt︠ ︡k and guide provides the underpinning knowledge to support all teaching assistants workin︠ ︡ Level 3 of the National Occupational Standards.

HA BOP

This new editi︠c ︡orates and responds to all new materials and initiatives required to meet the revised and exp︠a ︡— ︠ ︡07 standards. Taking into account current initiatives including Workforce Remodelling and ︠ ︡ Child Matters agenda, the book can be used to support NVQs or other teaching assistant︠ ︡ Level 3, or simply to supplement good practice.

The Essential G︠u ︡rienced Teaching Assistants:

- actively engag︠ ︡ *1* ︠ ︡der in activities, developing reflective practice while giving the theoretical background t︠o ︡ STOC︠ ︡sed work;
- gives insight a︠ ︡ DFR (︠ ︡tion about pupils' individual needs;
- helps teaching ︠ ︡evelop curriculum-based skills to enable more effective pupil, teacher and classroom sup︠ ︡
- emphasises th︠ ︡ *1* ︠ ︡ assistants are team members, supporting the school and being supported by the school;
- enables teachi︠i ︡ ︠ ︡ts to operate more independently, using their knowledge and initiative.

Contributions fro︠ ︡st advisers ensure that the ideas and techniques are up to date, relevant and the best practice. ︠ ︡ses of education are covered, from the early years to later secondary years, and references are ma︠ ︡urces of further information throughout the book.

The Essential Guide for Experienced Teaching Assistants is invaluable in supporting both study and everyday practice. It will also be useful to training providers, teachers and school managers supporting teaching assistants in their professional development.

Anne Watkinson is an ex-head teacher and LEA senior advisor who now works independently as a consultant on the role and development of teaching assistants. She has worked in this capacity for both the Department for Children, Schools and Families and the Training and Development Agency for Schools.

The Essential Guide for Experienced Teaching Assistants

Meeting the National Occupational Standards at Level 3

Second Edition

Anne Watkinson

with contributions by

John Acklaw, Carol Connell, Carole Jones, Peter Nathan and Ian Roper

Routledge
Taylor & Francis Group

LONDON AND NEW YORK

First published 2004 by David Fulton Publishers

This edition published 2009
by Routledge
2 Park Square, Milton Park, Abingdon, Oxon OX14 4RN

Simultaneously published in the USA and Canada
by Routledge
270 Madison Avenue, New York, NY 10016

Routledge is an imprint of the Taylor & Francis Group, an informa business

Typeset in Palatino by RefineCatch Ltd, Bungay, Suffolk
Printed and bound in Great Britain by MPG Books Ltd, Bodmin

British Library Cataloguing in Publication Data
A catalogue record for this book is available from the British Library

Library of Congress Cataloging in Publication Data
Watkinson, Anne.
  The essential guide for experienced teaching assistants: meeting the national occupational standards at
level 3 / Anne Watkinson. – 2nd ed.
      p. cm.
  Includes bibliographical references and index.
  1. Teachers' assistants – Great Britain. 2. Teachers' assistants – Certification – Great Britain.   I. Title.
LB2844.1.A8W378 2008
371.14'124–dc22   2008029464

ISBN 10: 0-415-46049-2 (pbk)
ISBN 13: 978-0-415-46049-1 (pbk)

Contents

Preface

This book aims to provide the basic underpinning knowledge to support teaching assistants (TAs) in all phases of schooling when undertaking study at Level 3 on the National Qualification Framework. It supports the *National Occupational Standards for Supporting teaching and learning in schools*. These are the revised standards relevant to TAs which are operative from March 2008 and which can be accessed from the standards website: www.ukstandards.org. The first edition underpinned the first set of TA standards published in 2001. The revision and hence the second edition reflect the changes in the standards and in schools since then, such as Workforce Remodelling and the Every Child Matters agenda. They also reflect both the greater variety of jobs that TAs do and the actual level at which they are working in schools. This second edition is therefore greatly expanded from the first edition. It also recognises the changes in use of ICT in the general population and in schools; all TAs will need to be computer literate now.

It assumes that you, the TA, are already working in a school and wish to learn more about the job you are doing. If you are considering undertaking a Level 3 qualification, references to the new standards are made throughout, but it will be equally useful to those not undertaking formal courses. It contains ideas for you to try out and some examples of TAs at work. In actively learning about the work you do, you will gain in confidence and understanding of the purpose of the tasks you are asked to undertake. If you wish to undertake any activities in your school, it is important that you talk over any practical issues with someone in authority in the school but it is also valuable to discuss any issues of interest to you with another professional. This may be a colleague, your line manager, or the class teacher with whom you are most closely associated. The school may appoint someone formally to be your mentor, so that you can discuss any issues which arise as you read or use the book. If you are undertaking any course, it is essential to have some kind of mentor within your school. At Level 3 it is also expected that you are able to undertake some of your own research and read much more widely than this text alone.

Involving you, the reader, in your own learning will help you understand better how pupils learn, how to further develop skills to support the teacher and various aspects of the curriculum. It firmly embeds practice of the TA within a whole-school context, enabling you to understand your role in supporting the school, and taking appropriate responsibility for aspects of care, health, safety and wellbeing of pupils with whom you come into contact, and to play your full part in the school team. However, some of the new standards are very specific and skills based. For these you will need practical training on the job and access to specialist understanding and knowledge beyond the scope of a book. Increased knowledge will give you increased confidence to use your initiative and experience appropriately, to support teachers usefully, to help pupils learn and access the curriculum. Undertaking active learning with the school's support will enable you to become part of the learning community of the school, fulfilling the school policies and participating in the formation of the whole-school ethos. You will also be developing professionally.

Acknowledgements

I would particularly like to thank:

- Carol Connell, Assistant Principal – Inclusion (SENCO), The Colne Community School for her additions to and oversight of the SEN part of Chapter 8 previously written by John Acklaw, previously a freelance Chartered Educational Psychologist, now retired;

- Carole Jones, Primary Strategy Consultant, School Improvement and Advisory Service, Essex County Council for Chapter 11;

- Peter Nathan, Independent Consultant, for Chapter 9; and

- Ian Roper, Lead Senior Adviser for mathematics and Numeracy Strategy Manager, School Improvement and Advisory Service, Essex County Council for Chapter 14.

I could not have written the book without them.

I would also like to thank:

- Hilary Cook, of Highfields Primary School and her staff, Tim Palmer of St. Osyth C of E School and staff and Jill James of Colne Engaine C of E School and staff for allowing me time to discuss their work with them and watch them, and I thank them and the children for allowing me to photograph their schools so freely;

- the pupils and staff of Colne Community School for allowing me to use photographs taken in their lessons; and

- the many other schools and TAs, whose practice and friendship has been a constant inspiration throughout my work with them.

As ever, I thank my husband Frank, for his endless patience and encouragement, domestic help and support with my ICT systems.

Photographs

Figures

Tables

Abbreviations

AAC	Alternative and augmentative communication
'A' level	Advanced level
AE	Adult Education
APL	Accreditation of prior learning
APP	Assessing pupil progress
BECTA	British Education Communication and Technology Agency
BESD	Behavioural, emotional and social development
CLL	Communication, language and literacy
CPD	Continual professional development
CRB	Criminal Records Bureau
DCSF	Department for Children, Schools and Families
DfES	Department for Education and Skills
DSP	Designated Senior Person
DT	Design and technology
EAL	English as an additional language
ECM	Every Child Matters
EFL	English as a foreign language
ELS	Early Literacy Support
EMA	Ethnic Minority Achievement
EP	Educational Psychologist
ERA	Education Reform Act
ESL	English as a second language
EWO	Educational Welfare Officer
EY	Early years
FE	Further Education
FLS	Further language support
G & T	Gifted and talented
GCSE	General Certificate of Secondary Education
GTC	General Teaching Council
HE	Higher Education
HLTA	Higher Level Teaching Assistant
HMI	Her Majesty's Inspectorate
ICT	Information and communications technology
IiP	Investors in People
INSET	In-school education and training
IQ	Intelligence quotient
JD	Job description
K	Knowledge and understanding criterion
KS	Key stage

LA	Local Authority
LSA	Learning support assistant
LSC	Learning and Skills Council
NAPTA	National Association of Professional Teaching Assistants
NASEN	National Association for Special Educational Needs
NC	National Curriculum
NICE	National Institute for Health and Clinical Excellence
NNS	National Numeracy Strategy
NOS	National Occupational Standards
NQT	Newly qualified teacher
NVQ	National Vocational Qualification
Ofsted	Office for Standards in Education
OMS	Oral and mental starter
OU STAC	Open University Specialist Teacher Assistant Certificate
P	Performance criterion
PE	Physical Education
PEP	Personal education plan
PGCE	Post Graduate Certificate of Education
PIE	Plymouth Inclusive Education
PPA	Planning, preparation and assessment
PSHE	Personal, social and health education
QCA	Qualifications and Curriculum Authority
QTS	Qualified teacher status
RE	Religious education
SATs	Standards assessment tests (or tasks)
SCITT	School-based initial teacher training
SDP	School Development Plan
SEAL	Social and emotional aspects of learning
Sebs	Social, emotional and behavioural skills
SEF	School evaluation form
SEN	Special Educational Needs
SENCO	Special Educational Needs Co-ordinator
SET	Southend, Essex and Thurrock
SIP	School Improvement Plan
SLD	Severe learning difficulties
SMART	Specific, measurable, achievable, realistic, time related
SSWG	Support Staff Working Group
STL	Standards for teaching and learning
SWOT	Strengths, weaknesses, opportunities and threats
TA	Teaching assistant
TDA	Training and Development Agency
PMLD	Profound and multiple learning difficulties
WAMG	Workforce Agreement Monitoring Group
ZPD	Zone of proximal development

Introduction

The reason for this book

YOUR IMPORTANCE as a teaching assistant (TA) has been recognised over the last ten years and your numbers have increased dramatically. The government has put considerable resources into the recruitment, training and support of systems for professional and career development, including facilitating pathways to teaching for those who wish it. National Occupational Standards (NOS) for Level 2 and Level 3 assistants were introduced in 2001 and a Higher Level Teaching Assistant (HLTA) status introduced in 2003. The rewriting of the NOS (TDA 2007) has coincided with the embedding into schools of a number of important initiatives, so the time is right for second editions of the books to support assistants in their work. This book supports those studying at Level 3.

The first set of standards seemed complicated and were written as a result of study of the varied role of TAs, consultation with focus groups and advisers. The role has not become easier to define in the intervening years: TAs have undertaken more responsibilities as well as operating effectively at the various defined levels. There are now learning mentors, cover supervisors, many specialist TAs and senior TAs in addition to the HLTAs. Although there are still no national qualification requirements for TAs, the value of training and celebrating the training with qualification recognition is recognised increasingly by school staff.

Since the first edition of this book, the literacy and numeracy strategies have gone into secondary schools, and a primary strategy is attempting to give schools greater freedom to define their own curriculum. The very title of the introductory document *Excellence and enjoyment* (DfES 2003a) indicated the need to release schools from the straitjacket which the subject strategies had become. The secondary curriculum as a whole has been reviewed, the primary curriculum is under review. This emphasis on curriculum content and the accompanying testing regime has narrowed horizons for school teaching staff, but this has not brought about a narrowing for the TAs. A new Early Years (EY) framework has also started in September 2008. The introduction of Workforce Remodelling (DfES 2003b), an attempt to lighten the workload for teachers, has increased the schools' dependence on assistance, not only from TAs but also from administrative staff. ICT (information and communication technology) has become increasingly dominant in the last few years, not only because of the development of the technology itself by schools and the general population, but also because of government funding. Most classrooms now have interactive whiteboards, schools and classrooms are linked with the internet through wireless connections, all teachers and some TAs have their own laptops. TAs are now expected to be computer literate and often to communicate with other staff and deal with school matters electronically. Policies and procedures are available on an intranet, along with plans and resources. Much of the government produced support material is now only available on-line.

There has also been a move towards more joined-up thinking between service providers for those dealing with children and young people. Some high-profile child abuse cases, notably that of a little girl, Victoria Climbié, highlighted that lack of communication between Local Authority (LA) departments was a major factor in the failure to support the child. A very important document called *Every Child Matters* (ECM) (DfES 2004a) outlined the philosophy which was felt desirable. Instead of focusing on the curriculum and its delivery, it focused on the needs and rights of children. Children are defined as those younger than 18 years old. The details of this initiative and its implications for local government, and more particularly for schools and their staff, will permeate this edition. It focuses on the softer outcomes of child care and education rather than hard-edged, testable, target-orientated ones. It underlines the fact that while schools are more than children's homes and education is more than care, unhappy children cannot learn. Low self-esteem, poverty, ill-health and the like prevent children from reaching their potential. This has now been followed by a ten-year *Children's Plan* which 'aims to make England the best place in the world for children and young people to grow up in' (DCSF 2007a:5).

The new guidance available on-line from the TDA (Training and Development Agency) (www.tda.gov.uk) written to support the new NOS, emphasises that the standards are written to support the new initiatives and lists the particularly important ones. Along with the major ECM initiative have come several smaller ones which all make their impact felt in schools. Short inspections, focused on the school's own self-evaluation; moves to look at the value a school adds to its pupils' achievements rather than crude test and examination result lists; providing for children before and after school hours; attempting to assess for and personalise learning rather than stick with the 'one size fits all' model have all contributed to a more autonomous climate for school governance. School budgets have been increased in real terms, enabling them to be more adventurous with staffing and resource provision. School buildings have improved, including making provision for TAs in the staffroom. It is rare now to find the teaching and support staff separation that was common ten years ago, although, sadly, it does still exist.

The National Occupational Standards

The original standards for TAs were consulted on and tried out over a period of well over a year before they were published. These new standards were also widely consulted on and, of course, the experience gained with the original ones was invaluable. The title of the new standards, *Supporting teaching and learning in schools* (TDA 2007), reflects this better than the job title by which the original standards were known. Teaching/classroom assistant was the generic title used to cover all the variety of names used by schools. The term preferred by the then Department for Education and Skills (DfES 2000) is 'teaching assistant', but Scotland, having its own education system, preferred classroom assistant, hence the dual nomenclature in the original standards. The way the TA role fits in with others in schools as it is understood by the TDA is shown in Table 1.1.

TABLE 1.1   The support staff framework as seen by the TDA

Administration	Learning support	Pupil support	Site staff	Specialist and technical
Exam officer Finance General administration	Cover supervision Early years Special needs Sports coach Teaching assistant/ bilingual support	Behaviour/guidance/ support Care staff Midday supervisor/ playworker	Catering staff Premises staff	ICT Librarian Science/design and technology

Acts of Parliament and codes of practice are sometimes changed for use in Scotland, Wales and Northern Ireland. Some differences between the four countries may be noted in the text, for instance in referring to the requirements of the National Curriculum (NC) but not all, so do check if you are not working in England. The other main difference in the development of these new standards was that the management of their development was with the TDA, not the employers' organisation which is the National Training Organisation for local government employees. This has meant that people involved in teaching and learning were heavily involved from the outset of the revisions. Some of the new units for TAs are in fact not new except to be included in this award. They come from the child care, playwork or social work sectors, for instance, and reflect the diversity of the role a TA can be called upon to play.

NOS are given in different levels corresponding to the National Qualification Framework – see Table 1.2. If you want to know more about this go to www.qca.org.uk where you will find further information and links to awarding bodies. All nationally recognised qualifications (at least in England, Wales and Northern Ireland) now figure somewhere on this framework.

Study for a national vocational qualification (NVQ) at Level 3 equates to that of 'A' levels so study at this level should be advanced. It is intended for those working across a range of responsibilities within an institution, able to use their initiative within certain boundaries. Those seeking HLTA status were envisaged to be at a Level 4 ability (second year undergraduate) and any training course should reflect this. Of course the foundation degrees for TAs are at Level 4. Qualified Teacher Status (QTS) implies not only graduate status, but also the professional qualifications needed by a teacher. Some degrees in teacher training institutions lead to the acquisition of both, and some require the recipient to take a further year's study to obtain a Postgraduate Certificate of Education (PGCE) or other teaching qualification. All newly qualified teachers have to undergo a period of at least one year's induction, which is monitored before they are fully accredited as qualified teachers. More details of these higher levels in the teaching profession can be found at www.tda.gov.uk.

TABLE 1.2 The National Qualifications Framework

National Qualifications Framework (NQF)		Framework for Higher Education Qualifications (FHEQ)
Previous levels	*Current levels*	*Levels and Examples*
Level 5	Level 8	D (doctoral) Doctorates
	Level 7	M (masters) Master's degrees, postgraduate certificates and diplomas
Level 4	Level 6	H (honours) Bachelor degrees, graduate certificates and diplomas
	Level 5	I (intermediate) Diplomas of HE and FE, foundation degrees and higher national diplomas
	Level 4	C (certificate) Certificates of HE
Level 3 A levels		
Level 2 GCSEs Grades A*–C		
Level 1 GCSEs Grades D–G		
Entry level		

It is on this website that you will also find detailed guidance of how to use the STL standards and gain NVQs or equivalent qualifications (TDA 2008). The guidance contains information for aspiring candidates on the actual process of undertaking an NVQ, how the standards match with the current understanding of roles in school, and suggestions for a training needs analysis. It explains things like accreditation of prior learning (APL) – how you can use qualifications you already have towards the qualification including how some Level 2 units transfer to Level 3. There is also guidance on how the standards can be used in schools for advertisement or interview processes or gap analysis in performance reviews.

The standards themselves

The standards are divided into units, some of which are considered essential for any TA in any kind of school. If taking an NVQ, these six units are considered 'mandatory'. Each level also contains optional units which at Level 3 are grouped in five areas of school work. Candidates for an award have to choose four of these optional units which can come from any group, so long as not more than two come from group 5. Some units appear in both Level 2 and Level 3 such as *Keeping children safe* [3] and *ICT* [8].

Each unit starts with a brief summary description of who the unit is for, what it is about, what it contains, what other units the unit in question may be linked to, where it may have originated from and its status in the qualification. Then follows a really useful glossary of terms for the unit. Each unit has at least two elements, and some have three. These are sections covering different aspects of that part of the TA role and they give what you would need to show in order to prove your competence in that area of your work. Each element is subdivided into 'performance indicators' which are numbered P1, P2, etc. Each unit also has a list of the knowledge and understanding which you need to know and understand in order to be considered to be working at this level. These are numbered K1, K2, etc. A few of the K indicators are subdivided again into a,b,c,d, etc., parts. Each numbered indicator or criterion defines what has to be evidenced in any qualification process. Some standards also have a separate list of the scope of activity which the standard covers.

In other words, the NOS are very detailed, covering 99 pages for Level 2 and 300 or so for Level 3. Hence they are not reproduced in this book, and you must get a separate copy for yourself from the standards website (www.ukstandards.org.uk). The NOS titles are given in Table 1.3 along with some indication of where you might find material in this book to support the contents. Only the mandatory elements are covered in detail, and thus their titles also appear in Figure 1.1.

Even if you are not going to take the qualification, these standards provide useful reference material and food for thought and discussion. There is much repetition and cross referencing inherent in the standards: for instance, the need for 'understanding legal frameworks' or 'following policies in that area' or 'referring to other adults' or 'using appropriate language' will appear in many standards. The first edition of this book had detailed NOS references given in square brackets in the text to every indicator or criterion in the standards, but such is the detail of the new ones that this is not possible here. However, each unit and many criteria will be referenced. All criteria in the mandatory units are referenced somewhere. Referencing is done numerically in square brackets. The aim is for this book to be of more general use to those working in schools rather than a direct support for gaining the evidence for any one unit. Hopefully, should you be undertaking a course or compiling a portfolio (see Chapter 2 for details of this way of keeping your work together), this book will ease your burden.

The standards are not themselves NVQs. They are, however, used as the structure and content of NVQs. The examination boards produce the instructions and syllabuses for

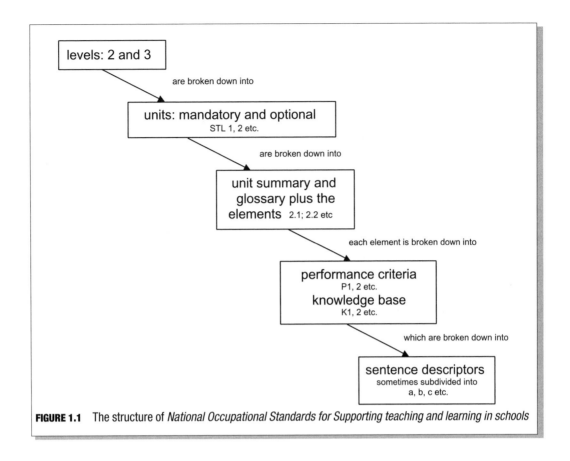

FIGURE 1.1 The structure of *National Occupational Standards for Supporting teaching and learning in schools*

candidates and centres to follow in order to obtain an NVQ Level 2 or 3, and some are also producing their own awards based on these standards, which are not NVQs but are nationally recognised. Details of all these can be found by following links on the TDA website, in the support staff section. NVQs are a way of achieving qualifications without taking formal examinations, where your competence is assessed by your workplace performance as well as your answers to questions about knowledge underpinning that performance. Different centres have different ways of questioning candidates: some do it verbally, others do it by assignment. Most have a mixture of methods to suit different types of unit or your circumstances as a candidate. You should be able to opt for the most appropriate method for your way of working. Search around your area for the further education (FE) or adult education (AE) college that is offering a course using your preferred mode of learning. Video or audio tape recording of your understanding should be acceptable if writing is difficult, although in the case of TA NVQs it is difficult to see how a candidate with writing difficulties can help pupils with their reading and writing, which underpins all other subjects. Technically, you should not need a course to undertake an NVQ as they were designed to be a recognition of workplace competence, although you do need to register with an assessment centre (TDA 2008: 8). However, few people undertaking a particular level have all the competencies already and most also need guidance on providing appropriate evidence. Many schools now have in-house assessors registered with a centre, which has eased the process considerably. Some senior TAs have not only done their Level 3 award but gone on to become assessors of the award within their schools.

Underpinning the NOS there is a set of values and principles which have been agreed. In the first set of standards these were published at the beginning of the whole thing and were reproduced in full at the end of the first edition. These values and principles now permeate the whole body of the standards and so are not available as a separate entity. They include the expectations of TAs in their ways of working with people, pupils and the legal and local

TABLE 1.3 Level 3 units and standards, with chapter references

Unit no.	Unit title	Element no.	Element title	Main chapter sources
MANDATORY				
1	Help keep children safe	3.1	Prepare and maintain a safe environment	7 & 10
		3.2	Deal with accidents, emergencies and illness	7
		3.3	Support the safeguarding of children from abuse	7
		3.4	Encourage children's positive behaviour	7
18	Support pupils' learning activities	18.1	Support learning activities	11, 5 & 6
		18.2	Promote independent learning	6
19	Promote positive behaviour	19.1	Implement agreed behaviour management strategies	7
		19.2	Support pupils in taking responsibility for learning and behaviour	7
20	Develop and promote positive relationships	20.1	Develop relationships with children	3
		20.2	Communicate with children	3
		20.3	Support children in developing relationships	3
		20.4	Communicate with adults	3
21	Support the development and effectiveness of work teams	21.1	Contribute to effective team practice	4
		21.2	Contribute to the development of the work team	4
22	Reflect on and develop practice	22.1	Reflect on practice	2
		22.2	Take part in continuing professional development	2 & 15
OPTIONAL				
Group A – Supporting pupils' learning				
8	Use information and communication technology to support pupils' learning			12
23	Plan, deliver and evaluate teaching and learning activities under the direction of a teacher			10 & 11

(continued)

TABLE 1.3 Continued

24	Contribute to the planning and evaluation of teaching and learning activities	10
25	Support literacy development	13
26	Support numeracy development	14
27	Support implementation of the early years' curriculum	12
28	Support teaching and learning in a curriculum area	12
29	Observe and promote pupil performance and development	11
30	Contribute to assessment for learning	11
31	Prepare and maintain the learning environment	10
32	Promote the transfer of learning from outdoor experiences	10

Group B – Meeting additional support needs

33	Provide literacy and numeracy support to enable pupils to access the wider curriculum	13 & 14
34	Support gifted and talented pupils	7
35	Support bilingual/multilingual pupils	9
36	Provide bilingual/multilingual support for teaching and learning	9
37	Contribute to the prevention and management of challenging behaviour in children and young people	7 & 8
38	Support children with disabilities or special educational needs and their families	8
39	Support pupils with communication and interaction needs	8
40	Support pupils with cognition and learning needs	8
41	Support pupils with behaviour, emotional and social development needs	8
42	Support pupils with sensory and/or physical needs	8
43	Assist in the administration of medication	4
44	Work with children and young people with additional requirements to meet their personal support needs	3, 7 & 8

Group C – Providing pastoral support

45	Promote children's wellbeing and resilience	4, 6 & 7
46	Work with young people to safeguard their welfare	3, 6 & 7
47	Enable young people to be active citizens	12
48	Support young people in tackling problems and taking action	12
49	Support children and young people during transitions in their lives	6
50	Facilitate children and young people's learning and development through mentoring	3
51	Contribute to improving attendance	3, 6 & 11
52	Support children and families through home visiting	4

(continued)

TABLE 1.3   Continued

Group D – Supporting the wider work of the school

16	Provide displays	10
17	Invigilate tests and examinations	11
53	Lead an extra-curricular activity	12
54	Plan and support self-directed play	12
55	Contribute to maintaining pupil records	11
56	Monitor and maintain curriculum resources	10
57	Organise cover for absent colleagues	3
58	Organise and supervise travel	10
59	Escort and supervise pupils on educational visits and out-of-school activities	10
60	Liaise with parents, carers and families	4
61	Provide information to aid policy formation and the improvement of practices and provision	4

Group E – Working with colleagues (no more than 2 from this group)

62	Develop and maintain working relationships with other practitioners	3 & 4
63	Provide leadership for your team – **OR**	2 & 3
64	Provide leadership in you area of responsibility	2, 3 & 12
65	Allocate and check work in your team	3
66	Lead and motivate volunteers	3
67	Provide learning opportunities for colleagues	3
68	Support learners by mentoring in the workplace	3
69	Support competence achieved in the workplace	3

frameworks. They refer to the kind of professionalism expected of a person working in schools in a multicultural society in the twenty-first century.

Who this book is for

Working at Level 3 is demanding both practically and theoretically. Undertaking a study in the generalist areas of school work, such as described in the mandatory units, will stand you in good stead should your job change. If you are working in a special school you might want to enter mainstream schools. Whether you stay in your current school or change, you should still know the basic principles which underpin the general ways in which education and schools work. It is important for TAs in any school to understand the characteristics of the development of average children and how to keep them safe, to recognise that pedagogic expertise applies in all sectors and curriculum entitlement is for all children whatever schools they attend. The new standards recognise that there are specialisms within mainstream schools, such as SEN, curriculum areas, different phases or settings, or mentoring.

Only you can learn about your job. Knowledge and understanding cannot be fed to you without you digesting it, taking it in and using it. You must take personal responsibility for your continuing professional development. You may want to show off your acquisition by undertaking assignments for others to read or even enter them into some kind of awards system, but fundamentally, all adults are still learners, and responsible for their own learning and progress. This also is described in the mandatory units.

How this book can be used

This book can be read and acted on in the sequence in which it is written, which may take some time if you stop and reflect on ideas, or carry out some of the activities, but even then it is not intended to be a course on its own. You cannot take a vocational course successfully without actually working at the job: that is what they are designed for. Some units are specialised or very practically based and you must contact a specialist to work with, to go through each criterion with them, for instance when working with a physically impaired child or invigilating examinations. Books can only point you in directions. You should always make sure that someone in the school is aware that you want to better yourself and increase your knowledge and understanding of the way in which you can support teaching and learning. Sharing your ideas and thoughts on the content with others is also important. This book can be your back-up text for an award. To get the best from any book or a course it is important to do it with someone experienced in the ways of your school so that you can share your ideas and feelings with them – you need an in-school mentor. Working at Level 3 you really should consider gaining qualifications in English and mathematics at least to Level 2 standard (GCSE or equivalent) if you do not already have them, in order to support pupils properly in any subject.

The real intention of the book is that it can be a foundation reference book. Use the index to find what you need, read that bit, look for the ideas of essential and additional reading and follow up your dipping into this book with more searches for information. One of the teachers may have a book at home and there is considerable material now downloadable from the internet. Do any associated activities, think through the questions posed and how they relate to you and your job, and make any notes for your own future reference. Discuss the reading with others in the school or on your course and remember anything you feel is important to use in your daily work. Not everything you will want to know will be found in this book – few books can ever provide such reference. You will also need to read more widely than this book or any basic book supporting the standards. At Level 3 you are expected to be able to use libraries and the internet for further information and consider it critically. The new standards cover a wide area, the whole gamut of teaching and learning, to cover the possible range of activity of today's TAs. Your best option is to seek out the member of staff responsible for the area in which you are particularly interested, talk to them, share ideas and ask their advice and help with resources and further reading. Some ideas for further reading are also given at the end of each chapter, with full reference to them at the end of the book.

The book is not written to follow the standards, but as a textbook to support working in schools. This is deliberate. While there are some references to working in the early years, the main context of the book will be that of compulsory schooling age, that is from 5 to 16 years old. The intention is that reading this will give you a grounding in the way good schools work to support teaching and learning in an holistic way. The hope is that you will understand the general principles of teaching and learning and of school organisation from this book rather than have a step by step guide to completing a particular unit for your award. Thus the book should be of wider and longer use than just supporting the NOS. It starts with looking at yourself, then your relationships with pupils and other adults. Your place in the school is then considered, how you support it by following procedures but also how its systems protect and support you. Understanding pupils as children and young people developing comes next and then how you can support their learning and needs. This is followed by how you support teachers in class and the curriculum subjects which it is hoped the pupils will learn.

One of the changes in the new standards that is very significant is that the level of understanding required at both levels is higher. This reflects the increased pressure on schools to raise standards, not only of pupils but of competencies of staff. The level of competence required of teachers is also higher than it used to be. There is a lot of new material in this book adding to that in the previous edition, chapters are fuller and there is an additional chapter on other aspects of the curriculum that TAs work in.

There are activities for you to try, shown in framed boxes. These can be photocopied to work on separately and changed to suit your circumstances if you wish. Try out some of these exercises to give you examples of things mentioned in the text you are reading and this will help you internalise the meaning. In addition, you will find a few examples or mini case studies. They are all based on good practice that I have seen in the many schools I have worked in or visited. All the names have been changed to preserve the participants' anonymity. After you have tried out the ideas for yourself, you will begin to recognise examples of good practice within your own school, and may be able to write a few scenarios of your own. It could be that you find examples of ways of working that puzzle you or are quite different from those described here. It is then vital that you have someone with whom you can discuss these matters, to find out why things are done in that way in your school. There will be a good reason for the differences, which will provide yet another learning point for you. All schools are different, even if they are in the same geographical area, of the same size and age, and take in similar aged children. People make them different, just as homes in a row of similar houses are all different.

Questions to ask yourself as you start

- To whom can you turn in your school to act as a mentor while you read this book and/or study for a Level 3 qualification?

- With whom can you discuss issues outside the school, bearing in mind confidentiality?

- Where might you find further reading or study materials in your locality?

- Is there a local group you can join to discuss ideas with?

- Do you know about the practices of and around TAs in other schools?

- What do you know about national initiatives and associations which could support you in your job?

- Who can tell you about local courses and qualifications and whether you can get financial help or advise you on career and professional development?

- To whom would you go if you had a personal problem?

- What does the LA in your area provide? Where are the local colleges?

Essential reading

National Occupational Standards for Supporting teaching and learning in schools (2007) TDA.

Guidance on the National Occupational Standards for Supporting teaching and learning in schools (2008) TDA.

Interesting to dip into

DfES (2003a) *Excellence and enjoyment: A strategy for primary schools.*

DfES (2004a) *Every Child Matters: The next steps.*

DCSF (2007a) *The Children's Plan: Building brighter futures: summary.*

Useful websites

www.tda.gov.uk

www.ukstandards.org.uk

www.qca.org.uk

2

Starting with yourself

Study skills

WHATEVER YOUR INTENTIONS, whether you want to take an accredited course, eventually train to be a qualified teacher, or just consolidate your position as a really good TA, you must consider yourself as a learner, continually developing. This may even be written into your job description. You need to develop ways of personal organisation, reviewing your experiences to date, addressing any wishes or needs for development and developing or honing your study skills. You need to develop the habit of reflecting on your practice and continually developing professionally as well as personally. There is more detail about study skills in the Level 2 book (Watkinson 2008a). A Level 3 qualification will require some sustained study at an advanced level. You should be able to read through your own work and be critical, not only of content but also of style and use of vocabulary. You should be developing a breadth of educational vocabulary and use some of the jargon with understanding. You should be reading regularly about your work and researching topics, using the internet wisely and discriminatingly. Make notes as you read; small 'Post-its' are very useful to mark pages you want to come back to, or quote, rather than pencil underlining. You should be in regular discussions with colleagues about your work.

When you read

- Do you understand what the passage/chapter/book is about?
- Do you think why a particular passage attracts your attention?
- Does it ring true with something in your experience?
- Do you make a note of your experience as well as a note of the thought in the reading?
- Do you disagree with the comments? Then think why.
- Do you want to talk with someone else about an aspect of what you have read?
- Will it change what you do in your work at school, how you behave or what you think of certain practices? Why? How?

Keeping materials together

You need a ring binder accompanied by card pocket files to collect things together – a portfolio. Do construct a personal file for yourself if you do not have one already, with a section for your personal details and a section for your school's details. Use later sections for your progress in your job and any procedure of review within your school. Any course of study will need its own file, and any accreditation process will need a separate one which will be submitted to the assessors or examiners. Material can be photocopied from your personal file or a course file, if it is relevant to the accreditation you are seeking. Just remember, you cannot be assessed on materials which you have obtained from elsewhere, handouts or photocopies of pages from books, as these are the work of other people, unless you annotate them with notes about how these points are relevant to you. Assessment is on evidence of your competence and activities, not that of others.

Do ensure, if you put any notes regarding pupils in your portfolio or diary, that you anonymise or depersonalise them; that is, you should refer to the pupil by a fictitious name or just a letter. This also applies to any references to pupils or people in any assignments which you undertake. Keep a diary or notebook with any thoughts from the beginning. When you are looking for evidence for assessment, photocopy the page of the diary, highlight the relevant passage and put a reference to the NOS unit, element and criterion or a qualification item reference in the margin. This book is set out in that fashion, the square bracketed numbers referring to the 2007 NOS. For example, by keeping a proper record of your performance reviews with a self review and its outcome targets you will have completed much of STL 22. More of that will follow later in the chapter.

Personal qualities

You need to know yourself, your experiences, expertise, strengths and weaknesses and how this can all be used to make a contribution to your school, but you also need to understand this for yourself. All of us during life have to take stock at times, evaluate what we can and cannot do and where we would like to be. You may have done this at school when deciding what subjects to take in examinations or even whether to take examinations at all. One of the joys of working as a TA is that there are opportunities for people to make serious life changes with support and avenues to start afresh. Taking an NVQ or a related award is also an ideal way to do this slowly and thoughtfully, and to build on existing strengths and not feel you have to start from scratch. The HLTA status award was designed to be exactly that, a recognition of experience gained without studying for a qualification. Before reviewing or making decisions you must start from where you are now, considering your strengths and weaknesses, and the context in which you find yourself. Then you can reflect on the list and decide how to move forward. It is not an option to stand still when working in schools as the clientele is always changing – the pupil base, and the initiatives for outside and inside the schools are always pushing to improve practice, to raise standards. Coasting or being considered just 'satisfactory' in Ofsted terms is no longer good enough. No member of staff can be a drag on that progress.

Table 2.1 shows a simple SWOT sheet (strengths, weaknesses, opportunities and threats) that you can use. Take a blank A4 sheet, fold it into four quarters, each quarter like the diagram. Fill in the top two boxes first, just thinking about you; the bottom two boxes give you the context in which you find yourself. By doing this, you are taking a good step along the road to reflective practice.

TABLE 2.1   A SWOT analysis sheet

Strengths	Weaknesses
Opportunities	Threats or barriers

Take your personal qualities first before thinking of any competence or knowledge issues. Watching TAs over many years, it is clear that those with confidence (without being feisty) who are prepared to give of themselves for the good of the pupils are the best TAs; this is what support is about.

Some things to consider

You need to be:

- sensitive to others, their feelings, aspirations, what interests them and what makes them work better, whether it is pupils or other staff. This will enable you to enhance their strengths as well as developing your own;

- empathetic with the situation of others, especially for all those who are learning – staff and pupils: you should be a learner yourself;

- respectful of others' beliefs and background, with a commitment to the school in which you are employed;

- assertive without being aggressive, able to express yourself without being unpleasant, to have your say without being rude (watch out for eye contact, posture, voice control and hand gestures; they can all indicate your feelings);

- approachable or available, meaning that people will look to you to help – the essence of your job;

- comforting to those in distress (note: there are ways of doing this appropriately; see the section on child protection in Chapter 7);

- able to go one step further than that required in any job, someone who always 'oils the wheels' of the organisation, accepting reasonable challenges;

- someone with good manners. A careful and responsible attitude to the job not only sets a good example to pupils but shows that you understand the importance of education and caring for others; avoid blaming people;

- someone who has patience when working with slower children and kindness for those who are struggling;

- developing the intrapersonal skills of self-awareness, appropriate self-confidence, reflection, contemplation, compromise;

- developing creativity, enabling yourself and others to innovate, encouraging independence in others, particularly pupils.

Do you:

- have an outgoing personality, without dominating, which enables you to make friends, share ideas and contribute to the teams within the school?

- have interpersonal skills, accepting pupils and people even if their behaviour is unacceptable; knowing how to behave?

- recognise stress in yourself or others, develop the ability to cope with it or seek help?

Another aspect of yourself that is well worth reflecting on is the area of your beliefs and values. We do not always realise how our upbringing, background, culture and religion (or lack of it) actually influence how we think, act and react [22K5]. Beginning a new course of study or aiming to be a senior TA is a good time to do this. You will not just be carrying out instructions from others, you will be expected to show initiative and leadership qualities and influence other staff as well as the children. You must be clear about your own values so that when considering those of the school you know whether you are in tune with the way in which the school is aiming. One of the most important things that affects how well a school operates is its ethos and how far the staff work as a whole-school team. This does not mean changing your beliefs or values but it does mean recognising what they are, what the school's are, and where the similarities and differences are and whether the differences are important to you. It is really important that you talk any issues over with a line manager at an early stage. These could be issues of dress (there have been instances of TAs refusing to change into appropriate clothing for PE (physical education) on religious grounds); words or phrases used (do you speak ungrammatical English because of your origins although you are trying to teach correct grammar to the children?); behaviour (are you comfortable to attend assemblies?) or relationships (would you always treat boys and girls the same?). You are working with children and young people at a very malleable time of their lives. Some values one hopes are universal: honesty, integrity, care for others, responsibility, punctuality, truthfulness, and so on; but others are more culturally based, like openness or manners. You may disagree with the policies and procedures of the school, or even with the legislative framework in which the school operates. If the differences are great or irreconcilable, you may have to decide whether you can continue to do this kind of work. These kind of conflicts occur throughout our lives so a personal check is always helpful before any event rather than during it [22K7].

You also need to know your academic qualities, what kind of learner you are and what you do not know and need to find out about. You need to recognise your own skills and levels of knowledge and understanding, and which of these is needed to fulfil your appointed role. You must understand how your own experiences and achievements contribute to those of others. Knowing yourself also includes knowing how to maintain your own health and safety when dealing with pupils and your own capabilities to deal with an emergency. It is your responsibility to share with your line manager any health problems you have that might affect your work, and that applies to emotional problems as well. School staff have also been known to keep to themselves severe causes of stress due to domestic circumstances, not realising that most school managers and governors are able to be flexible. Honesty on your part along with a reputation for hard work and commitment will usually be met with understanding.

Being a professional

You are a professional now and need to consider what that means in terms of:

- loyalty to your school and employer and supporting the existing ethos and values of the school;
- what you do if there is a conflict between your family and home needs and your school commitments;
- what channels you have if you do have a disagreement about how things should be done;
- what you do if you see things done by your colleagues or the pupils which you do not like or consider inappropriate;
- expectations of yourself and others;
- being a role model in your behaviour, your learning strategies, your speech, dress, timekeeping . . .

Being a professional means that you think about what you do.

You need to:

- always reflect on whether you can do better next time or whether there is a different way to do things;
- accept responsibility for your own practice;
- be able to have rational and reasoned discussion with your colleagues and line manager about changing things;
- be accountable and constructively critical, and share ideas and developments;
- recognise your limitations and your boundaries so that you can start from where you are.

[22K6]

Professional knowledge

The school

You need details of the place in which you work, the context for your job, and you must understand the principles which underlie effective communication and collaboration. You have to work within the legal context of the school and the school's own policies. Chapter 4 goes into the details. You should familiarise yourself with all the main roles and responsibilities within the school and how you fit into any hierarchy. Schools have a variety of management structures for TAs and as the role has diversified so has the variety of systems of management. Most TAs have been traditionally organised through the SEN (special educational needs) department, with TAs working directly with individual pupils under the SEN coordinator (SENCO) because that is how the funding came into the school originally. The wider role of TAs supporting teaching and learning is reflected in the diversity of the standards themselves. The tables in the NOS guidance available on the TDA website, showing which standards might be relevant to which jobs, show the range of nationally recognised roles. In practice, one person can take on several roles in a school, and getting to know the children or young people well may even combine these roles at any one time.

An example

A young woman employed as a learning mentor in her contract in a primary school was able, while showing me round the school, to discuss management strategies with a colleague, then a timetabling problem with a child who had only 50 per cent attendance, to find certain resources for a teacher, to encourage a group of pupils struggling with their ICT at the back of the ICT suite, to discuss another child's problems with a visiting behaviour management teacher, to discuss the work of the TAs in the school with me, and then to end the morning taking a club activity at the beginning of the lunch break.

Some schools have allocated TAs to subjects, to be managed by the subject leaders or heads of department, with liaison routes through the SENCO. Some TAs are allocated to a specific teacher to be classroom assistants. One school did this but reallocated their TAs each year according to the SEN proportion in each class indicated by their previous term's assessments. Other schools cannot do this because of the great mobility of the pupils – they have a high proportion of travelling children or parents who are military personnel. Some schools have allocated their TAs to year groups or key stages, hoping to get the best of all worlds: the support of pupils, teacher and the curriculum.

A really useful list is to be found in the DfES (Department for Education and Skills) now the DCFS (Department for Children, Families and Schools) induction materials in the induction file (TDA 2006a, 2006b, 2.2–2.7). It covers the following areas:

1 Do you know the key facts about your school setting?
   This includes items about numbers of pupils, teachers and support staff and key stages, any specialisms or defining characteristics of the school.

2 Do you know about the local community?
   This includes items about the locality itself and who makes up the community, employment patterns and community activities.

3 Do you know what the governing body does and who the governors are?

4 What regular visitors from the local authority, other services, agencies or teams come to the school?
   This includes what contact the TA may have with such people.

5 How is the school organised?

This includes class groupings, guidance on systems and procedures, policies, resources, internet access etc.

6 Are you familiar with school procedures?

This refers to a school handbook and procedure on health and safety, confidentiality and child protection, security, expectations of behaviour management.

7 How does the school provide for pupils' differing needs?

This is about access to the Code of Practice for SEN, and resources and people who can support SEN or pupils with EAL (English as an additional language).

8 What do you know about the curriculum?

This asks about familiarity with key stage demands of the NC, the strategies, assessment procedures and inclusion implications, and also about SDP/SIP (school development/improvement plan) and accountability strategies including inspection.

9 What is your school/LA doing in relation to the ECM agenda?

This asks questions about each of the five areas.

10 What training and development opportunities are available in your school/setting or local area?

The secondary induction includes a separate section asking 'What do you know about qualifications?' (This is referring to the qualifications the school offers pupils, not what is available to the TAs.)

Compile a responsibility tree for your own school

- Find out who the senior managers are and for what are they responsible. Who has responsibility for:
  - leading each NC subject?
  - religious education (RE)?
  - personal, social and health education (PSHE)?
  - citizenship?
  - SEN? (Does the SENCO and what that entails line manage all the TAs? If not, who does?)
  - pastoral care of pupils?
  - gifted and able pupils?
  - maintaining the various resource areas such as:
    - the library?
    - the information and communications technology (ICT) equipment?
    - the outside study areas?
    - reception area and displays?
  - clubs or extra-curricular activities?
  - health, safety and security?
- Who represents the staff on the governing body, especially the support staff?
- Who liaises with visiting therapists, community leaders, local businesses, other local schools, pre-schools or colleges?
- Who runs the parents' association (assuming there is one)?

Your job

Your job description should state what you are required to do to support pupils, teachers, the school and the curriculum; to whom and for what you are responsible; and what the school will do to support you. There is an exemplar job description for a senior TA in the TDA NOS guidance, but it does not include the school support of the TA. It is important that you understand your job description as to where your responsibilities start and finish. It should define not only your direct role but also your role and responsibilities with regard to health, safety and security and there is much more about this in later chapters of this book. You must always be working under the direction of a teacher, whether or not that teacher is actually present in the room with you. The final responsibility for the learning of the pupils in the school is that of a qualified teacher, whether or not you have planned the activity, prepared the materials, carried out the task and fed back what happened; whether or not it is decided that you can liaise directly with the parent, or contribute to an assessment report on the pupil. Several of the standards refer to you working within boundaries. These may be limitations of your knowledge, understanding and skills, or within the limits of your job description. It is important that you know yourself and your capabilities and do not try to undertake more than you can do, and that you only undertake things for which you have been made responsible. Nevertheless, it is hoped that you are intelligent and at Level 3 can use your initiative where appropriate. If you feel this involves more than you were originally employed for, talk to your line manager. In most cases senior staff will be delighted when people offer to do more, but it could be that it is actually someone else's job already, or it is inappropriate for reasons which only they can see. People working at Level 3 competence, with such jobs specified in their job description, should be paid more than those working at Level 2 competence, who are contracted to do jobs with less responsibility. This may be a problem. With the new single status agreements made between the LA as employers and the unions, grades of pay should be clearly matched to levels of responsibility. Ask questions if you are troubled about any of this, but beware; depending on the personnel history in your school, you could be opening up a 'can of worms'.

In looking at your own job description and the responsibility tree you have drawn up, see where your role lies in relation to others and track how any one person contributes to the learning of pupils [22.1P6]. For some this will be direct and obvious – for those of you who work in the classroom in lessons with the pupils – but for some roles in school it will seem less obvious. Some of you will be midday assistants as well as TAs and will quickly realise, as you learn more about school curricula and how pupils learn, that midday assistants contribute greatly in two particular areas. One is the obvious one, that of enabling those in direct contact with pupils in class to have a well-earned break and come back to afternoon school refreshed and prepared; but the other is that in helping pupils with learning table manners, socialising, cooperating, sometimes with emotional traumas or physical mishaps, or enabling them to understand fair play, taking turns, using game rules, you are enabling pupils to learn life skills, crucial in their development and ability to make the most of their classroom experiences. Without site managers and cleaners, the learning environment would soon deteriorate; without office staff, the teachers could not cope with the outside world and thus would not be able to teach (any small school headteacher with class responsibility and few administrative hours will affirm this with feeling!). The contribution that support staff other than those directly involved in the classroom are making is now recognised by the TDA with induction materials and occupational standards to match the variety. Some of these jobs may even entail being on the senior management committee; often this is so with the job of bursar.

Often standards or job descriptions talk of 'appropriate' support or help. You have to find out what this means for you in your situation, by asking. Too often in the past things have been left to people's intuition, but it need not be so. Explicit instructions can be given and do help to prevent misunderstandings. It often appears that this section is left out of job descriptions or is not operative. Too often the TA is left to learn the job by osmosis, by interpreting what they see; teachers assume you know what to do, managers assume the teachers will direct the TA appropriately. One of the drawbacks of the general recognition of the role is the assumption that everyone knows what TAs can or should do and few actually talk about it. Make sure you talk about it and find out what kind of support /induction/CPD (continuing professional development)/paid planning time is available.

Self-review

Part of your responsibility as an adult is that you are now responsible for your own development. You not only want to do your best as a basically competent TA, but you want to develop to be recognised for your experience and advanced competencies [22K1]. This is where you not only look at your own characteristics but at what you are employed to do and your capabilities in relation to the defined job [22.1P1]. It is not up to you to decide what you do on your own. Any job description should be achieved through negotiation, and should be reviewed with you at least annually. Standard 22 is mandatory at Level 3 so you cannot undertake this award unless your school is fully prepared to do this. It is thankfully rare these days to find TAs without job descriptions but it is still common to find TA performance review systems that are fairly perfunctory. It is not enough to have an annual sheet sent round or a meeting of all of the team with the headteacher to discuss 'how well has this year gone'. You are entitled to having an informed more senior colleague consider your work seriously, and the work you do for the pupils can only benefit from this. Your reviewer could be a more senior TA or a class teacher with whom you work regularly. You can think about what responsibilities you want to take on in future and what you need to do to maintain your present circumstances, if that is where you wish to be. This self-analysis is part of being employed, and needs to be updated regularly.

There are many mothers and even a few fathers, who, over the past 40 years, have come through the playgroup movement since its inception or as volunteer help in primary schools when their children attended, later to be employed in schools, who then find they are capable of taking not only basic examinations but degree courses and going on to become teachers, even headteachers. There are young people turned off examinations by their own school experience who, undertaking the apprenticeship route, find the NVQs fit their needs and even excite them to go further. There are others who recognise such pathways are not for them; they realise the work involved, the academic strengths needed, the responsibility and time involved in such development are too great; in their words they just want to be a good TA. Try the SWOT analysis mentioned earlier [22.1P2]. This standard also suggests that you measure your progress against best practice benchmarks. You can complete a checklist such as that below and add it to your personal professional portfolio. There are also some examples of real sheets developed and in use in schools. Some of you may even be asked to be the reviewer of some newly appointed TAs, as at Level 3 award you may be the senior TA of a team of Level 2 or induction level TAs.

Possible constituents of a self-review

- successes and appreciation from others;
- job satisfaction and lack of it – fulfilling your existing job description;
- relationships with pupils, colleagues and others associated with the school [22.1P3];
- understanding of the learning process and special educational needs;
- teaching skills and contribution to the learning objectives of the teachers;
- relevant curriculum knowledge and understanding;

- contributions to pastoral and physical care and behaviour management;

- understanding of and contributions to school life;

- professional development opportunities taken: training courses, meetings attended, personal study under-taken, in school or out of school;

- setting and achieving of any personal targets;

- areas for change, development or improvement – adjustments to job description, and career development issues or ideas.

(Watkinson 2002:85)

You can see that taking stock of the above items actually reminds you what you have achieved. The whole process of NVQs where you are recording or showing what you can do – not being tested on what you cannot do or know – is a very positive self-valuing process. Having an annual review reminds you what you have being doing well and often things are forgotten: you only remember easily the things that went wrong. The NOS them-selves can make a useful checklist of looking at what you do. [22K3].

The above paragraphs assume that all goes smoothly in career development, whether moving upwards or expanding understanding at a desired level. Of course, this is not always so. Sometimes you will make mistakes, your relationships with other staff could become sour or difficult, or personal circumstances intervene in work-based situations – you may have bereavement or other emotional problems, you may have developed a serious illness, or a close member of the family may have done so, or you could have money problems. You may just find that the demands being put upon you are too great for your ability. You might feel you need more communication about something – this is quite common for support staff, as historically they were left out of staff meetings. Whatever the problem, you need to think whom to tell and share it with, or what you can do about it. Letting relationships fester is no solution. Coping with domestic problems beyond your control will be sympathetically listened to; ideas for improving the working practices in which you are involved should be listened to, provided you are tactful and constructive.

Also, circumstances change, and alter what you are capable of [22.1P5]. Having children dependent on you makes a lot of difference to your time commitments. If you have a fam-ily, they do grow up and may release you to undertake more responsibility or a new course. This means you have to review your personal objectives. Not only that, the educational scene is constantly changing with new initiatives, ideas for teaching and learning, new resources. The school circumstances may change. The building of a new estate in your neighbourhood can radically alter not only the number of pupils attending the school, but also the nature of the background of those pupils. The installation of a new industry or the closing of a large factory can create all sorts of problems as well as opportunities for different qualities in staff. The arrival of one new pupil with particular SEN can alter the opportunities for yourself.

An example

Margaret, a TA in a small village primary school, had started work in the school as a volunteer when her children started school. She loved the job and showed capability and enthusiasm. When the opportunity to pay Margaret for a few hours a week came, she was taken on to the staff. A young girl started at the school, Jane, who was a wheelchair user. Jane needed 'full time' (25 hours a week) cover in order that her physical needs could be catered for. Margaret was offered the job. By that time her own children were old enough to enable her to undertake these longer hours. Jane later needed first an electric typewriter to help her write and then a laptop computer. Margaret had been a typist before her marriage, and adapted the reading scheme words to a typing tutor and taught Jane proper keyboard skills at a time when the other pupils were learning to use a pencil. She taught herself computer skills. As soon as any courses became available for TAs she asked to go on them, particularly ones with special needs included in them. She even asked to go on courses which were supposed to be for teachers, and with the cooperation of the school and the tutors did so, to the benefit of all concerned. Later, as Jane got older, Margaret had to decide whether she would go on to Jane's secondary school with her or change her job. She decided her village and family affiliations came first, and also that Jane's need for independence would be best served by her having various adult carers, not just one. As this meant changes in Margaret's role, becoming a general TA rather than one with SEN specialities, Margaret started to organise the school's ICT resources and became an invaluable troubleshooter and source of expertise. She never went on to higher education, of which she was quite capable, deeming herself 'too old' (her words!). In her retirement she promised herself to undertake a GCSE course in mathematics, understanding of which she felt she was lacking.

Performance management

Appraisal – or professional review – is a formal opportunity for TAs to discuss their performance and professional needs with their line manager [22.1P4]. Appraisal is meant to be a dialogue, with the person appraised and the appraiser both contributing freely. Some (many?) TAs may not be familiar with this process, and it may need to be made clear in advance that an appraisal is not some form of one-way report delivered by the manager. The appraiser should clearly acknowledge what the TA does well, and provide an opportunity for the appraisee to raise any problems or concerns that they may have about the way their job is developing or what they are expected to do (DfES 2000a: 34).

Your appraisal is an opportunity to revisit the job description and see if it still applies. It is a time to assess your training needs and any queries you might have about performing at Level 3, having responsibilities that reflect your competence, and where you need to concentrate to gain evidence of further competence. It should be a time to discuss your self-review – you only have to share what you want to share with another person – and maybe decide which form of accreditation for any training you might undertake would be best suited to you and the school circumstances [22.2P1]. You can also discuss what kind of contribution you could make to the life of the school, or any developments or initiative with which the school is involved. Any notes you have made in your personal/professional portfolio will be useful, and any records of training you have undertaken, meetings you have been to and thoughts you have had. If certain courses are agreed which mean you must make changes to your timetable or will not be paid, both of you must take that into account. The school will also have priorities, particularly for their budget and may or may not be able to support you financially in any agreed process, but they should provide general support, opportunities and resources for any targets that you jointly set at the end of the appraisal dialogue. Together you can match your skills, knowledge and understanding and your potential for development against the school policies and objectives. The school will have a development plan (SDP) which will have set priorities for the year ahead and allocated funds to support them. It will also have to take account of any government initiatives or directions; for instance, the introduction of the national strategies and initiatives. The strategies have made a considerable difference to the way TAs are both used and trained. National moves towards greater inclusion of pupils with SEN affected the use of TAs, resource provision and training opportunities, both in special schools and mainstream ones. You need to keep yourself informed of what is going on in your school, in the LA, and nationally. Your personal objectives and school objectives have to be balanced [22K11]. Also, you should agree a time to review those targets. The process is cyclical, probably on an annual programme.

Some schools recognise that equal opportunities in employment mean that if teachers are observed at work, so should support staff be. If this is done, you should be quite clear when it is happening, as should the class teacher in whose class you are working at the time. You should be able to see any notes made and discuss any comments at the dialogue time. The dialogue should be done in paid time, in a comfortable private place, even off the premises if you both agree. The only record of the meeting that should be made is when and where the observation and dialogue have taken place and any outcomes, targets or training programmes that are agreed [22.2P2]. Appropriate targets are often described as being SMART: specific, measurable, achievable, realistic and time-bound. Unrealistic vague targets, which could only be achieved after a lot of changes or considerable time, are useless [2K9].

While the school should provide this review system, you must take account of what is said about your performance, discuss constructively any targets suggested for you, and carry out any agreed programme to the best of your ability. You should keep a record of ideas and opportunities offered and those which you have come across. Schools know it is in their own best interest to have highly competent and trained staff, and recognise the low pay scales on which many of you operate, so will help with fees if they can. All school staff not only have a right to CPD but will benefit from it which in turn means higher expectations of each other and the pupils. It is always worth discussing finance at your review.

Do also remember that you do not have to depend on your school line manager for personal or professional debate and support. Your school may have appointed a mentor for you within the school – someone to go to for such debate outside any formal review process. The class teacher with whom you feel greatest rapport may help; if you are on any course, the tutor is usually willing to discuss matters; if you are undertaking an NVQ assessment, the assessor should discuss your progress and ideas and plan ahead with you. Some courses, such as the Open University Specialist Teacher Assistant Certificate (OU STAC) course, were known to formally pair students, and part of the course is set round visits to your paired colleague's school. Such pairing often creates lasting friendships as well as an opportunity for professional debate. When sharing information about your school, any staff or pupils, do remember to ensure that confidentiality is maintained. While you should be able to have this professional dialogue to help you sort out ideas on strategies and courses to help you progress, at Level 3 you should be able to take responsibility for searching out opportunities for yourself. The local library, FE college and any local higher education (HE) colleges will have details of local courses. Try the internet and Google in what you are particularly interested in and see if there are online courses. The TDA website will give you links to support any nationally recognised accreditation possibilities and routes to teaching [22K8, 10].

Being a reflective practitioner

Pollard (2002) in his book *Reflective teaching* explores many ways for teachers to look at their own practice. While much of the book is unnecessary for a TA there are some useful bits to read. Some schools have a copy of this in the staffroom or a teacher may have one. Just read the first chapter and the opening page of the other chapters. The first page of each chapter is a diagram showing the contents of the chapter. Some of these sections may interest you to read or even follow up with your mentor or class teacher. The author believes Dewey's characteristics of 'reflective action', as distinct from 'routine action', can be applied to teaching. These are:

1 an active concern with the intention and consequence of your actions;

2 your action (or teaching) is a cyclical or spiral process, where you continually monitor, evaluate and revise your practice;

3 the need to develop competence;

4 attitudes of open-mindedness (listening to others), responsibility, and whole-heartedness (energy and enthusiasm);

5 judgement and insight;

6 collaboration and dialogue which lead to professional development and personal fulfilment;

7 an ability to be creative with materials or frameworks developed by others [22K2].

It is tempting in this age of the internet to think that information is easily accessible and that an attitude of continuing to develop or learn or question is not necessary, because the answers are available. But Barber (1996) says:

> Information on its own is nothing. Information only provides access to power when it is linked with reason and thought. For information to be useful, people must make selections from it. To connect diverse strands of it together, to ask intelligent questions of it and to reject parts of it which, though they are there on the screen, in the book or on the paper, appear inaccurate. Even then, thought and information need to be linked in a chain of reasoned argument.
>
> Developing a questioning attitude, making connections, arguing with reasons all takes a bit of practice. It is not about being argumentative or confrontational for the sake of it.
>
> (p. 181)

Developing a constructively critical view

- Try reading the same account of an event in two different daily newspapers, preferably broadsheets rather than tabloids. Formulate your own views on the subject, then look at their editorials and see how they have slanted their views and see if you agree with them – or not.

- When you next watch a film or a play, think about it afterwards. Why do you like it? What did you not like – the story, the acting, the location, the length? Would you recommend someone to go and see it and why? What would you do differently if you made the film?

- If you have the time(!) you could join a book reading group. They usually meet once a month, after all reading the same book, and discuss just these sorts of questions. Ask at your local library if you are interested.

A reflective practitioner examines their learning, achievement and aspirations, identifies areas for development, undertakes research and can justify their actions and conclusions [22K5, 6]. This is hard and it really helps if you have another view on your practice and people with whom to discuss your ideas and feelings. Use the NOS and any other models from your reading or experience to compare with your ideas and actions. 22K4 has a useful list of strategies or techniques which can be used in reflective practice.

Then think about the answers to those questions, put ideas together, challenge yourself and colleagues in what are called critical friendships. This does not mean critical in the negative sense but analytical.

Leadership attributes

The processes described in this chapter of reflection, review and professional development are not a one-off thing, not something only done in the early years of undertaking a TA job, but will continue all your life. Learning never stops, so while in a job, professional development is continuous [22.2P4]. Schools are beginning to see their teams of TAs in the same light as teams of nurses in a hospital. Schools are used to teachers having hierarchies and specialisms; hospitals have them for both doctors and nurses but schools have been slower to recognise the value of organising and training their support staff in the same way. The NOS, HLTA status and foundation degrees are excellent for preparing people to fit the various roles. Many schools with teams of TAs are realising that leading and managing the team does not have to be done by a teacher – they are the equivalent of medical consultants in the teaching system.

Leadership and management skills are not easy. Working with people is not easy. Teachers themselves are not taught to manage people, only pupils. There is more about working with other people and leading a TA team in the next chapter. Consider Table 2.2 below. Because you are in a school, dealing with people rather than machines or goods, you do not just deal with implementation and operational issues, the means and the systems. You may have a vision of what you want to do, and what the school wants you to do, and you will need to think strategically, discuss ideas, consider change and changes. You will be concerned with achieving an end – the development and achievement of pupils and staff, possibly also parents and governors, not just the processes which lead to that end.

West-Burnham (2004:3) also considers the links between leading and managing and administration.

Leadership	**Management**	**Administration**
doing the right things	doing things right	doing things
path making	path following	path tidying
complexity	clarity	consistency

'Generally, the roles and responsibilities of school leaders cover a range of strategic and operational areas including: setting the strategic direction and ethos of the school; managing teaching and learning; developing and managing people; and dealing with the requirements of the accountability regime' (PricewaterhouseCoopers 2007:v).

Skills required for good leadership are soft skills – not knowledge based but the ability to build relationships, and teams. The traditional view of leadership is that of power through hierarchical control. The following phrases are taken from various sources and my own observations (Watkinson 2008:21,22). Good leadership appears to be much more about style and behaviour than knowledge and particular strategies.

Leadership is not about:

- control, ensuring that you 'win' arguments;

- taking advantage of the position;

- suppressing any negative feelings so that you always look 'in charge';

- being negative or overly critical of others;

- showing that you know better because you have been better educated or have a higher status;

- avoiding embarrassment, feeling vulnerable or incompetent.

TABLE 2.2   Leadership and management compared

Leading is concerned with:	**Managing is concerned with:**
■ vision	■ implementation
■ strategic issues	■ operational issues
■ transformation	■ transaction
■ ends	■ means
■ people	■ systems
■ doing right things	■ doing things right

(West-Burnham 1997 quoted in Collaborne and Billingham 1998: 1)

Can you recognise any of these attributes in yourself?

- engagement – the ability to mobilise people to tackle tough problems;
- being personable, approachable and accessible;
- being aware of the dynamics of your organisation, its systems and relationships;
- motivating and empowering others;
- being flexible rather than dogmatic;
- role modelling, being a lead learner professionally and personally;
- allowing yourself to show ignorance, or incompetence or vulnerability at times;
- being able to stand back, reflect and learn from experience;
- being self-aware – reflecting on what you do and sharing those reflections with others;
- having core values which you act out in practice rather than imposing on others;
- seeing the bigger picture;
- being decisive if necessary, consultative where possible;
- being able to pay attention to detail, including maintenance and development;
- being optimistic, enthusiastic and resilient;
- retaining confidence and maintaining calmness;
- encouraging a climate of trust;
- having vision and communicating it to others.

Good leaders are people who communicate through:

- what they say;
- their example and action;
- policies, programmes and practices that enable other people to be able, responsible and worthwhile;
- motivating other people even by the way they listen.

Hopefully you have experienced working with such people.

Questions to ask yourself

- Do you have a personal professional portfolio? If not, construct one for yourself.
- Do you have an up-to-date job description? If not, why not?
- Are you clear about the boundaries and possibilities of your role?
- Have you had an appraisal or performance review? If not, and you have worked in the school for more than a year, why not?
- Have you found out about the main roles and responsibilities of others in your school?
- What have you read lately? Did you share your comments on it with anyone?
- Why do you want to work with children or young people?
- What value systems do you adhere to? Are they the same as those of the school in which you work?
- What personal attributes can you bring to the job?
- Where do you turn for help and support for yourself?

Keep these in mind as you read further.

Essential reading

DfES (2000) *Working with teaching assistants: A good practice guide.*

National Occupational Standards for Supporting teaching and learning in schools (2007).

Guidance on the National Occupational Standards for Supporting teaching and learning in schools (2008).

Some further reading

Balshaw, M. and Farrell, P. (2002) *Teaching assistants: Practical strategies for effective classroom support* (especially Chapters 7 and 12).

Barber, M. (1996) *The learning game: Arguments for an education revolution.*

O'Brien, T. and Garner, P. (2001) *Untold stories.*

Pollard, A. (2002) *Reflective teaching: Effective and evidence-informed professional practice* (especially Chapter 1).

Ritchie, C. and Thomas, P. (2004) *Successful study-skills for teaching assistants.*

TDA (2006a) *Teaching assistant file : Primary induction.*

TDA (2006b) *Teaching assistant file : Secondary induction.*

Watkinson, A. (2002) *Assisting learning and supporting teaching.*

Watkinson, A. (2008a) *The essential guide for competent teaching assistants: Meeting the National Occupational Standards at Level 2.*

Useful websites

www.ukstandards.org.uk

www.teachernet.gov.uk/teachingassistants

www.tda.gov.uk

3

Relationships

The basic principles of good relationships

THERE ARE SOME PRINCIPLES that underlie good relationships whether they are professional or social: treating others as you would like to be treated, having respect for the other person or people in the relationship. They are built on a sensitivity to differences and an ability to make compromises and cooperate [20K1].

Effective relationships are helped by:

- a mutual accountability, whether doing the asking or being asked to complete a task of some kind;

- mutual trust;

- qualities such as punctuality, truthfulness, honesty and reliability, building up the necessary trust;

- a recognition of your own mistakes – apologise and learn from them;

- effective communication. This means not only listening, but also giving clear, appropriate and if possible unambiguous instructions or messages; even simple things like not mumbling when in doubt will help;

- being explicit (politely) about needs and misunderstandings; implicit messages can be misunderstood, causing hurt or delay. Write things down for yourself and others where you can, being as accurate and concise as possible;

- assertiveness without aggression;

- positive attitudes such as trying to see the good in people or pupils, trying to understand, smiling where you can; for instance, ask for things or give instructions in a positive – not a negative – manner;

- good manners – try to thank for things wherever possible, without being a 'creep';

- cooperation and collaboration rather than conflict – although this does not mean always agreeing with others;

- avoidance of damaging conflict and unnecessary confrontation – aggression and attention seeking do not get the same results as cooperation;

- sharing problems, and not allowing worries to fester;

- common aims, objectives or goals – such as in a fundraising group, or a group trying to put on a play – which make people recognise the importance of burying differences to 'get the show on the road';

- shared values or similar backgrounds;

- frequency of contact, helping people to get to know each other more, both what the common interests might be and what areas of potential disagreement there might be, and therefore how to avoid them;

- a lack of cliques, where groups of people become inward looking and exclusive;
- celebrating differences – the ability to speak more than one language, cook different dishes, have a differing style of dress or home furnishing, or read different books is something to be proud of, share or show an interest in.

Consider two relationships you know well, one with a close relative and the other a work relationship. Look at each in the light of the above list.

- Are they different? How?
- Do you agree with the list?
- If not, where do you differ?
- Can you add to the list?

It is not important that all relationships conform with one person's list (mine or yours) but that you consider what makes things work well for you and what does not, then try to make them all work well. Your relationships with the pupils in your care are crucial, as are those with all the adults with whom you come into contact in your job. You cannot work in isolation, nor can other members of staff. You need to understand how your relationships with other members of staff enable the whole school to work better. Level 3 TAs are deemed capable of leadership and management either of teams of TAs, of a specialist area, of a group of volunteers or of working with people from outside the school: specialists, parents, members of the business community. Success in all these roles depends on having good relationships with people, understanding their roles and needs and enabling them to succeed better because of you.

Take a copy of the organisational chart or tree of the school staff which you have built up from reading the previous chapter.

Circle the people with whom you come into contact daily, weekly and termly, even yearly, with different colours. This will give you an idea of where to concentrate your efforts in making sure relationships are effective.

Take two more colours and track the paths of your line management and accountability (both those to whom you are responsible and those who are responsible to you) through the tree. Are they the same?

With whom do you have informal contact, and with whom do you have more formal meetings?

The climate and ethos of the school is largely reflected in the kind of relationships which develop. This climate is important in creating a learning environment which is supportive and effective, not just operating in a shell of a building with paper policies. Leadership, not just from the headteacher but from all those who have responsibilities, including you, sets the standards for how the school operates. The leaders can consult, supervise and show by example; they can respect others' contributions and delegate. You may be a leader in a small field for which you have responsibility, such as organising a resource area, or working with a group of pupils. What kind of leader are you? Collaborative cultures take more effort and time on the part of everyone in them, but have been found to produce more effective organisations. They prevent fragmentation of jobs and duplication, and this has a beneficial effect on pupils.

Learning and interpersonal intelligence

In the section on learning you will find more about the theory of multiple intelligences, suggested by Howard Gardner. He makes the case for human beings having different kinds of intelligence and nominates seven different types. Subsequent psychologists have suggested other dimensions than these seven. They are not discrete 'things' or areas in the head but ways of thinking. Each of us has varying capabilities, and they are not fixed. We can recognise them, develop them and use them. Along with linguistic, musical, logicomathematical, spatial, and bodily kinaesthetic, Gardner proposes interpersonal and intrapersonal intelligences or skills or capabilities. These refer to our ability to relate to other people and to understand ourselves. By recognising what we find easy or hard – some people find music helpful when learning, some find mathematics and logic hard – we can see how to help our own ways of learning by utilising methods we find easy, or where we can concentrate effort on things we find difficult.

Having good interpersonal intelligence means that you find relationships with other people easy, you are sensitive to atmosphere and willing to cooperate or share. You may, however, be shy or have other traits which mean you find working with other people difficult. With the research that has been done on learning, following the ideas of multiple intelligences, have come ideas on how to recognise your strengths and weaknesses, and how aspects can be utilised or developed. 'Interpersonal intelligence makes use of core capacities to recognize and make distinctions among others' feelings, beliefs and intentions. Early in development, this intelligence is seen in the ability of young children to discriminate among the individuals in their environment and discern others' moods. In its most developed forms, interpersonal intelligence manifests itself in the ability to understand, act on and shape others' feelings and attitudes for good or otherwise' (Gardner and Wake 1996:211).

You can also see that interpersonal abilities need to utilise aspects of all the other 'intelligences'. They are, according to Smith (1996) highly developed in teachers, among others. To work in a school with pupils and the other staff, you will need to develop this area if you do not feel it is well developed in you already [21K1]. 'A person with a well developed interpersonal intelligence will enjoy paired and small group activities and collaborative learning. They will enjoy exercises which require looking at issues from a number of human perspectives, empathising, devising class rules – agreeing roles and responsibilities, interviewing adults other than teachers and participating in conflict management games' (Smith 1996:57).

Lazear (1994:19), building on this concept of intelligences, gives some activities to help develop and use interpersonal skills:

Exercises to stimulate interpersonal intelligence

- Get a partner to try to reproduce a complex shape or design you have drawn simply by describing how to make it. These are the rules: (1) Give verbal instructions only. (2) Your partner may not look at the drawing. (3) Your partner may ask you any question. (4) You may not look at what your partner is drawing.

- Explore different ways to express encouragement and support for other people (for example, facial expressions, body posture, gestures, sounds, words, and phrases).

- Practice giving encouragement and support to others around you each day.

- Practice listening deeply to someone who is expressing a view with which you disagree. Cut off the tendency to interpret what the person is saying and to express your own views. Force yourself to stay focused on what the person is saying. Try to paraphrase his or her thoughts to verify your own understanding.

- Volunteer to be part of a team and watch for positive and negative team behavior (positive team behavior includes the things that help the team work together and be successful; negative behavior includes the things that impair the team's efforts).
- Try disciplined people-watching, guessing what others are thinking and feeling, their backgrounds, professions, and so on, based on nonverbal clues (for example, dress, gestures, voice tone, colors, and so on). When possible (and appropriate!), check your accuracy with the person.

You can see that by practising some of these skills yourself, and with your family and the pupils with whom you work, family life and decision making can be enhanced, and sophisticated proceedings such as school councils can result. Developing good interpersonal skills will enable your own personal and working life to be more fulfilled and help the pupils with whom you work to grow up into communicative, more confident adults. You will be an effective team player and member of the school community.

Respect and voice, rights and responsibilities

Britain has a long history, at least two thousand years, of tolerance of invaders, migrants and asylum seekers; even previous enemies have eventually settled here, married and become part of our heritage. In recent years considerable legislation has built up to protect the rights of individuals and try to ensure that we can live together on our crowded islands. Embedded in the laws and studies of what works and what helps are certain principles. Basically they reflect what makes good relationships and prevents escalating conflict. Around the ideas and principles has also grown a vocabulary and much literature. The standards reflect this growth, but also the importance of the principles.

The Human Rights legislation has been the most contentious because people have apparently used it to get away with actions which others feel are wrong. However, enshrined in it is the principle that we all have rights because of being alive. We have the right to be recognised as an entity and be treated by others as we would like to be treated. But, in order to make this work we need to treat others similarly. If we want respect we must both give respect and earn it. This applies to small children and young people as well as adults. If we want to be heard then we must also listen. There is a very interesting body of research building up to show that where even small children are given a voice, consulted and allowed choices they can be sensible, show great perception and respond [3.4P3; 20K10–14] (DCSF 2008b). This can range from simple behaviour management choices in bringing up children – 'finish your first course or go without your second course' – to designing play areas and school councils. Some teachers are using pupil voice to help them determine how successful their teaching methods are. Children do have to learn as they grow up that with rights and voice also come responsibilities: to abide by majority decisions, to carry out tasks they have agreed to, to abide by rules made for their safety [20K16, 17, 23, 26–29].

Equal opportunities and anti-discrimination legislation and the concerns about inclusion, both of those with disabilities and those of differing backgrounds or beliefs or differences, all originate from the basic principle of a right to a decent life [20.1P4; 20K4]. Defining all the parameters of what that means is a task which will never end. It is part of our human nature to defend ourselves, to discriminate in our choices, to raise barriers to communication, to become aggressive or frightened when threatened, to 'survive as the fittest'. This is true for small children playing, youngsters taking tests or drivers on the road challenged by others. Our natural competitiveness and defence of ourselves, our family and home makes it hard to tolerate differences of opinion or apologise for our actions. We are all different and individuals. As part of educating children and young people we need to see their rights, listen to their voice but also show them by example and discussion that tolerance and respect is not 'sissy'. It will enable them to live and work together with others [20K6, 7]. We have to help them understand and celebrate differences. Conflict resolution is not about one side winning but about communicating, listening, negotiating and often compromise. It takes time and patience. If good relationships are established in the first place, it is much easier to have constructive dialogue. Bullies are often children or people who have not themselves been respected or listened to so they resort to verbal or physical abuse to draw attention to themselves. Discrimination and choice should be based on rational, open reasons, not on prejudice [20.1P3]. The importance of these concepts is reiterated in Chapter 6 when discussing the importance of each child being encouraged to be independent. Standard 44K1–8 gives many of the key factors which need to be considered when dealing with any children, not just those with additional requirements.

The report *20:20 vision* (DfES 2006a) suggests that 'Reflective schools view "pupil voice" as far more than establishing a pupil council'. They are engaging pupils actively in shaping learning and teaching, for example, by:

- using pupils as learning resources for one another, helping their peers to learn and develop, within the classroom and beyond;
- inviting pupils to work with teachers in curriculum teams to review schemes of work and develop plans for improving learning and teaching;
- asking pupils to provide feedback on particular lessons, either through general surveys or by training them as observers of lessons;
- conducting regular surveys on the quality of the school experience and how it could be improved, sharing the results with all pupils;
- involving pupils in the selection process for new members of staff.

(DfES 2006:21)

Working with pupils

This has two aspects – your relationship with the pupils with whom you work, and your facilitation of their relationships with each other. It could develop into you listening and even advising them about their relationships with other adults or pupils outside the group, but this is really more about counselling. Some TAs are interested in this aspect of school work and undertake proper counselling training and are recognised by senior managers for these skills. The proposals for support staff working as learning mentors include aspects of this work with pupils. It can be time consuming and challenging but very valuable if the pupils come from family circumstances where time is not made for anyone to listen to their concerns. Even if you are simply asked to run a circle time group you should still undertake appropriate training to ensure you do not make the situation worse.

When working with individual children your relationship with them is important. It should be a professional one, friendly, receptive to their ideas and suggestions, but enabling them to carry out the teacher's intentions. The aim is to increase the pupils' independence, not their dependency on you. It feels good to be wanted and sometimes tempting to be a substitute parent or pal, but do keep a watch on this. Schools as a whole are *in loco parentis* but you must consider your personal purpose and role. Sometimes, that role includes carrying out intimate procedures for pupils, such as dealing with incontinence or menstruation. You must be familiar with the school's policies on child protection, confidentiality and health and safety [20.1P7]. A pupil may, as a result of having a close relationship with you, reveal circumstances occurring out of school which may be quite harmless and interesting but could indicate matters which you should refer to someone else [20K2, 3, 5]. Do read the child protection notes in Chapter 7 carefully if you have not studied them at Level 2.

It is interesting to consider how the pupils see you. Why not ask? You should be providing a role model for them, and for some pupils this may be different from their out-of-school relationships. This could be particularly important, for instance, if you are male and a pupil you are working with has a single-parent mum.

Considering the relationship you have with your pupils in groups is not necessarily about managing those groups. Check all the items mentioned above in thinking about relationships in general and apply them to the pupils you work with.

Good relationships with pupils

Do you:

- listen to what they have to say?
- question them to explain more if you do not understand?
- try to see their point of view?
- give positive feedback and encouragement?
- facilitate their ability to contribute to a game or discussion?
- encourage them to cooperate when working in groups?
- explain rules and how they can be observed?
- ensure each one in a group can take part appropriately, that each has a turn?
- enable the pupils to recognise and learn from their mistakes without losing face?
- make goals, aims or targets explicit and give praise when they are reached?
- look for similarities and celebrate differences?
- share joys and problems, yours and the pupils – establish rapport and understanding?
- look for opportunities to promote self-reliance, self-esteem and self-confidence?
- always show respect and good manners to all the pupils you work with?
- show a consistent and positive role model to the pupils in your relationships within the school?

[20.1P5; 20K8–14]

You need to consider the age and stage of development of pupils when you are working with them. The stage may not be related to their learning ability or age, as home backgrounds and opportunities for seeing and participation in situations with good relationships will differ widely [20.2P1]. The role models offered and the experiences of social behaviour will differ from family to family. Many children come from homes where games are not played, even simple card or board games. This is not necessarily a sign of a deprived home, for many wealthy parents are too busy with their jobs or social activities to spend time with their children. You may need to encourage children to talk, question, offer their own ideas and make their own suggestions or you may need to curb their dominance if they are used to always getting their own way [20.2P4]. Having a different language from other pupils or yourself will inhibit communication, as will lack of appropriate vocabulary, which may be due to background or learning problems [20.2P5; 20K15]. The behaviour of others in a family or group can influence group dynamics and prevent good relationships developing. Peer pressure or members of the family needing or demanding attention through illness can divert adults in the family from giving attention where it should be given; disruptive or even very noisy groups or family members can all influence the ways in which pupils develop their own interpersonal skills. Some pupils may have communication and interaction problems and need special help. Some of you may be working in speech and language units. The SENCO should be able to help you if there are pupils with SEN [20.1P6]. Standard 46 is about working with older pupils with STL 46.3 particularly emphasising the need to create a relationship of trust and openness if they are distressed.

Young children coming to school for the first time may have particular problems with relationships, and those changing schools, from a small rural primary to a large comprehensive, or from a school near home to one a bus ride away or even to a boarding school, will also be vulnerable. For these groups of children and young people it is about moving from the known surroundings to the unknown and from probably small, more intimate relationships to a much wider world [20K8]. Young children are very self-centred, and see themselves as the link to everyone else, but an average pupil at the end of Key Stage 2 has a much greater understanding of the 'give and take' of normal relationships. Only children may find sharing and taking turns for adult attention more difficult than those from families with more children. Children with changing relationships between their parents or carers will have a different view of adult relationships from those from more stable backgrounds [20.1P2].

Dealing with transitions is seen as such an important thing in itself that Standard 49 is devoted entirely to this and it is referred to again in Chapter 6. It is also one of the separate sections dealt with in the Common Core of skills and knowledge suggested for support staff in any care situation (DfES 2005). It is worth remembering that all of life is about change and coping with change and so our role in supporting children and young people in school is to see change as a possibly positive thing, something to be enjoyed, to get excited about as well as fear. The fear is real – we have all experienced it, but we also know it passes. We also know the kind of support that helped us – empathy rather than trying to hide things. We are all more vulnerable at such times, and those already vulnerable through various circumstances will be more so [20.1P1].

While this section is not focusing on sexual relationships or sex education, those of you working in secondary schools will be working with young people exploring this aspect of their lives, and may well have to deal with the results of sexual relationships, whether they are going well or not. If you have a close working relationship with a pupil, it may well be to you they bring their questions about sex and the problems of their love life. You do need to know the sex education policy of your school, whether you can enter into debates about HIV and AIDS or contraception, and where you should direct the older pupils for more specific advice.

There is some very useful material on the importance of working with children about their relationships in the Health for Life books, which used to be used in many primary schools for their health education materials. Book 2 (Williams *et al.* 1989:260–3) gives some useful background on various developmental aspects of relationships and the emotions and feelings experienced by children aged 5 to 11 as explored in investigations of 22,603 children in 11 LEAs. This book also gives many pages of ideas for exploring feelings and relationships with Key Stages 1 and 2 pupils. You should not do these with pupils on your own, only as part of activities directed by a teacher, but there is much to make you think about how these difficult areas can be explored sensitively. The book gives worksheets and questions for all these ages, and many of those for older primary children could be adapted for secondary pupils who are experiencing problems. They focus on five main areas – special people, friends and friendship, feelings, memories and growing up, and special places. The ideas on consulting children, getting them to draw situations if they cannot write or talk about them are very useful.

This material may still be available in your school and still has great value. It has been rather eclipsed by the SEAL materials (social and emotional aspects of learning) which are readily available on the internet. The SEAL project also started in primary schools, but is now also available for secondary schools. It seems that the combination of television and computers with a raised incidence of maternal working and dysfunctional families has made such material more necessary than ever [20.3P1–4; 20K8–14; 18–22].

As TAs you are in the best position to help pupils make and sustain worthwhile relationships. Take every opportunity to play games of all sorts, in play activities in class with little ones, in the playground or as part of group activities. These help explain the purpose of rules, taking turns and competing without becoming aggressive. Just spending time talking with a pupil or group of pupils can be productive; communication is vital to good relationships. If pupils are not used to this – leading solitary lives with their own television, videos and computers, not participating in family meal times – they have to develop the skills needed. You may need to question subtly to clarify points or make sure you have understood, particularly if the children are not used to talking to others [20.1P3]. The popularity of texting and chat rooms may well be explained by the lack of personal communication in homes. Even in more advantaged homes, the opportunity for discussions does not always coincide with the need because of busy timetables [20K18–22].

This role has been developed into the 'Learning mentor' role, again with its own standard [STL 50]. This refers to supporting children and young people to assess their own strengths and weaknesses and how these relate to their learning and development, while supporting their motivation and self-confidence. When undertaking any mentor role or participating in a mentor/mentee relationship, it is always important to be clear about the respective roles and what expectations either person has of what may result. It is about having time,

PHOTOGRAPH 3.1   A learning mentor helping a child sort out his timetable

respecting each other's point of view while being as open as possible about what you think. Standard 51 – contributing to improving attendance – is not just about knowing all the technicalities of registration but about being the sort of person who can contact pupils and families tactfully and sensitively. The aim will be to increase purposeful attendance where all parties want to improve. Clearly how you relate to pupils and adults is crucial in such circumstances.

Also you need to consider the environment in which you are working or playing with pupils. Noise, space, comfort, even lighting can all create a sense of well-being or anxiety. Hunger or disruption can affect what you are doing; the rise of breakfast clubs has been an attempt to address this problem. The move to improve the content of school meals and the withdrawal of vending machines have been a response to recognising that diet is a factor in emotional and social behaviour, even in learning capability. You cannot influence the pupils' backgrounds or what is going on outside school to make them behave well towards each other, but you can listen and try to understand [20.2P2]. They may be being bullied on the way home or even abused at home. Even if you live in the community and know the family, it is not your place to interfere at that level. If you have concerns, you must share them with a teacher, even the named teacher for child protection if you feel your knowledge warrants it. You are a member of the school staff; you must be guided by the school protocols and policies, particularly regarding confidentiality [20.1P7]. Sometimes you need time to get pupils' confidence, but do ensure that you are not creating a dependency which is detrimental to the long-term independence of the pupils concerned. Relationships of all kinds have to be built but also sustained. All the factors that prevent the development of interpersonal skills before you meet the pupils could affect your relationships.

Looking at group dynamics [20.1P6]

Ask for a time to observe a group at work on a collaborative task or playing. Draw a map of where each member of the group is standing or sitting. Then for a period of ten minutes or a quarter of an hour:

either, make a list of members and tally when each member speaks;

or, draw a line on your map each time someone speaks, showing the line of communication;

or, tape-record the conversation, noting who is speaking each time so that you can transcribe the tape later;

or, look out for all the incidences of non-verbal communication.

■ Did any one person dominate? Why?

■ Did anyone not contribute at all? Why?

■ Was there any off-task activity or discussion? Why?

■ Did any outside things influence what was going on?

■ Did it matter where the group members were placed?

■ Did the group break into any sub-groups? Why? Did it help the task?

■ What sort of intervention, if any, would have made things work better?

■ Was it an appropriate activity for group work?

Relationships with teachers: partnership

The relationship between you and the teacher in whose class you are working is a working relationship which may even become a friendship. The teacher takes the responsibility and it may seem at first glance to be a boss–worker or power relationship. They just tell you what

PHOTOGRAPH 3.2   A TA working with a small group

to do and you get on with it. You will have been working long enough in schools to realise that this is a very superficial way of viewing how you need to work together. Nevertheless, it is important that you take time to make the working relationship a human relationship; teachers and TAs should form a partnership based on understanding each other's roles, purposes and limitations. You need to talk with and listen to the teachers you work with, spend out-of-class contact time with them, if only in the corridor on the way to or leaving a lesson. Normal chat about the weather, families, homes or hobbies can cement relationships and prove to each partner that the other is human. The school should allow you to use the same staffroom as the teachers, although this is occasionally a problem where space is at a premium. Similarly, cloakrooms, toilet areas, car parks all provide common ground for beginning conversations. On top of this, the school should ensure that you both have paid non-class contact time to discuss curriculum matters and pupils' needs properly, to plan together what has to be done.

You will find, even in the same school, that each teacher has their own characteristics, and you as a TA are likely to work with several in a week, and possibly even in a day. Many schools have realised that allowing the teacher and TA continuous time together, even in some cases allocating one TA per class, has a beneficial effect on working relationships. On the other hand, varied experiences and working with different adults can increase your understanding of the different ways of tackling similar problems, giving you a range of ideas of how to operate. You must be seen to be an example of good working relationships not only by any assessor for a Level 3 accreditation but also by the pupils, for they will note subconsciously that this is how grown-ups work together, resolve their problems and hopefully enjoy their time together.

Whatever you do in school should be under the direction of a qualified teacher. The status conferred on them by their qualifications does mean them taking responsibility for the learning of pupils whether in a class or a subject. You will often find yourself doing tasks that include teaching or working with a small group out of the sight of the class teacher. Whatever the situation, however, that teacher still takes responsibility for the progress of the pupils and ensuring that your role with them is as effective as possible. This can create tensions with the teacher either if you feel under-used or if you are given more responsibility than you feel comfortable with. Even with the introduction of HLTAs the regulations for using support staff to relieve the teachers' workload (DfES 2003c) indicate that, whatever level you are working at, there will still be supervision of your work, and ultimate responsibility for teaching and learning of pupils will be with the teacher. The main problem seems to lie where communication and relationships with the teacher under whom you are working are not good. It takes two to make a partnership, even where one is in charge, so part of the responsibility for making this work for the good of the pupils is with you. Do make time to discuss any problem or concern with the relevant person. It could be to do with your job description, the space you have been allotted to keep your things, your timetable or contract, or the pupils or materials with which you are working. If there is a real problem you must seek out your line manager, and if that is the same person then a senior manager or headteacher.

The case studies which Lacey (2001) quotes are taken from a study which she undertook of learning support assistants (LSAs) in special schools. Read the chapter about teacher and TA partnerships (pp. 100–12). She concludes by saying

> The partnerships between teachers and assistants that are effective, have to struggle in the face of many adversities. When they work, the partners are supportive of each other and of the children. They have sufficient time to plan and evaluate how best to work as well as efficient systems for communications . . . This partnership appears to be built upon mutual respect and trust, support of each other and a shared understanding of how to meet pupils' learning needs. It is underpinned by clear lines of communication, commitment to providing planning time and the security of a permanent job supported by a career structure and relevant training. Nothing less is sufficient.
>
> (Lacey 2001:112)

If you work with children who have severe or profound and multiple learning difficulties (SLD or PMLD) or work in a special school, you will find the report *On a wing and a prayer* (Lacey 1999) also very helpful reading. She gives an audit for partners wishing to look at how they spend their time together, developed by a group of teachers and assistants:

- Estimate how much time you spend together planning, reporting back, in meetings and in children's reviews in an average week.

- Make a note of the sort of topics covered.

- Gather together any planning and record sheets you use. Describe your roles in specific lessons.

- Estimate how long you spend on different parts of your roles (just the bits that are to do with working together, e.g. how long the teacher spends on writing plans for LSAs, or how long LSAs spend on filling in record sheets).

- Estimate how much time is spent on unplanned activities (e.g. a sick child).

- Estimate how much time LSAs spend not actually supporting anyone (e.g. teacher-led activity when LSAs are listening, but are not actually supporting an individual or a group).

- Estimate how much time LSAs feel that they are 'teaching' (e.g. rephrasing something in the lesson; asking questions to make children think; explaining why they have got something wrong).

- Estimate how much time LSAs are supporting individuals or groups (e.g. keeping a child on task; pointing out the different steps of a task).

■ Estimate how much time LSAs are supporting the teacher (e.g. 'controlling' disruptive pupils; conveying to the teacher when pupils don't understand or need a different approach).

(Lacey 2001:103)

Estimating how much time is spent on different aspects of the work of LSAs can help in the joint reflection of how to develop the effectiveness of that work.

You will need to discuss certain basic things with each class teacher with whom you work about the boundaries of your roles in their room. You may be inferior in terms of academic qualifications, although this is not always so. Whatever your and the teacher's backgrounds are, you can contribute to the partnership; it is not a one-way process, and I am not referring to feeding back after lessons. You will have differing life experiences as well as previous or current work experiences. Many newly qualified teachers (NQTs) lean heavily on their TA to find their way around the conventions of a school, which everyone but them seems to know about. You have to be tactful, but that is the essence of promoting good relationships: a sensitivity to know when and where and how to say things so that they help and do not upset.

Another useful way of looking at the partnership is that described in the development of mentoring between a more experienced teacher and a trainee. Maynard and Furlong (1995) talk of the transition from 'apprenticeship', or the collaborative model where all you need to do is work alongside an experienced practitioner, through the 'competency model' where you get systematic training, to the 'reflective' where you and the teacher switch from focusing on your or their skills to a focus on the learning of the pupils and what is best for them. You and the teacher become 'co-enquirers'. Clearly, such a partnership is developmental and based on those elements of trust, respect and common aims talked about at the beginning of this chapter.

You have to be reliable in carrying out your part of the partnership; you should be punctual, accurate in relating anything that you have observed or heard, undertaking only those tasks that you understand and can do. If you say you will make something, or find something or make contact with others, then you should do it or immediately let the teacher know if circumstances intervene to prevent you. A phrase often used when promising to do things is to remember your 'yes' is only as good as your 'no'; only promise what you can carry out, otherwise refuse.

Your relationships with the teachers with whom you work are not just important for your and their sense of well-being, or even for the direct enhancement of learning strategies for the pupils, but your mutual personalities and compatibility will affect the atmosphere in the room. Make yourself aware of possible signs of tension, particularly when working with a teacher new to you. You are the 'additional adult', and not many teachers have had training in using support in the classroom. Sometimes teachers feel exposed to view by having another adult in the room, and they can feel their role is threatened if you seem to 'take over' parts of the lesson even with some pupils. Your demeanour – say, a grim face if you have a headache – can influence how the teacher perceives the partnership. They could feel they would be better off without you! Respect and good manners mean you should be quiet and quieten your group if the teacher addresses the class. If you feel there are problems, talk about them. They may feel having to plan for you actually makes their job more onerous rather than less.

Think of two partnerships which you know well, one good and one which seems weak. They could be from a marriage, a business, people who enter games together such as tennis or bridge, or who go on holiday together.

■ Can you list their characteristics against the list at the beginning of this chapter?
■ Does the weakness affect the second partnership's function?

- What could they change to improve the partnership?

- What is stopping them?

- What is it about the first partnership that makes it work so well?

- Do any of these thoughts affect your school working relationships?

Relationships with other adults

One of the distinctions of developing as a TA, and maybe a distinction between a Level 2 and a Level 3 TA, is the wider group of adults with whom you not only come into contact, but work. You will not just be working with a single child or with a particular teacher or set of teachers but may be working with parents, teams of TAs, visiting agencies such as specialist teachers or social workers. All the same principles still apply with adults as with children: respect, good communication strategies like listening, negotiation, clarity along with honesty, reliability, consistency and so on. It is not always so easy to recognise when adults have communication problems as they may well have developed strategies to cope with and even hide their disability. Deaf adults, particularly those without visible hearing aids, are not always easy to spot. With any person hard of hearing, you need to remember not to shout but to articulate clearly, maybe speak a little more slowly and stand where the listener can see your mouth to lip read [20K30–32]. As you work with a wider and wider group of people, you will recognise that not all of them have the same agenda as you [21.1P9, 10]. Part of your role will be to show by example how to develop and maintain good relationships, and encourage and support those you come into contact with in maintaining their relationships with each other [20.3P5; 20.4 P1; 20.4P3, 4]. There is more detail of the various groups in the next chapter on the school team.

Being part of a team

You may be part of a TA team as well as the whole-school team, particularly in a special school or a secondary school, where the numbers are larger. Even in the smallest schools now there are several TAs, so you are likely to be part of such a group. You may be part of an SEN team or a subject team in a secondary school, or even a year group team, such as the Early Years team. This means you can form relationships with people who may have similar problems and joys to yourself and probably similar training needs, at least where supporting your particular school is concerned. You will also be part of a large group called support staff [21K2].

Teams are not just groups of people working together; they have common aims and purposes and in schools if the group can meet, communicate and have good relationships they will achieve a consistency of practice [21K1]. It means teaching methods and discipline will be consistent and not confusing for pupils [21.1P1]. It means individual pupil needs can be shared and problems aired, where all the team members have respect for and trust each other and observe proper codes of confidentiality. Teams need members to play an active part, to speak openly and honestly, to know when to put themselves forward for tasks and when to take instructions from others [21.1P2, 3]. This takes thought and sometimes patience or initiative. An ideal team person can listen, yet contribute when they have something to say or do, and help others achieve their tasks. Each has their role to play in a team, has individual characteristics and strengths of use to the team purpose [21K5]. As people are different, from differing backgrounds and experiences, there will be a range of possibilities within the group. If you consider what you can contribute, try to find out what the others can contribute as well, and how this can make things go more smoothly [21.2P6, 7;

21K3, 4]. In order for the team to work, they do need to meet from time to time, ensure they understand what they are trying to achieve, learn more about the methods needed to achieve it and review the relevance of this to their day-to-day working practices [21.1P5, 6; 21.1P3–5]. Lacey (2001: 58) suggests that 'what is needed is a combination of the best long term personal education with the relevance of institution based projects, with particular help for participants in transferring learning to practice'.

Examples of good practice

A team of TAs in a primary school met for half an hour every Wednesday morning during assembly as well as informally in the staffroom. It was they who suggested using a common feedback form in every class for the teacher, as they went into different classes from time to time. The teachers were highly delighted and the ICT-literate TA produced the trial templates for the whole school to use.

Another primary school TA team met every half-term with the head, and then had the odd meeting with the SENCO. They so enjoyed these meetings they asked for a regular weekly session. They determined together what the agenda for such a meeting could be and the head allocated financial resources to support these meetings after school. As they had been in the habit of voluntarily helping the teachers clear up at the end of some days, they found they could manage their family circumstances for a short time once a week to ensure they could attend the meetings. The head considered the financial outlay well worth the cost in terms of increased team spirit and professional development. Learning together had welded the team and enhanced the learning opportunities for the pupils.

TAs in a secondary school had been appointed over the years to address individual pupils' needs. The SENCO had always line-managed the team successfully but began to realise that, as the team grew, so did the expectations of the teachers as to what they could be asked to do. She asked the TAs to discuss the problem. She was prepared to put in some extra training in curriculum areas and was already sounding out the heads of departments with the idea of having their input on the training. The idea came up of having the TAs more team based in subject areas, but she was reluctant to let go the SEN element of the team. The TAs pointed out that there could be up to three of them in one classroom with a teacher if the pupils with SEN happened to be seated together for certain subjects. The SENCO, again with discussion with her line manger, the TAs and the heads of department, decided on a full review of the systems of support. This entailed a review of job descriptions, resource base, training programmes and IEP fulfilment programmes. It took a year to complete, but the end result was a series of TA teams, each based with a subject department or group of them, and each having a team leader who met regularly with the SENCO to ensure individual pupil needs were met. Reviewing the strengths of the team members meant that each TA could be placed where they were most able to contribute, and each teacher got a support system addressing both the needs of the pupils and the classroom or laboratory circumstances. Parents were unhappy at first, because of the break-up of the individual attention for their child, but slowly they realised the benefits of the team approach.

There can be weak or difficult members of the team, and part of the strength of a group is that the stronger ones can support the weaker ones in times of stress. Each member can feed back to another when things have gone well. It is up to the team leader to see that individuals pull their weight and are not continually carried by the rest. Being part of a team means that, if you are ill, there should be someone who can take over your work at short notice. You should always keep sufficient records, securely, preferably in a way decided by the team so that they can easily be interpreted and your work can be continued in your absence [21.1P4; 21K12–15].

Sometimes differing personalities can cause conflict but differing opinions can be healthy, provided discussion is constructive. As a team member you need to speak your mind appropriately as well as listen to your colleagues and acknowledge their views [20K33; 21K6]. You can see that, in the example given above, there could easily have been conflict if no one in the TA team wanted to work in a laboratory, or if the review had found some of the TAs were actually redundant, because of the doubling up in some lessons where it was not necessary. Such situations have to be handled sensitively and within proper personnel guidelines to ensure that people are not hurt unnecessarily by potentially negative situations [21K9–11]. You also need to distinguish between professional and personal relationships. While friendships may develop when working in a team, they should not take precedence over the purpose of the team or the way in which it works [21K7]. You will probably have a team leader, and as a more experienced TA you may become a leader of a small team.

If so, this should be written into your job description, paid time given to you to perform what is required and the rate of pay commensurate with the responsibilities required of you [21K5]. A team leader may have to take decisions and ensure that the rest of the team abide by them, or by decisions made by the team collegially. The same procedures should apply to teams as to individuals; that is, if there is misunderstanding or even conflict which the group themselves cannot resolve, then the next in the hierarchy should become involved – your line manager if you are individually concerned. As in any situation you should be honest and accurate in your dealings with superiors, not stretching the truth because you do not like someone. There will be reviews of the ways in which the team works, because circumstances have changed, the membership of the group or the needs of the pupils have changed, or there are new initiatives coming along [21.1P1]. You can use this opportunity to share your ideas; as an experienced person you will have much to contribute and can help the group move forward constructively [21.1P7, 8; 21K8].

Relationships within and between the school teams

The good practice guidance (DfES 2000) has a section about teachers and TAs working cooperatively and learning together, which requires meeting together largely outside the classroom and needs joint commitment and partnership. Another section looks at TAs' attendance at functions, the involvement of governors, parents and visiting advisers in liaising and linking with TAs, and liaison within the schools between relevant senior staff and TAs; and yet another is about meetings, liaisons and communication. All of these will require the understanding, funding and action of the senior management team. Although this document is meant for managers it is available free from the DfES and can be downloaded from their website (www.teachernet.gov.uk/teachingassistants).

MacBeath and colleagues give the five key features of good relationships in schools as:

- there is a shared sense of teamwork among all staff;
- older pupils help younger ones;
- bullying is not tolerated;
- parents and governors feel welcomed and valued in the school;
- people address one another in ways which confirm their value as individuals.

(MacBeath, Boyd and Bell 1996:36)

These things could all take place if each individual was committed to it, but 'Teamwork leads to better decisions and speedier completion of work through the pooling of expertise and the sharing of tasks' (Hargreaves and Hopkins 1991:37).

Leading a team

Attributes of a leader were discussed in Chapter 2. Standards 62 to 69 are very helpful in delineating some of the skill and knowledge you would need for this aspect of your work.

Standard 57, organising cover for colleagues, also contains many similarities. Managing resource areas, libraries or events calls for different skills and specific knowledge of the area concerned but similar strengths of reliability, questioning, imagination and creativity that you should bring to your everyday job. The personal characteristics required for leading a team were discussed in the previous chapter. Standard 63 is specifically about this, with a useful list of behaviours which they suggest underpin effective performance. Standards 64–67 are all about leading or managing people and have similar lists of behaviours. Some attributes are common to each of these standards. Taking all the attributes mentioned in Standards 63, 64, 65 and 67, ask yourself:

Do you:

- recognise the opportunities presented by the diversity of people?

- find practical ways to overcome barriers?

- inspire others with the excitement of learning?

- articulate a vision that generates excitement, enthusiasm and commitment?

- create a sense of common purpose?

- take personal responsibility for making things happen?

- make complex things simple for the benefit of others?

- encourage and support others to take decisions autonomously?

- act within the limits of your authority?

- clearly agree what is expected of others and hold them to account?

- prioritise objectives and plan work to make the best use of time and resources?

- make time available to support others?

- state your own position and views clearly and confidently in conflict situations?

- show integrity, fairness and consistency in decision-making?

- seek to understand people's needs, feelings and motivations and take an active interest in their concerns?

- recognise the achievements and success of others?

- take pride in delivering high quality work?

- model behaviour that shows respect, helpfulness and cooperation?

- encourage and support others to make the best use of their abilities?

- remain vigilant for possible risks and hazards?

- confront performance issues and sort them out directly with the people involved?

- say no to unreasonable requests?

You need to be able to plan for you and for your team, understand their objectives as well as your own, what kind of support, advice, resources and training they might need and what kind of standards they should work to. You can see the commonality between this set of standards so it is easy to see why the TDA are limiting the number of these standards which can be taken for an NVQ qualification to two.

If you are responsible for your team's performance management and target setting, do ask to get proper training yourself for this as it can be a very sensitive area. Standard 65 is particularly about allocating and checking work. Make sure that both you and your appraisee understand the proper procedures, protocols and purpose of such a situation so that it does not cause undue conflict. It is most important that you and the appraisee have copies of the school's policies and that you do everything 'by the book'. The potential for problems is greatly increased if the process is formal. You should have copies as a member of staff being appraised anyway, but when you become an appraiser it behoves you to go through it even more carefully. You should also have a copy of the discipline and grievance procedures, but this is often not looked at until there is a problem. If you want to be properly prepared to deal with problems or hopefully prevent them happening, it is vital that you read these policies and question anything you don't understand or disagree with before any event. You are then aware of the processes. Always ask for help from a more senior member of staff if you need it. Unions can be helpful sources of advice, documentation and maybe even training. Teachers and heads are relatively new to these processes compared with industry or businesses, so don't be afraid to seek help and advice. It is someone else's life and work that is at stake.

Standard 64 is about leading in a particular area of expertise, where you are more in the role of teacher than line manager, you are having to impart skills and knowledge rather than enhance another's performance. Standard 67 is very similar but is more about providing a knowledge base than a skill base. Take to heart all the points on learning style and methods meant for you in this book and consider their needs. Standard 66 is about leading and motivating volunteers. Motivation is important in whatever you do. Leading volunteers can be difficult in that they do not have the training, may not have the skills that you have, and will be much less aware of the health and safety issues involved in a task than you are. A particular case which may come your way is briefing and leading a group of parents on a school trip. While the teacher will be in charge, they may leave this aspect to you so you must make particularly clear what is expected. Volunteers also really appreciate being valued and thanked for their effort simply because they are unpaid and have volunteered. Simple things like a tea party or a letter can mean a lot.

Standard 68 is about mentoring a colleague. This is a very worthwhile exercise as you will know well; hopefully you are being mentored yourself for your Level 3. You can do the same for a colleague undertaking a Level 2 award or the literacy and numeracy Level 2 qualifications. Standard 69 is about becoming an assessor for the NVQ itself, again something which is becoming more common as NVQs and similar qualifications are more widely known. As it is an official position, where the award (or not) of a qualification is at stake, it is essential that all the proper procedures, documentation and criteria are followed implicitly. As you are most likely aware, the procedure is a paper chase but the exact defining of a task can be a most helpful discussion point.

Questions to ask yourself

- With whom do I come into contact at my workplace?
- Do I need to give more thought to how I get on with the other adults in general?
- Are there any colleagues I need to spend more time with or try to understand better?
- Do I have favourites among the pupils and does it show?
- Do I have any problems with adults or pupils which I should talk over with someone?
- Do I know of any problems with pupils relating to each other that I should report to someone?
- Would I like to specialise in this area and get training in counselling?
- Of which teams am I part?
- Am I playing my part?

Some further reading

DfEE (2000a) *Working with teaching assistants: A good practice guide*.

Dunne, E. and Bennett, N. (1994) *Talking and learning in groups*.

Lacey, P. (2001) *Support partnerships*.

Vincett, K., Cremin, H. and Thomas, G. (2005) *Teachers and assistants working together*.

Watkinson, A. (2008b) *Leading and managing teaching assistants*.

Williams, T., Wetton, N. and Moon, A. (1989) *Health for life: Health education in the primary school*.

Useful website

www.teachernet.gov.uk/teachingassistants

Working in the school team

Being part of the whole-school team

AS WELL AS BEING PART of the TA and classroom teams, you are a member of the whole-school team. You need to know where you fit into the hierarchy, who does what and when, how the systems and structures of your school work for communication and consultation. Chapters 2 and 3 suggested that you put together a school staff structure, so you should know to whom you can go for help in various aspects of your work.

The governors have the responsibility for the standards of the school and the ways in which those are carried out, and also for the budget and the staffing. For the everyday running of the school, they appoint a chief executive, a professionally trained person – the headteacher. The head will be assisted by various deputies or assistant heads depending on the size of the school, and will delegate much of the teaching and business side of the school to various staff. There will be a teacher who is head of department or coordinator for each curriculum subject or aspect, such as health education and SEN. There will be someone to whom you can go about health, safety and security matters, equipment repair, ICT support, finance problems or other areas of school work. There may be other posts of responsibility such as inclusion coordinator or head of pastoral care. You must find out to whom you go for what and when. You must cooperate with them when needed and develop as good a working relationship as you can, always abiding by the policies and procedures within the school.

Look at this list and check how you feel about it, and then discuss it with your mentor. Is there anything you two together can do to improve any ways of working in your school?

Teams are working well when:

- members are clear what needs to be done, the time-scale involved and who is to do what;
- members feel they have a unique contribution to make to the work of the team;
- a climate of trust encourages the free expression of ideas, suggestions, doubts, reservations and fears;
- individual talents and skills are used effectively;
- members are able to discuss alternative approaches and solutions before taking decisions;
- there are established ways of working together which are supportive and efficient in the use of time;
- progress is checked regularly and members are clear about whom they report to and when.

(Hargreaves and Hopkins 1991:137)

Some schools have tried teambuilding techniques, similar to those found in some industries and businesses. Sometimes they can provide a bit of light relief on an otherwise intense in-service education and training (for teachers) (INSET) day, and participating in these, or any school based meeting, will help you feel part of the whole school. If there is a consultation of any kind, do make an effort to take part; you should have your say in formulating policy as well as carrying it out. Any kind of working together helps. Balshaw's (1999) book is designed for SENCOs and other TA team leaders and is largely made up of exercises that teachers and TAs can do together to enhance their working relationships. She gives a health warning that schools need to have a collaborative culture before embarking on the exercises; otherwise they could throw up discussions that some people feel uncomfortable with.

Collaboration:

- creates a commitment to a common purpose among governors, head and staff and the school's partners;
- improves communication and reduces misunderstanding;
- fosters creativity in finding solutions when problems are discussed;
- enhances motivation;
- prevents individuals from becoming isolated;
- generates a sense of collective achievement;
- supports teamwork.

(Hopkins and Hargreaves 1991:137)

Kerry (2001:60) talks about promoting 'creative dissatisfaction' through what he calls 'superteams'. These are teams who:

- constantly re-visit what they are trying to achieve;
- are persistent;
- set high expectations and standards;
- are highly committed to each other and to the task;
- communicate effectively with others;
- are proactive;
- bring in others to help the work of the team;
- prioritise and hit their targets;
- are never fully satisfied.

Your effectiveness and potential is not just down to you, it is also a question of how things work in the school. A lot of research on how organisations work – schools and others – was published in *The fifth discipline* (Senge 1990). This book was seminal in explaining how good organisations work. In 2000 he followed it up with *How schools learn*, based on the use of the first book in schools (Senge *et al.* 2000). His main premise is that organisations or schools that continue learning as a whole team are successful. He divided his arguments into five main disciplines:

- Each individual needs *personal mastery* of the tasks that they are employed to do. Everybody should be involved in continuous professional development assisted by performance management which need not be heavy.
- Everyone should participate in the *shared vision*. Any of you who are in a school which has achieved Investors in People status will understand this. Knowing the statement in

the prospectus is not enough. It means everyone knowing what is important in their school and for their school. It will influence ways of appointing staff as well as what staff to appoint. It is about following the collegiate values, which could mean that you compromise on your personal values or even leave that school.

■ In the school there are ways of talking about everything that is shared, staff have *mental models* so that you can reflect on what has happened and discuss it, even if that is uncomfortable. For instance, comments from even simple performance reviews – asking questions about what you enjoy or do not enjoy about your job and what would make it better can surprise headteachers, but good ones will make changes because of them. It is about a shared understanding of vocabulary, use of resources and ways of treating people.

■ Things get done and new ideas can be tried out where there is *team learning* – small groups that work together to transform their thinking or mobilise their actions.

■ Senge called the fifth discipline *systems thinking* or joined-up thinking. This is where the teams talk and work together, where colleagues learn to understand each other, people are interdependent and no one person has all the answers. Schools that work collegially work well.

It is tempting to think that these systems all come from the top, the head or the senior management team, but they do not work unless you personally go along with the other four disciplines and follow the systems. You should be striving to have personal mastery, you must have vision and ideas, understand relationships, so that you help bring about change by discussing ideas, dealing with people. As an experienced TA, you can think strategically. Learning and leadership needs to be replicated right through the school so that it operates as a learning community, not a fragmented set of individuals. Where the school is secure in its aims, and has a positive ethos and collaborative culture, where relationships are good and team members can challenge each other with respect, the systems and procedures will provide the machinery to carry out the aims. Adults and pupils enjoy their time in the school and provide enhanced opportunities for learning.

Working with adults other than teachers

Parents can be totally self-centred or child-centred and make remarks like 'I don't care about the other 200 children, my child will do something different'. Visiting specialists can be arrogant or misunderstand the limitations of a building or its lack of resources and may underestimate the time required to carry out their directions. Governors may ignore you, members of your team may expect you to do more than you should. You will need patience, sensitivity and understanding but also firmness. The parent may not understand the health and safety issues behind a particular directive, the specialist may be new to the job, the governor following a different train of thought, and the member of your team having a domestic crisis [20.4P2]. Your life experience will help you deal with situations. If you are young and this is you first job or you are worried about a situation, ask for help from your line manager or from a teacher you get on well with. Don't bottle up anxieties, but instead share problems [20.4P5, 6; 20K30–33].

Visiting specialists

Not all your work will be with staff employed by the school. TAs increasingly work directly with advisers and specialists visiting the school, again under the guidance of teachers. This is particularly true if their job is concerned with pupils with SEN. You may be trained by physiotherapists or occupational therapists for particular tasks like exercises needed daily to maintain flexibility or assist pupils with conditions such as cystic fibrosis. Not all visiting agencies are educational professionals; these two just mentioned are employed by health authorities. Some are educational professionals: teachers or TAs who are members of SEN, inclusion or behaviour management teams, educational psychologists, educational welfare officers (EWOs) or similar. The ECM agenda and the 2004 Children Act have specifically decreed that schools should work more closely with professionals from other disciplines. All LAs now have a department called Children's Services or similar where family social workers and education professionals come under the same umbrella. Children's Trusts are expected to be set up in all areas by the end of 2008. These bring together all services for children and young people in an area, and there may be several in any one LA, especially if the areas are large. The idea is that they will support those who work every day with children, young people and their families so that they experience more integrated and responsive services, and specialist support. People will work in multi-disciplinary teams, be trained jointly to tackle cultural and professional differences.

Schools or children's centres are recommended to become the centres for this local liaison, to include social workers, the police and health workers. So, school staff will become increasingly familiar with joined-up working regarding both particular children and planning. What kind of progress has been made in this direction will depend on your local circumstances. Standard 62 is specifically geared to those of you who do a lot of this kind of work. If you are in a special school it is likely that a great deal of your time will be spent in liaising with one professional or another in order to gain the expertise necessary to support the pupils.

All of the things mentioned in terms of good relationships apply whether the person you are working with is inside or outside the school team. The main difference to working with school staff is that the visitor will have a line manager outside the school and be working to their agenda, not the school's. They may not have the school experiences that you have had and so not realise the possibilities or restrictions that can apply. On the other hand, they will have visited many different schools and have a good repertoire of alternative ways of doing things. By talking, sharing and cooperating you will learn a lot and help your colleague increase the value of what you do for the pupils in our care. There may be particular protocols or procedures to observe, additional to those in the school, so you do need to be clear about the groundrules that will apply to your joint working. It is worth spending a little time on this at the beginning of your work together, just to make sure you understand how you will work together. You also need to recognise your own limitations if decisions are needed and when you should refer to a class teacher, a SENCO or other manager.

The following descriptions are very general and may vary from school to school and certainly from area to area.

- Educational psychologists (EPs) are experienced ex-teachers who have a first degree in psychology and additional training for their role. If working with the LA, they will have a group of schools for which they are responsible. They can give advice, even training, but their role is usually diagnostic and consultative.

- Psychiatrists and psychotherapists are medical doctors, working in the health service, and you are unlikely to have contact with them.

- Special needs support teachers are ex-teachers who have considerable SEN experience in mainstream or special schools, and may well have postgraduate SEN qualifications. They usually belong to an LA team and visit several schools in the course of a week. They can give advice and training and often work directly with pupils or with teams of TAs.

- Therapists will work under the health service. The three main types visiting schools are speech therapists, who can help with language acquisition as well as the actual formation of sounds by pupils; physiotherapists, who help with physical mobility problems; and occupational therapists, who also help with coordination problems, helping pupils access normal life routines.

- Educational Welfare Officers (EWOs) are employed by the LA and monitor school absences and do home visits to support families with problems. They may also be involved in child protection issues.

- Social workers who work with children will come under a social services section of Children' Services. They used only to be involved in schools over child protection issues but increasingly are working proactively with schools and families.

- The police may visit the school on a community policing/liaison role – a 'meet the local bobby' kind of visit, doing the 'never go with strangers' and similar talks – but this type of work is very patchy and depends on local resources. Some schools in very difficult areas may have a police presence for staff protection or issues involving weapons from time to time, but this is still rare. Otherwise, police visits will probably be in connection with a specific incident and they will probably involve the appropriate senior manager.

- Other visiting advisers or specialists such as librarians or ICT technicians used to be dealt with only by teachers, but increasingly specialist TAs may well be the communicating point with them. They may be from the LA, or working for some private company or freelance.

It is vital that you also have lines of communication with the pupil's tutor or class teacher to ensure that appropriate information from your work with any visiting specialist is regularly passed on, and records are kept up to date. You will have to use your judgement about this. A teacher will not want to know of minor changes to regular routines but must know if there is any deterioration in the condition of the pupil detected by the experts, or any changes to routines that will affect the pupil when they are not with you. You must keep accurate and clear records of any meeting or work with such specialists where the teacher is not also present, and these should be accessible to the teacher or SENCO in the event of your illness or departure. They must also be kept in a secure place, as obviously such records are confidential to the school. As well as leaving records, ensure that someone else knows how to support the particular pupil or resource base about which you have been consulting the outside adviser. This may be in written form or by demonstrating a skill that you have been taught.

Visits of governors, inspectors and assessors

You will find that you are either talking to or being observed by someone from this group of people from time to time. Their purpose will vary to an extent but they are all concerned with your wider accountability. You are directly accountable to your class teacher, line manager or the person who has been appointed your supervisor under the proposed regulations. Your assessor may be an in-school person but is quite likely to be someone from the college or organisation where you are studying if you are aiming for a Level 3 qualification. The governors and inspectors are concerned with the effectiveness of the teaching and learning in the school, of which you are part. All three may directly observe you and record what they see and give comments. Assessors should share this with you completely; their purpose should be your increasing competence and confidence. Talking to them is part of your training.

Governors will probably talk to you and the class teacher and may write a visit note for the headteacher, of which you could have a copy. Inspectors may observe your work as part of an observation of the teacher. Only very occasionally do they make a direct observation of you. Of course, with revisions of the Framework for Inspection which occur every few years and the continuing spotlight on yourselves, observations may increase in frequency although with short inspections there is much less lesson observation anyway. Inspectors will not show you their written record, but should give you feedback if you request it; they do this with teachers. None of these people should be intimidating and, if they are, you should tell your line manager immediately. They should all be working to various codes of practice, which direct them to be properly professional in their approaches to staff. Intimidation does not produce the best results from those being observed and could be detrimental to your work with pupils. If you are able to talk to them, be honest and open and listen to what they have to say; they usually have a lot of experience of various kinds and may have some helpful ideas for you. Keep a dated note of any visits, the occasion, purpose and outcomes, along with a copy of any related paperwork.

Working with parents and carers

Standard 60 deals with relating to parents, carers and families and is a particularly useful one to read through even if you are not specifically undertaking a liaison role. It lists a variety of communication methods and differences which can create barriers, all of which apply to any relationship with adults. It talks particularly of being professional, respectful, open, welcoming and non-judgemental in order to develop trust. It itemises matters like the importance of location and timing in providing conditions which help discussion. The proverbial cup of tea or coffee can make all the difference to breaking down barriers of shyness or even anger. It is very important that you observe all the proper protocols of confidentiality set by the school when talking to parents, not gossiping. Make sure that you are understood. You may feel like a colleague parent, but you can slip into school jargon after quite a short time working in a school. Keep notes and records properly. It is really helpful if you can have day-to-day contact with parents so that you can share the good things, then if you do have to contact them about a problem, the relationship is already on a trusting footing. Often TAs can be a very helpful link with parents as you often come from the community yourself and so you will understand the various contexts from which the families come. Increasingly schools are receiving children from diverse cultures and backgrounds, so always be sensitive to these. Family traumas can affect a parent coming to talk about their child, and this can make them seem aggressive when actually they are anxious. Also remember that children of quite a young age may be carers themselves.

If you are home visiting [STL 52], as part of working as a parent/carer, family liaison worker [STL 60] or dealing with attendance matters [STL 51], you have to be particularly careful not to be judgemental and to recognise that you are in someone else's home, whatever you may think of their decor, tidiness or way of life. However, you may discreetly pick up clues as to why the child or young person concerned is behaving in the way they are. In all that you do, you must recognise that you are working with pupils who are someone's children. You may be a member of the school who is *in loco parentis* – acting as a caring parent while the child is with you – but this does not give you 'parental rights'. Home has a significant central role to play in all our lives. School only provides contact for between 25 and 30 hours a week for 38 weeks a year for 10 years of a child's life. Around that time there may well be lengthy periods of care from nurseries, child minders, clubs and friends' homes, but these will all be controlled by the home, not the school, except perhaps for nursery classes, breakfast and after-school clubs and games. Every family will have different needs and traditions. The vast majority of parents have the best intentions for their children, even if they sometimes appear misguided.

The Children Act 1989 gives parents rights and responsibilities, intending that families are to be respected and given help in coping with the difficulties in bringing up children. The school will deal with matters concerning parental rights and who is eligible for these in the cases of separation and changing of partners in the child's home. You must be guided by more senior school staff if there is any doubt over matters of care. Very occasionally there can be disputes over responsibility which spill over into school, as when acrimonious divorces end up in 'tug of love' problems, court orders and even very rare cases of abduction by one partner of children from the school. It is not your place to try to intervene, but do follow instructions in the rare cases of anxiety. Information and access must only be given to authorised people. Be very clear what can and cannot be communicated and what the school policies are on releasing pupils from the school.

The teacher should have written permission for the child to leave other than at the ends of sessions, and at that point there will be clear procedures for pupils leaving, especially the younger ones or where transport is involved. There will be clear policies and procedures within the school for parent–school relationships, some schools even having a formal signed agreement as to the various roles, rights and responsibilities of parents, pupils and the school. Make sure you have a copy of this and understand its significance for your work. Establish your role and boundaries in dealing with parents as early as possible. Always report difficulties and pass on requests to the class teacher or tutor concerned, possibly in writing and dated to ensure that they get the message – post-it notes are invaluable for such quick communications. Keep a careful diary of visits or meetings, with dates and a brief note of why the event took place and of the outcome. Parents or carers should be aware and be able to read anything you write and have agreed with you any action that you or they are to take.

The relationship of parents and carers with TAs varies with the school and the needs of the pupils. Where the pupil has distinct physical needs, it makes sense that the TA liaises directly with the parents or carers to report on any changes in their needs. In some cases of supporting pupils with SEN, it becomes more useful and appropriate for the TA to deal directly with the parents. In other schools, there is little or no direct contact between the TAs and parents. If you are hoping to show your competence in this area for accreditation purposes [Standards 51, 52 and 60], you need to be working in a school that recognises the possibilities of TAs liaising directly with parents or carers. Carers may be of different status: they could be daily child minders who bring and collect pupils from the school; they could be foster parents, grandparents or partners of one of the blood parents. It is not your role to sort this out, but it is your role to know with whom you are dealing and what each person's responsibility is before embarking on prolonged conversations. You could be betraying confidences, and putting yourself in a compromising situation.

Check with the class teacher your exact role and what information is relevant and allowed for you to pass on to the parents from school. Also, remember to communicate with the teacher whenever you feel parental information should be passed on to them. This is particularly important when there are changes in parental circumstances, which, however positive, may affect the emotional state of the pupil and hence their capacity to work well at school or maintain their normal relationships. Do not get into conversations that rightly should be held with the teacher either about a pupil's academic progress or about more domestic matters. It is definitely not your place to make any comment on the home situation to parents, however strongly you feel. If you are worried about the welfare of the pupil, discuss this with the class teacher or tutor, not the parents or carers, and take their advice. Different cultures have differing standards, values and practices, and you and other school staff must have regard for home background and parents' wishes. For instance, there may be questions of dress, or modes of address and preferred names. You must be guided by the teachers in these matters, and any concerns should go through them.

In some schools, communication can be by note, such as with the pupils in a unit for the hearing impaired, who are bussed to school. Here, for instance, notes could accompany the hearing aids if there were problems. Do word any notes carefully, remembering to use the minimum of educational jargon, and having regard for the language needs of the parents concerned. Sometimes TAs are closer to the parents in that they often live in the vicinity of the school and may be parents of children in the school themselves. The way in which you talk to pupils and deal with situations that might arise in front of the parents can give positive images of child care and respect for the pupil. Develop positive relationships with parents whenever you can, showing respect and giving reassurance.

An example of good practice

In Hawthornberry Secondary School, the TAs are part of the SEN support team, and part of their defined role is to liaise with parents regarding day-to-day needs. They sit in on any visit of the parent to the school where logistically possible, although sometimes they may have responsibilities elsewhere in the school. Some do primary school visits and home visits with the SENCO, and attend the induction meeting for parents. They have full copies of the IEPs, provide reports for SEN reviews, and attend the review meetings. TAs are present on parents' consultation evenings and are available to liaise directly with parents over the implementation of specific teaching programmes designed for individual pupils. Where the pupil has severe physical needs, requiring intimate help from the TA, the TA completes the home/school diary, as does the parent, monitoring any significant changes in the pupil's condition or circumstances. This same diary is completed where the TAs are providing the physiotherapy assistance in the lunch break, and messages from the physiotherapist are often passed on in this way. Where the parents are in full-time employment and release is difficult for direct parent–therapist communication a TA can act as a useful go-between, without worrying the teachers. The diary also acts as a record in the event of TA illness.

Now mobile phones are so ubiquitous that the TAs are, by arrangement, able to contact the parent or carer at the beginning of a day if there is an unexplained absence or at the end of the day if it has been a good one or there has been a problem. In some cases, with the knowledge and written permission of both parent and tutor, a TA has accompanied a pupil to an out-of-school appointment such as for an eye test. Some of the TAs have been involved in the parent literacy class run by the school one afternoon a week, which has helped to cement relationships for the future. Two TAs come from the same ethnic group as a large majority of the school population and this has been invaluable for communication with parents whose English is not yet fluent enough to cope with school jargon, and for internal school discussions on the needs of a community with differing cultural backgrounds.

The Code of Practice (DfES 2001) suggests that TAs be included in IEP reviews, and the training of TAs for secondary schools promotes this kind of involvement. The chapter on working in partnership with parents (pp. 16–19), while meant for SENCOs and other senior managers, is worth reading to get a flavour of the way in which this should go. It defines parental responsibility and recognises the importance of the partnership of parents and school. It promises positive attitudes, user-friendly information and procedures. For instance, it suggests (p. 17) that:

To make communications effective professionals should:

- acknowledge and draw on parental knowledge and expertise in relation to their child;
- focus on the children's strengths as well as areas of additional need;
- recognise the personal and emotional investment of parents and be aware of their feelings;
- ensure that parents understand procedures, are aware of how to access support in preparing their contributions and are given documents to be discussed well before meetings;
- respect the validity of offering different perspectives and seek constructive ways of reconciling different viewpoints;
- respect the differing needs parents themselves may have, such as a disability or communication or linguistic barriers;
- recognise the need for flexibility in the timing and structure of meetings.

TAs have not voiced problems over themselves being parents of children at the school, although one problem which then faces TAs is how to deal with enquiries from anxious parents who see the TA as a source of information on what goes on in the school. This reinforces the importance of knowing and following the school code of confidentiality.

Working with volunteers in school [66]

This is very like working as a team leader so look at the sections in the previous two chapters which refer to characteristics needed of you personally as a team leader and the relationships you may have with other adults. There is one big difference: you will not be involved in any formal kind of performance review. If you are concerned about what the volunteer is doing you may be able tactfully and privately to suggest they do it differently, but you should refer anything other than minimal concerns to the class teacher. This is not 'telling tales'; it is the pupils who will suffer if things go wrong. Be as helpful as you can and praise wherever possible without being patronising. Think about getting pupils to organise a thank-you party.

They will need guidance on school policies and procedures, maybe even copies of some, and may well need help in finding their way about, finding resources and developing techniques just as you did when you started. You may be in the position of actually training volunteers, either generally or for a specific outing or event. Just be as organised as you can; they must have a proper briefing. For instance, have paper lists prepared, and make sure they know all the appropriate health and safety procedures and have access to communication systems. Be proactive, you are the professional. You could even consider going through Standard 3 with them at some point. Check with your line manager that they approve.

School policies and procedures

As the whole-school team will consist at the very minimum of about ten people even in the smallest school, and could consist of several hundred people, written policies and guidelines are in place to ensure consistency and compliance with the law. Parental and volunteer involvement in schools, governors' and parents' rights and responsibilities, along with the increasing recognition of the need to take heed of the views of pupils, mean that consultation and paperwork have become a regular part of school life. This means that you, as a member of staff, must make very sure you know your role and responsibilities within the system and take opportunities to participate in debates about any changes. These policies and procedures may seem bureaucracy gone mad, but they do provide the skeleton on which the flesh of the body of the school can fix and so become a working organism. They lay out everything from the common aims and purposes of everyone associated with the school – essential to enable the teams to have their purpose – to the ways in which individual pupils are to be treated in varying circumstances. They also act as protection if there are complaints or accidents. If things have been done according to the policies, then there is no cause for complaint.

The main document determining the work of the school is the School Development or Improvement Plan (SDP/SIP). This is the business plan of the organisation and should be reviewed annually. As part of this review, there should be a cycle of reviews of all the policies in place in the school. The total number of these will be considerable, and you do not need to know the content or have them all. A master copy should be available for anyone to consult when required, but there are some policies which you do need not only to have but also to know and understand. Many schools now have all the policies on their intranet, with standalone computers in the staffroom so that there is access for anyone to consult them.

It is really interesting to look at the list below to consider what is legally required against what is necessary. Most of the standards require that you know and understand the:

- setting's procedures for . . .
- laws governing . . .
- regulations associated with . . .
- relevant legal requirements for . . .
- policies for . . .
- legislation, guidelines and policies which form the basis of action . . .
- awareness of good practice in . . .
- school policy and practice in relation to . . .
- agreed principles for . . .
- school's agreed code of conduct in . . .
- roles and responsibilities of yourself and others for . . .

Whatever the standard is, it is up to you to make sure you familiarise yourself with policies, procedures and practice. If you are not sure, then ask. The list below is not exclusive, nor does it list the most important ones for TAs. For instance there has to be a pay policy for teachers – is there one for support staff? Health and safety will contain many sections, most of which you need from the beginning, concerning emergency procedures and prevention procedures. No teaching and learning policy is required by law but most schools have them, guiding staff as to how teaching is to be done, as well as what is to be taught in the school. Target setting is required but assessment procedures are not.

Many schools do not have a specific policy for the use of their TAs except perhaps as part of the SEN policy; practice has grown up rather than being determined. It was hoped that the Workforce Remodelling exercise would clarify the roles of all support staff, but some schools seem to use TAs like sticking plaster to solve problems rather than employ people to fulfil a whole-school methodology. This may be an area in which you can take a lead as you grow into a senior role.

Some major school policies (those marked * are legally required as at January 2008)

- Health and safety*
    - health and hygiene, safety and security
    - risk assessments*
    - child protection*
- Curriculum*
    - English
    - mathematics
    - science, ICT, etc.
    - collective worship*
    - sex education*
- Teaching and learning strategies
    - assessment

- target setting*
- record keeping and confidentiality

■ SEN*
- systems for individual education and behaviour plans (IEPs and IBPs)
- independent learning

■ EAL
- pupil discipline (including anti-bullying)*
- what constitutes unacceptable behaviour
- dealing with conflict, restraint procedures
- rewards and consequences

■ Equal opportunities
- inclusion and access
- valuing cultural diversity
- racial equality*
- accessibility*

■ Management issues
- teachers' pay*
- performance management*
- any TA or support staff policies
- discipline, conduct and grievance*
- review of staffing*

■ Pupil issues
- registers*
- admissions*
- attendance targets*
- exclusions*

■ Parent and carer issues
- prospectus*
- home school agreements*
- freedom of information*
- complaints procedure*
- charging*
- annual report*

■ Governor issues
- instrument of government*
- minutes of meetings*
- allowances*
- register of business interests*
- school companies (where relevant)*.

Being a healthy school: health, safety and security procedures

One of the most useful exercises to do with young pupils, or those who have difficulty in expressing themselves verbally, is to get them to draw pictures. There are some excellent examples of this in *Health for life* (Williams, Wetton and Moon 1989).

You might like to try this for yourself

- Can you draw a healthy person? Describe one in words if you prefer.

- Now look at your drawing and answer a few questions for yourself.

  - Does age, gender, ethnic origin or religious belief matter?

  - Is diet or exercise important? Is being healthy only about visible, physical appearance?

  - Is mental capacity important? Does one have to be intelligent to be healthy?

  - Does happiness or sadness affect health? Does state of mind affect health?

  - What is a healthy mind? Is it part of having a healthy body?

  - Do attitudes to others and relationships matter?

  - Is family background, education, financial stability important?

  - Can a person in a wheelchair be healthy? Can a poor person be healthy?

- Now can you define a healthy school?

- What are the important factors affecting the all-round health of a school?

Although the following section is about obvious health issues, such as dealing with accidents and first aid, do not forget the importance of relationships which enable the school to function in a healthy way in the broadest terms. Schools should be providing not only an environment which is safe for exploring and growing bodies but also a learning environment for enquiring minds.

All employees have a duty to observe the in-house organisational requirements in this area [3K2]. There is considerable legislation governing health and safety at work, based on the 1974 Act and subsequent legislation such as the Management of Health and Safety at Work Regulations 1992. These indicate that establishments must have health and safety policies and carry out risk assessments for people, equipment and off-site activities. It puts the responsibility for health and safety on employers, which in the case of schools may be the LEA, the governing body, trustees or owners, depending on what type of school it is. The Health and Safety Executive produce some useful information leaflets and have local offices. However, all employees have a responsibility to observe local policies and take all reasonable precautions to keep themselves and others using the premises safe. This includes being personally vigilant for potential risks to adults or pupils. It does not mean you necessarily have to mend things or make things safe on your own, but you need to ensure that pupils in your care observe proper procedures. Your responsibilities regarding health and safety may be spelt out in your job description. The requirements for all staff in the areas of health, safety, security and supervision will be in writing somewhere; you need to find these.

All schools will have an appointed health and safety officer among the staff, usually a teacher, often linked with union affiliation. They will advise you if you have queries, and will take concerns to the appropriate quarter if you have any. Helping to keep children safe is a common mandatory standard for Level 2 and Level 3. The knowledge and understanding section is long and comprehensive, and rightly so. This stand must underpin all that you do, remembering your definition of a healthy school: it is not only about disinfectant, PE and school meals – important as they are – but also about care and attitudes and relationships [3K3]. You should know about the location of first-aid boxes, how to protect children and adults against accidents and how to use different equipment in emergencies. The standards apply to all pupils, whatever their special needs, to all colleagues and other adults or children who may be in the building, and to all areas of the school: in and out of the classroom, outside the school buildings and in places you might visit with pupils on an educational trip [3.2P5].

Even if you are not undertaking these units for accreditation purposes you should read this standard and be able to perform to all the four sets of criteria [3P1–4]. These items are required of all employees either by law or for the protection of all the people within the organisation.

Emergency and accident procedures

Before you even go to a classroom, you should know about fire alarms and procedures [3K1]. This includes how to evacuate the building, what to do if there is a bomb scare, an intruder or a missing child [3K16]. As a visitor to the school, you are usually asked to sign in so that the people responsible know who is in the building if there is an emergency. As a member of staff, it is assumed that you are on the premises if the timetable indicates you are. You need to familiarise yourself with the fire alarm points, the whereabouts of extinguishers and fire blankets and their use. Remember, if you are in laboratories or wherever hazardous liquids are about, there may be different kinds of extinguisher to use. Water should not be put on oil or electrical fires; it can make matters far worse. Carbon dioxide extinguishers or fire blankets will be available in vulnerable situations; check out how and when they should be used.

Usually the fire alarm is the signal for any evacuation of the building, whatever the cause. You need to ensure that any pupils in your charge behave appropriately at such times, 'silence' and 'walking only' usually being paramount. Both of these measures reduce panic as well as being something positive to maintain. All rooms should have evacuation instructions. If they do not, tell someone in the office.

If you are appointed to support a pupil with special physical needs, make sure you know where all their equipment is, and what you do with it in emergencies. An emergency could be personal to them or could arise in an evacuation procedure. A wheelchair may need a special route out of some areas, such as by a lift. Alert the SENCO if you have any worries [3K4].

First aid

All schools will have at least one appointed person responsible for ensuring that correct procedures are followed and probably a fully trained first-aider [3.2P2]. You need to find out who these people are and where they may be found at different times of the day. Cover of some kind should be available at all times when people are on the school premises. You do not need to have first-aid training but it helps, and schools usually have sessions every so often which deal with resuscitation, choking and bleeding and other simple procedures. Be wary of getting information from the internet or from books on home medicine unless you are sure of their validity, as some methods are not helpful. The Red Cross and St John Ambulance run courses in any community and will usually come to a specific venue to run a course if sufficient people are interested. These associations also publish useful manuals about first aid, at work and at home, for adults or children, some of which are available as

CD-ROMs. The details can be found on their websites. The school designated first-aider will have at least some of this training, and you will be told when and how you should use them. Common sense and experience, particularly of bringing up a family, can help you, but you must know your limitations both personally and within the procedures of the school [3K15]. You may become that trained first aider, or be made responsible for administering medicines [STL 43].

There may be a school nurse visiting on occasion or, very rarely nowadays, a school doctor. Visiting therapists such as occupational therapists, speech therapists and physio-therapists can be very helpful in giving information on how to cope with pupils with particular needs. There may also be religious or cultural 'dos and don'ts' with some pupils or staff, such as problems with removing certain items of clothing, and you need to be aware of these [10.2:v]. The important thing is not to panic, but to make a quick assessment of the situation. Usually your first port of call in any emergency will be the class teacher, but you may find yourself in a learning area out of sight of such a person. You need to know who can help and how to summon assistance. Find out where the trained first-aiders are situated, where people who deal with sick pupils are located, where first-aid materials are kept and who has access to them.

You should ensure you can recognise all the following emergencies, and know what to do, and what not to do:

a severe bleeding

b cardiac arrest

c shock

d fainting or loss of consciousness

e epileptic seizure

f choking and difficulty with breathing

g falls – potential and actual fracture

h burns and scalds

i poisoning

j electrocution

k substance abuse.

(LGNTO 2001 Level 3:46)

- Look for danger: you may have to deal with this.
- Remove any danger: only move the casualty if absolutely necessary.
- Assess the casualty: check for consciousness, open the airway, and check for breathing and pulse.
- Get help as soon as you can.

You should know what to do if a pupil has an accident, or if you have an accident, and you should know the procedures for dealing with the results of illness as well as with the sick pupils [3.2P3]. Remember that simple things such as reassurance and maintaining some privacy and calmness will help, whatever the situation [3.2P1, 4]. Afterwards, you may need to clear up vomit, urine, faeces or blood and you should find out about protective clothing for yourself, such as surgical gloves, whether to use sand, sawdust, disinfectant or not, and where to locate a site manager or other help. Sickness or accidents to one person can be a health risk to others.

Checklist

- Do you know your own limitations in first-aid skills?

- Do you know what is expected of you by the school?

- Are there any cultural or religious limitations to your possible actions of which you should be aware?

- Do you know to whom to turn for help?

- Where is the first aid box kept?

- Should you use it?

- What do you do when you have finished using it – whom do you tell about replacing items?

- What would you do if any of the above list happened to you? Or happened to a pupil in your care?

[3K13]

All incidents and accidents should be recorded somewhere in the school, along with the action taken, the time and cause, so be sure you ask about this as well when informing yourself about your appropriate action [3.2P6]. The reporting of major incidents can then be dealt with by the appropriate person. You should record incidents in which you are involved; check the requirements for your school. Most schools have notes which can be sent home, signed by someone in authority, to tell parents or carers of incidents in school. It may or may not be your responsibility to inform parents directly; it will depend on the pupil and the nature of the incident. For instance, bumped heads are always considered important, as symptoms of concussion can develop many hours after the incident, so the parents or carers need to be on the lookout for any problem, but the note may need to be signed by a senior member of staff, not by you.

Some chemicals and medical materials are not allowed in school, and all medicines should be properly secure. Do not administer medicines or apply ointments or plasters unless you are sure that it is all right to do so. Never use your own creams or lotions on a pupil. Always record your actions.

Child protection issues are more fully discussed in Chapter 7.

Equipment, materials and buildings

Prevention is better than cure and it is part of your responsibility as a member of staff, particularly one dealing closely with children and young people, to ensure your surroundings are hygienic and safe. You will need to get to know the routines for keeping the place tidy and clean as well as who is responsible for the environment – probably the site manager or caretaker – the equipment and materials including stock control, and allowing access to the premises and store rooms [3K10]. Be firm about school routines, but be careful. It is not your place to criticise or denigrate family customs, but to carry out the procedures recommended for your school. Gentle reminders can help; some pupils appear to have become used to people clearing up for them – that is not your job, but the safety of others is! You need to be a good role model where tidiness is concerned [3.1P6].

You may have to visit toilet areas to ensure they are being used properly; you may need to ensure young pupils wash their hands after using the toilet or before handling food [3.1P7]. Make sure you know the appropriate places for you and your pupils to eat or drink in your school. Remember families differ in their standards of tidiness and hygiene at home. Some religious groups have strict rules about eating particular foods, so be careful when commenting on the content of lunch bags. You need to be careful what foods you bring into the classroom for consumption, not only because some children have allergy problems but also because there is increasing concern over providing healthy diets [3K14]. Some schools have strict rules about handling soil or animals, most leave it to common sense; that is, wash your hands well after handling either [3.1P5]. Fewer schools actually keep animals these days but many still do. Do familiarise yourself with their care in case your particular pupils are interested. The RSPCA has a lot of information about the proper care of animals in schools as well as at home. This includes aquaria and ponds, as well as the more obvious creatures such as mammals. Some people are allergic to animal fur and even caterpillar hairs so always ask before bringing any animals to school yourself [3K9]. There is more about the learning environment, electrical and ICT safety in Chapter 10.

There may be occasions when gender is important; for instance, you may have care of a female pupil who begins to menstruate yet has not got any protection with her at school, or even to whom the event comes as a surprise. This can occur as young as eight years of age. Whatever gender you are, make sure you know the school's arrangements for accessing emergency supplies of protective clothing and disposal of soiled materials, and, if you are male, identify whom to go to for help should this condition become apparent to you. Some physically disabled girls may need intimate help at this time. Seek clear advice before undertaking this.

Make sure you report any problems with pupils carrying out your hygiene rules or creating unsafe situations to a teacher or to your line manager, as well as any hazard which you find while using any of the school's facilities. The named health and safety officer may need to be informed.

Health and safety procedures also include ensuring security procedures are observed, being alert for strangers and keeping locked the areas or equipment that should be away from general use [3.1P8]. Schools now contain much expensive equipment such as ICT and laboratory equipment, some of which is highly portable and desirable to thieves. Secondary schools probably have some dangerous chemicals and even radioactive materials in various stores. All of us have heard of the thankfully very rare but devastating acts of aggressive visitors to schools [3.1P2].

Risk assessment

This is not necessarily a complicated paper-based task for using dangerous chemicals or machinery but can become part of your everyday thinking. A simple example is teaching children to cross the road safely. You can teach them the Green Cross Code, but as they get older they will want to cross on their own, where it is not 'safe to cross', say from between parked cars. To do this they need to make a mental assessment of how dangerous the place is, how far they need to go out between the cars to see adequately after stepping off the kerb, whether they have the right footwear on to run, and so on. We take this kind of assessment for granted, but when in school we need to be alert for possible dangers, mentally assessing the risk of certain procedures. This does not mean not doing certain procedures which may be interesting or fun, but being sure before you undertake them that you have thought the process through [3K12; 45.2, 45.3]. Some activities, such as visits off site or use of certain chemicals, need formal risk assessments before they are undertaken. Risk assessments are routine procedures in science laboratories and DT (design and technology) areas.

- Keep a diary for a week of where you are working with pupils.
- Note any incidents – what did you do? Could these incidents have been prevented by any action you could have taken?

- Think of all the potential hazards that could have occurred during that week, e.g., spillages, falls, conflicts, injuries, breakages.

- How did you avoid them happening?

- Can you avoid more incidents in future by taking more care?

[3.1P3]

Communication systems

In order to familiarise yourself with the practice and procedures in the school you will have to watch, listen, read and ask questions. But things change either through a change in circumstance or by design. So there will be a constant updating of policies and new things will be introduced. It is vital that you tune in early to the communication systems with the school in order to keep abreast of news and changes. There will also be ways in which you communicate with others and keep records of your activities. Does your school do everything by word of mouth, paper-based systems, ICT or notice boards? If you think of the school as a live organism, then the communication system is like the blood circulation system. If you as a part of that body don't get your 'nutrients' then you will die. If other parts of the body are dependent on your actions, (as they are) they will be less effective if you do not communicate with them. It is worth carrying a small jotter and pencil with you or a small pack of Post-it notes so that you can write memos to yourself or leave a message.

You must also be aware of copyright laws when using the photocopier, and you must know the importance of accurate record keeping and the housing of records, the proper confidentiality of school issues, who to tell about what and the best way to tell them, and how to communicate with people outside the school staff. This includes whether you can use the school phone or your own mobile in the building, and the policy on the use of mobiles by the pupils for either school or personal business. Most schools are generous where personal matters are concerned provided they are asked and no costs are incurred. Appropriate ways of communication with parents should be clear, as should the procedures for contacting outside agencies. The use of email and access to the internet will also have its own guidelines, both for staff and for pupils. Use of and access to any school intranet may be necessary in some schools to keep up to date with school events or changes, and some schools also use email to contact parents.

You need to find out the best ways of communicating problems and who to turn to in different circumstances and where they might be found. Always be as clear as possible about the problem [22K30]. You also need to attend meetings and in-service days when applicable. These should be part of your contractual and paid time, as no one can operate properly in an organisation like a school without talking to and listening to colleagues and developing professionally within the organisation. If you are being asked to discuss work with pupils with teachers outside the pupil contact time you should make a strenuous effort to alter your working arrangements or even your contract to allow this. You cannot undertake work with pupils if you are not clear on the learning objective of the teacher and the circumstances of the particular lesson. It is also quite clear in the 'strongly recommended' guidance given by the members of the Workforce Agreement Monitoring Group (WAMG), which was based on the 2003 Education Act regulations and 2007 amended regulations that 'Supervision arrangements for all support staff undertaking activities to support teaching and learning should include time for teachers and support staff to discuss planning and pupil progress within the contracted hours of the support staff' (WAMG 2008 : 18). That is, you should not be talking to teachers about these matters in your 'goodwill' time.

Just a note of caution. In all your dealings with people inside and outside the school, particularly in using emails, do remember to keep your knowledge of school or class issues confidential. You are dealing with people's and children's lives. The only time you do not keep a confidence is if a child or person reveals a possible child protection issue when there are proper procedures to follow – see Chapter 7 on what to do in these circumstances.

Proactive communication

An experienced TA should be able to find out the communication pathways for instigating changes if you feel they are needed. You will see things that can be improved as you work longer in a place, so gain your confidence and discuss these with the appropriate people – your line manager or the head of department or class teacher. Politeness pays off, as does informing yourself well in advance of why things are as they are currently. There may be good historical reasons of which you are unaware. Standard 61 is about providing information to aid policy formation and the improvement of practices and provision, and is well worth reading if you are at all involved in consultation exercises or are considering requesting changes. The knowledge and understanding indicators give a useful list of things one has to consider when undertaking these exercises. A note on 61.1 states:

> **consultation** can include written, verbal, formal, informal, exchanging ideas and perspectives, making decisions, making recommendations and suggesting appropriate phrasing of policies and plans.

> **communicate** may include communication with individuals and groups within the school/community, colleagues outside the organisation, funders, management groups.

> **objectives and indicators of performance** that are quantitative, qualitative.
>
> (STL 61:2)

Finding measurable objectives and indicators of performance is always difficult in education where so much of value is difficult to quantify, and will be the hardest bit of such an exercise.

The main documents which affect school life are the SDP or SIP and the School Evaluation Form (SEF). The SEF is the evaluation of all the school's activities which forms the basis of any Ofsted inspection. The SDP/SIP is the school business or action plan which is drawn up as a result of the SEF and any other initiative the school wishes to introduce or is obliged to introduce. Find out when these documents are drawn up and by whom, and how any consultation processes operate. All members of the school community should be aware of their existence, how they affect their work and how they can inform their content. They must contain as much quantifiable data as possible for Ofsted purposes.

Questions to ask yourself

- Do you have copies of the policies that concern you?
- Have you read them? Do you understand your role in them?
- Have you identified the lead person for each of these policies?
- Do you need any training in first aid?
- Do you know what to do in an emergency wherever you are in the building, whatever pupils you are with, whatever you are doing?
- Do you know how the communication and consultation procedures work in your school?
- Are you prepared to participate in reviews and activities which help the school change for the better?

Essential reading

Standard 3 of the *National Occupational Standards for Supporting teaching and learning in schools* (TDA 2007).

Some further reading

Balshaw, M. (1999) *Help in the classroom.*

Balshaw, M. and Farrell, P. (2002) *Teaching assistants: Practical strategies for effective classroom support* (especially Chapters 10 and 11).

Blamires, M., Robertson, C. and Blamires, J. (1997) *Parent–teacher partnership.*

Bastiani, J. (1989) *Working with parents: A whole-school approach.*

DfES (2001) *Special Educational Needs code of practice.*

Williams, T., Wetton, N. and Moon, A. (1989) *Health for life: Health education in the primary school.*

Kerry, T. (2001) *Working with support staff: Their roles and effective management in schools.*

Useful websites

The Red Cross: www.redcross.org.uk

St. John's Ambulance: www.sja.org.uk

RSPCA: www.rspca.org.uk

Understanding how we develop and learn

The importance of studying how children grow and learn

LEARNING DEVELOPMENT has been a neglected area of study for those in teaching in recent years. The emphasis has been on curriculum delivery rather than how pupils learn. While it is clearly important that the teachers and TAs should know what they are teaching in terms of subject content, and that they should be both as accurate and as up to date as possible, there are two other factors always to be borne in mind: the way in which the subject matter is 'delivered' – the teaching methods, background and personality of the teacher (or TA, using 'teacher' in the widest sense) – and the characteristics of the learner – the one on the receiving end of the delivery.

This and the following chapters will look at various aspects of this matching process and how your understanding of these aspects will help you enhance the learning of the pupils with whom you work, starting with the learners themselves.

Learning development is much more widely used in considering the teaching and learning of pupils in the early years, where it used to be referred to as 'child' development; this very term has connotations of childhood and primary schools. It must be considered to cover the area of study from birth to adulthood, whenever that is supposed to be, and beyond. We never stop learning. When working in secondary schools or even tertiary colleges, an understanding of how the growth processes influence the way in which the pupils learn is important. Indeed, when undertaking new fields of study, most of us regress at times to methods learnt in childhood. The need to 'play around' with a new television, or 'fiddle about' with a new tool, is part of all our experience. Play is not confined to the early years, but is an essential part of learning. Standards 50 and 54 particularly refer to the play aspects of learning in schools.

Nor can we study the learning process in isolation; not only does the physical and emotional state of our bodies influence the way we learn and efficacy of our learning, but much of our intellectual development has a physical and emotional basis. Our social, cultural and spiritual selves also develop as we become adult, and continue to do so throughout our lives [18K5]. We are made up of all these facets, each influencing the others to produce a whole person. We have to try to see our pupils as whole human beings, yet in order to study the complexity which makes up the whole, we have to look at each facet separately. If these facets get out of balance, one develops but another does not, then the pupil, or adult, becomes frustrated, even disturbed. This can be seen sometimes in very bright children who are emotionally their chronological age, but socially immature. They can throw tantrums. Most children develop and grow normally and do so in a recognisable sequence which can be studied and which forms the basis of designing schools, equipment, teaching methods and curriculum. Thus in studying development you will understand the rationale behind most of the things we do, not only in school but in all our lives as shoppers, parents or home builders. Also, a study of what are called 'norms', the stages that researchers, medical

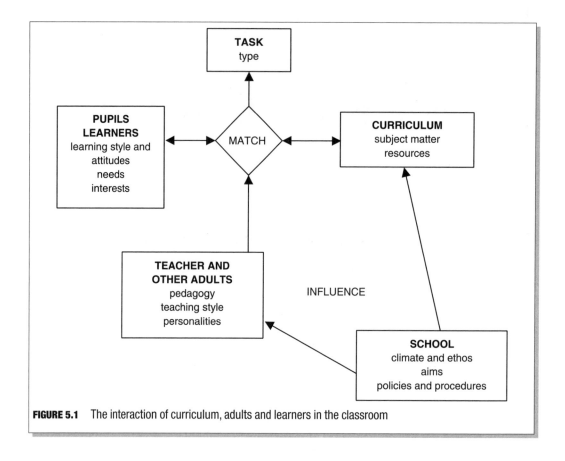

FIGURE 5.1   The interaction of curriculum, adults and learners in the classroom

practitioners and teachers have identified over the years, enables practitioners to understand better when things are not developing as they should. Many of you will be helping pupils with developmental delay in one area or another, and it will help if you learn more about normal development. The most obvious area to start with is that of physical development.

Physical development

A family photograph album will give you material to identify some of the norms of physical development. In Great Britain we are relatively well fed and clothed, with a modern medical service, and so most of us have the privilege of growing to adulthood normally. Many of you have children of your own, and have kept that height chart on the kitchen or bathroom wall and entered your family heights on each birthday. Some of you may even have kept up entries in your baby books, recording weight, first teeth, first walking and talking, toilet training milestones and so forth. Doctors and nurses have tables of norms and will check development at certain critical intervals, particularly when children are in infancy. The milestones of puberty are also marked by bodily changes. Physically, we are able to procreate in our early teens, yet we are not fully mature until our early twenties. Some might say it is 'downhill' after that; certainly we become less fertile. Mothers may have more complications in childbirth after 30 years of age, and menstruation ceases in the forties or fifties; sperm counts tend to drop with age. Boys tend to mature later than girls in many aspects of physical and intellectual development.

However, we all know that diet, exercise and environmental factors affect that growth pattern. In the so-called western world, people are living longer overall as well as being inches taller than their grandparents' generation. Understanding of disease, its causes and many cures have contributed to this longevity.

Looking at physical norms

Get out your family albums with photographs of either yourself and your family or your children. If you have them, find your children's 'baby books'. Ask other members of your family for some remembrances. Can you identify at what age the following happened? Try following the development of one child at a time. When did they:

- sit up on their own?

- turn over?

- crawl?

- stand up unaided?

- walk unaided?

- kick a ball?

- ride a bicycle?

- hold a pencil?

- draw a shape?

- draw a recognisable person?

- write their name?

- catch a ball with one hand?

- skip with a skipping rope?

- tie their own shoelaces?

As you do this with several family members you will begin to see a pattern emerging. Did the boys develop later than the girls in any of these respects? If you have friends or colleagues who would be willing to share their family material you can compare notes.

Early years practitioners will divide the abilities mentioned above into two types – gross and fine motor skills. The fine motor skills – those using just the hands – are the ones that schools usually identify as important, except in PE.

If you are particularly interested in physical development, either because the pupils you help have some physical impairment or because you wish to specialise in an area of physical education, you might like to ask a friendly nurse or doctor to let you have a look at their more specialised charts. The work of Mary Sheridan was invaluable in establishing some of the schedules which were used as paediatric tools in clinics and hospitals in studying children from birth to five years. You need to recognise the important stages in physical development, as they may impinge upon your work. For instance, girls can start to menstruate while at primary school. Tall pupils will need larger furniture to enable them to work in comfort. Many of you will be working with children with particular physical needs for which you need to understand how best to help them. So-called clumsy children may need more help in concentrating, others may need special furniture or equipment.

Genetic and environmental factors

There has long been a debate as to the source of differences from the norms. The main contenders have been inherited characteristics and environmental factors. The real answer is that both are responsible in closely linked ways. Our physical characteristics are dependent on our genes, the DNA which provides the code for cell development and distribution. But various things can intervene, either in the very protein which makes up the DNA or in the cells to influence the way in which the genes can operate. Irradiation from atomic bombs dropped in Japan at the end of the Second World War caused mutations of human genetic material which resulted in anything from death to minor physical deformity. Diet and environmental factors such as water or air pollution, housing, exercise or lack of it all have their effect. The environmental factors do not necessarily have a lifelong effect; sometimes reversal of circumstance can allow the body to catch up. You may be helping pupils who have come from countries where malnutrition was endemic; they may seem small for their age, listless and slow in learning. With proper diet and medical aid to rid the body of possible infection incurred through dirty water or bad housing, the pupils may grow and regain some of their lost ground.

There are also best times for certain development. Language acquisition appears to be easiest in the pre-school years, when children seem able not only to learn their mother tongue but also to become bilingual or multilingual with more ease. Some of the muscles of the palate used or unused in that period can make it difficult in later life to articulate certain sounds; for instance, people who have been brought up speaking in a Chinese dialect find it hard in adult life to articulate all the sounds that we use in the English language. Children seem able to learn to read most quickly between five and seven years of age. It does not mean they cannot learn to read at other ages, but the effort both they and the teacher have to exert will be greater. Some of this will be due to the maturation of the brain itself.

Intellectual development

The brain

Intellectual development or cognitive (knowing) development and the development of learning are dependent, just like the rest of the body, on genetic and environmental factors. Learning takes place in the brain. The physical development of the brain is going to influence what learning can take place, just as physical development of the limbs influences whether walking can take place. However, there is one major difference in the cellular structure of the brain from that of the rest of the body. With some exceptions and within some limitations, the number of brain cells does not increase as the brain grows but each cell will grow. There is also very limited regeneration of the cells if they are damaged. There have been some great advances in the treatment of stroke victims in recent years, with recovery of speech and movement previously thought impossible. The changes brought about by constant appropriate exercise are not due to new brain cells growing to replace those lost, as when skin heals or bone knits after a break has been mended, but to the ability of the brain messages to find alternative pathways.

There are many billions of brain cells, each with many connections to other brain cells. Electrical and chemical messages are transmitted at enormous speeds when we think or do anything. While we are alive, all the body systems are maintained in balance by the various parts of the brain, enabling us to breathe while we sleep, our blood to be pumped without our conscious intervention and our senses, such as hearing, to be alerted in emergencies. In order for this to happen, the blood has to pump oxygen and nutrients to the cells of the brain, which die in a matter of minutes if starved of them. Recent developments in scanning techniques have enabled doctors and scientists to study the physical basis of brain functioning while people are still alive. Previously, it was only possible to track some of the electrical impulses while people were alive and then study brain tissue after death. It is research such as this that suggests that we should keep up our intake of water between meals, to reduce the risk of dehydration and thus enhance brain function. Some schools have encouraged their pupils to carry water in bottles around with them. The water does not rehydrate the brain itself, the cells of the brain operate within a very specific, chemically balanced environment. However, dehydration can affect the bodily systems which supply the brain and thus affect things like concentration and tiredness.

If the brain cells are not increasing in number, and may well be decreasing in number as we get older, how do we go on learning? There have been many theories, and some of these have determined the way in which we teach and what we teach over the past century. As is the case with most research, the more we know the more we find we do not know, and currently we recognise the complexity of what goes on in the brain; no one theory fits all cases and we need to look at the variety of theories, and recognise some of the strategies that have developed from them. Different pupils, different subjects and different situations call for different strategies and using different parts of the brain. You will soon get to recognise the characteristics of the pupils with whom you work closely and adapt your techniques to fit them – things such as how long a pupil can concentrate without taking a break.

The brain is not one entity; the hindbrain is more like a swollen end to the top of the spinal cord. It regulates your heartbeat and breathing, the activities which go on even if you are unconscious. Part of the hindbrain controls your movements, coordination and balance, so important in learning to walk and talk. The middle part of the brain is responsible for memory, emotions and processing and managing information. The upper part of the brain, the cortex, the bit that looks like an outsize walnut without its shell, has the main thinking parts and personality. The right and left parts of the cortex do different things and there are pathways between the two sides. Buried inside the midbrain are some important glands whose hormones determine things such as our bodily clock, which triggers off hormones such as the sex hormones or thyroxine controlling our daily metabolism. So you can see how closely thinking and our emotions are to controlling other functions of our body.

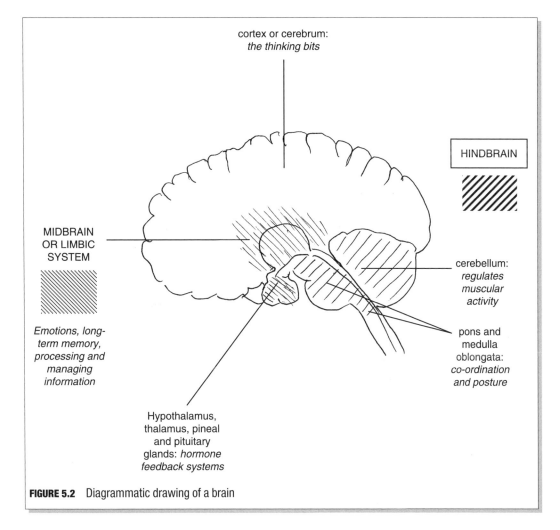

FIGURE 5.2 Diagrammatic drawing of a brain

What is more, the cell structure of the brain is distinct. Each cell in the cortex has many branches like a tree, and each of the branches ends in a join to a branch of another tree-like cell. It is estimated you may have 100 billion of these cells in your cortex. It is the connections between the branches which make the complexity of the brain, enable the memory to increase, enable us to learn skills and even, with thought, change our habits and behaviour. It operates with the mediation of minute electrical impulses and complex chemicals, rather like a massive computer. There are some more lengthy descriptions of the brain function and its relationship to learning in *Accelerated Learning* (Smith 1996:13–23) and *The Learning Revolution* (Dryden and Vos 1994:109–37). You can see that, with such a complex network, if some cells die or are damaged through an accident or a stroke, it is possible that alternative pathways can be found, provided the owner of the brain continues to exercise it. Obviously, it depends on the extent of the damage and the location. If it is possible to relocate pathways, it is also possible to establish new ones – the process of learning.

While an understanding of the biology and biochemistry of the brain is helping us establish the best physical conditions for learning, it still does not address the psychological aspects. Doctors treating people with personality disorders or mental illness use a combination of drugs, psychotherapy and even at times electrical stimulation, although the last is used much less frequently than, say, 50 years ago, when there were few drugs available other than those inducing sleep or hallucinations. Modern therapies take a much more holistic approach to mental illness, recognising that we are complex beings with body, mind and spirit, all of which can become unbalanced in different ways and all of which affect the function of each other. We all live in different social contexts, with different backgrounds, talents and needs.

Luckily, most of the pupils and parents with whom we work are not suffering from mental illness, but the principle is the same. Enhancing learning is not just a matter of having the right breakfast and drinking water, but these do make a difference. As with the whole body, exercise is important, indicating not just that elderly folk should go on trying to do their daily crossword or whatever, but that there are ways of practising thinking. Some schools

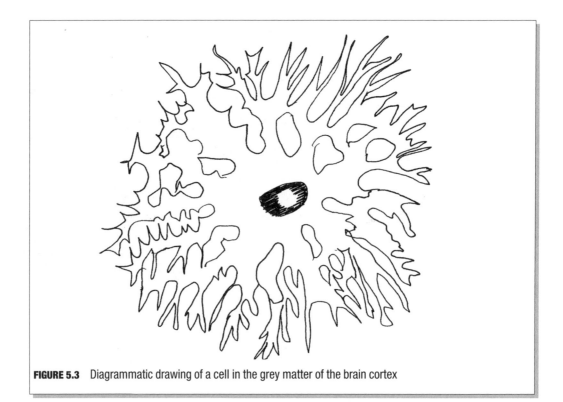

FIGURE 5.3 Diagrammatic drawing of a cell in the grey matter of the brain cortex

do 'brain gym', as a sort of club for certain pupils, although there is little but anecdotal evidence for its efficacy. Others introduce specific techniques such as those developed by Edward de Bono. He has published widely, with many ideas for lessons and games, and is responsible for phrases such as 'lateral thinking'. Unfortunately, thinking – activities like brainstorming, pupils offering differing opinions, discussion, challenge – takes time, when there is a mountain of curriculum facts to be delivered to pupils. However, without time for these activities, the pupils will not develop their own understanding of the facts being put forward and will not be creative, be problem solvers and grow in their learning capacity. It is a dilemma which all those working within the constraints of a set curriculum have to solve for themselves. One of the problems with these specific activities is that the pupils see them as separate exercises, interesting as far as they go, but they do not apply the techniques to their general work or lives.

Getting pupils thinking

Discuss with your mentor or a friendly class teacher how they solve the dilemma of balancing 'telling' time with 'thinking' time for pupils.

If they are willing (do not do this without discussing it with them first, and see Chapter 11 for observation techniques) observe some lessons and note how long the teacher spends telling the class things, how long the pupils are allowed to offer their opinions on the subject of the lesson and how long the teacher allows for silent thought before a task is undertaken.

Jot down any questions asked by the teacher.

After the lesson, go through these questions and sort them.

Which ones wanted factual answers (sometimes called closed questions)?

Which ones were asking for ideas or opinions (sometimes called open questions)?

Discuss your findings with the teacher you observed.

Current theories of learning and thinking

There is a distinction between thinking and learning, and many differing views on what constitutes learning. One definition of learning is 'that reflective activity which enables the learner to draw upon previous experience, to understand and evaluate the present, so as to shape future action and formulate new knowledge' (Abbott 1996 : 1). Senge's work on learning organisations was mentioned before and defines learning as 'nature's expression of the search for development. It can be diverted or blocked but it can't be prevented from occurring. The core educational task in our time is to evolve the institutions and the practices that assist, not replace that natural learning process' (Senge *et al.* 2000 : 57).

The Office for Standards in Education tried to define good and less than satisfactory learning in terms of observable behaviour in the 1993 *Handbook for the inspection of schools* (Ofsted 1993 : 9):

Where learning is good, most pupils respond readily to the challenge of the tasks set, show a willingness to concentrate on them, and make good progress. They adjust well to the demands of working in different contexts, selecting appropriate methods and organising effectively the resources they need. Work is sustained with a sense of commitment and enjoyment. Pupils are sufficiently confident and alert to raise questions and to persevere with their work when answers are not readily available. They evaluate their own work and come to realistic judgements about it. Where appropriate, pupils readily help one another.

Where learning is unsatisfactory, pupils are either insufficiently engaged in their work, or demonstrate undue dependence on the teacher or uncritical use of resources. They are reluctant to take initiatives or accept responsibility. They find it difficult to sustain concentration for more than short periods of time. They are unable to apply their learning in new context.

This definition was dropped in the 1995 handbook and replaced by definitions of pupils' responses, attainment and progress. Ofsted now concentrates on attainment and standards.

How well do learners achieve?

Inspectors should evaluate:

- the **standards** learners reach as indicated by their test and examination **results**, and other available evidence, taking account of: any significant variations between groups of learners, subjects, courses and key stages; trends over time; and comparisons with all schools;

- how well learners **progress** relative to their starting points and capabilities, on the basis of data and observed evidence, with any significant variations between groups of learners (e.g. by ethnicity, ability or gender), making clear whether there is any **underachievement** generally or among particular groups who could be doing better;

- whether learners achieve their targets and whether the targets are adequately challenging.

(Ofsted 2007a:11)

The problem is that learning itself cannot be seen, only the behaviour which shows itself during and after it has taken place. There are the heart-stopping moments of seeing 'the penny drop', but these do not constitute all that is going on; most is unseen. There is an assumption sometimes, that learning is one kind of thing. Thinking and learning are not the same. Learning can be anywhere on a continuum between an unconscious act, through conscious learning to sitting down and deliberately organising one's reasoning. It can use trial and error methods, reliance on experience alone through problem solving, following others as in an apprenticeship approach to the kind of academic disciplines practised in universities. Learning can induce habits, require facts to be memorised or involve learning about learning itself. Thinking is a mental process which can be random or purposeless and does not have to be communicated. School processes are where teachers try to influence what and sometimes how their pupils are thinking. You can think about improving your football and the theory of game strategy but you can only learn to play football by doing it. We should try to understand as much about the natural processes as possible, complicated as they are [18K8]. The measurable outcomes of learning, the products, the matter that can be tested, can be referred to as attainment, not learning itself. Learning is a process of change taking place in the brain. The brain's basic structure will be determined by genetic factors, but the capacity to learn, or intelligence, is not fixed. People used to believe that this power of thinking was finite, fixed and measurable, hence the development of intelligence quotient (IQ) tests such as the Standford-Binet test favoured in the middle of the twentieth century. There are some inherited parameters, as can be observed in the inheritance of aptitudes or talents, say, in music or dexterity for a craft, but such traits can be encouraged (or discouraged) by the environment in which children are brought up. Identical twins inherit many similar characteristics but can have quite different personalities, which affect their performance.

Recent ideas on learning have been influenced by the theory of Gardner who suggests that there is not just one intelligence, but multiple strands or aspects or dimensions or domains. There are different intelligences for different things, and you can be clever in one area only or several:

- verbal/linguistic: enables individuals to communicate and make sense of the world through language (e.g. as journalists, novelists and lawyers);

- logical/mathematical: allows individuals to use and appreciate abstract relations (e.g. scientists, accountants, philosophers);

- visual/spatial: makes it possible for people to visualise, transform and use spatial information (e.g. architects, sculptors and mechanics);

- bodily/kinaesthetic: enables people to use high levels of physical movement, control and expression (e.g. athletes, dancers and actors);

- musical/rhythmic: allows people to create, communicate and understand meanings made from sound (e.g. composers, singers, musicians);

- interpersonal: helps people to recognise and make distinctions about others' feelings and intentions and respond accordingly (e.g. teachers, politicians and sales people);

- intrapersonal: enables a capacity for a reflective understanding of others and oneself (e.g. therapists and some types of artist and religious leader);

- naturalist: allows people to understand and develop the environment (e.g. farmers, gardeners and geologists).

(Pollard 2002:150)

Smith (1996:60, 61) has some useful checklists for doing this sort of analysis and has designed them for children of different ages to complete themselves, using smiley faces for the younger ones. His book is full of little exercises and explanations of these various intelligences. The idea is that if we know what our own best way of thinking is, we can use it to help our own learning, and if we know how the pupils we work with are operating we can support them better. Another suggestion is that we may need rather to work on the areas we or the pupils function in less well, in order to develop pathways of thinking that are currently underdeveloped. Say, if we are not good at intrapersonal skills (working with others), maybe we should spend some time on developing them; or vice versa, if we always need to operate in a group, maybe we need to develop our ways of working on our own. Some people find aspects of one mode in which they are comfortable help them operate in another; for example, having music on while you learn something off by heart, even singing straight prose or lists of things.

Physical factors affect learning, just as they do any other activity. If we are tired or ill we do not learn as well as normal. Children and young people with a physical disability are liable to have to spend effort and time in dealing with the disability that more able-bodied people can put into intellectual activity. Visual or hearing impairment will impede or prevent access to written or spoken communication. The list is endless and those of you who work with pupils with special educational needs of a physical origin will know the kinds of effect these disabilities can have. For these children and young people, the role of a TA is to provide the support that takes away some of the hassle their physical condition causes to enable them to use their mental powers to the full. However, in some children the very lack of physical development of the brain in the womb may have resulted in a reduced number of brain cells, which may prevent full intellectual development.

The world around us – people, social interaction, rewards, as well as the physical conditions – can influence how we learn, and the world inside us – our physical status, personality, motivation and learning style – can also affect the process. We learn facts (knowledge), how to do things (skills), ideas (concepts), and about ourselves (attitudes). Learning together can result in greater achievements than learning in isolation. What we have learnt can lead to thinking and creating new ideas or solving problems.

Learning about our own way of learning can help us to improve, and assisting pupils to look at their own processes will help them to improve. Abbott (1997) explores the theories of intelligence and the building up of network pathways which enable memory to be accessed. 'All brain activity occurs spontaneously, automatically in response to challenge. The brain does not have to be taught how to learn. To thrive it needs plenty of stimulation, and it needs suitable feedback systems' (p. 4). 'The ability to think about your own thinking (metacognition) is essential in a world of continuous change. Through metacognition, we can develop skills that are genuinely transferable. These skills are linked to reflective intelligence, or wits' (p. 5).

Behaviourism

The hindbrain which controls the more reflex behaviour is the area that is susceptible to the Pavlovian, behaviourist training. Pavlov lived in Russia in the late nineteenth century and worked with dogs. He found hungry dogs would salivate at the sound or smells associated with food. We all know how we experience this if friends describe a new restaurant or recipe for our favourite food. We do it without thinking, without using the higher order part of the brain; it is a mechanistic thing.

Thorndike, in America about the same time, trained cats to use levers to get at their food. We train ourselves to use the clutch and brake to bring a car to an emergency stop when learning to drive. We are at first using our higher order brain, to think about what we are doing, but practising makes it become a more reflex activity. Skinner worked with pigeons, and recognised that repeating the stimulus strengthened or reinforced the connections. The mind, or the thinking part of the brain, is significant, but skills and memory pathways need this kind of reinforcement, and some school learning needs this kind of behaviourist approach – lots of praise and repetition.

Constructivism

Piaget worked in the 1930s and 1940s. He was a biologist by training but was fascinated by his own children, whom he observed intensely, recording and commenting in depth on what he found. His work has come under criticism because of his limited area of study, just a few children, but his influence has been profound. Being a biologist, he took a biological, developmental view of how thinking develops. Piaget became interested in thinking or intellectual or cognitive development. He recognised that thinking develops just like any other physical part of the body and goes through stages. However, he was dogmatic about the stages, saw only one type of development and considered that there was linear progression through the stages. We now appreciate that different aspects of learning and thinking develop differently, and the stages are not fixed or as age-related as Piaget proposed. Because of his more fixed ideas on the process of cognitive development, people thought that children had to go through the stages, and one had to wait for the right stage to teach certain things. This went along with theories that all one had to do in educating children was to wait and see, offer a rich learning environment and the child's exploration would do all that was necessary.

His developmental stages of concept development were as follows:

- Up to about 18 months old the infant is involved in developing skills of mobility and sensing his/her environment – the 'sensori-motor stage'.

- From 2 to 4 years is the 'pre-operational' stage – the child is only concerned with themselves (egocentric).

- By about 4 years they are 'intuitive' – thinking logically but unaware of what they are doing.

- From 7 to 11 years old, the child can operate logically, but still needs to see and work with real objects to learn and understand – the 'concrete stage'.

- Then the child is capable of 'formal' thinking about things without the 'props' – the 'abstract' stage.

This is why younger children need 'props' for their learning, things like blocks for counting, or artefacts and films about days gone by. Yet we know that even small children can have amazing imagination. Piaget ignored the context of learning, and did not ask how to facilitate or accelerate cognitive development. Very young children have all the parts of the brain functioning, formal thinking is possible for them, but often the more sensori-motor needs dominate.

Piaget also believed that learning was similar to digestion. We take in food, and digest it to make it part of ourselves. He spoke of 'assimilating' ideas and 'accommodating' them; they then become part of our own mental make-up. He also spoke of 'conservation', the ability to 'operate' internally with 'schemes'. This is how we carry out mental operations. He believed that children are born without substantive knowledge but have the definite means of coming to know the world. We construct miniature theories of how the world works; we may be problem solvers – testing strategies or 'schemes'. This all makes a lot of sense, in that we need to present children with ideas and facts in stages, give them props and practical experiences – the 'play' of children – and allow them time to assimilate [54K9, 35]. Standard 54 is full of detail on how you support children through play. The subject has been well studied and forms the basis of how the early years' curriculum is 'delivered'. Many books and materials are available to help you understand play and its importance in intellectual development as well as physical development.

There are some classic experiments regarding the conservation ideas of Piaget that we can do with children and which are fun.

Conservation of number

With a three-year-old who is just learning to count:

Ask them to count the fingers on your hand.

Do they match a number to a finger or do they count several numbers while resting on one finger?

With a five-year-old:

Try lining up two rows of 10 counters, one equally spaced and the other spread out. Ask which row has more in it.

Conservation of length

Take two pieces of tape, each about 20 cm long.

Put them together in parallel on the table in front of you, with the ends together.

Now pull one away to the left or right.

Ask if they are still the same length.

Conservation of weight or volume

Take a ball of plasticene or dough.

Carefully cut it in half, flatten one piece.

Ask if they are still the same size.

Or balance two pieces of plasticene on a pair of scales, demonstrating they are the same weight, and then flatten one piece. Ask if they are the same size.

Much of the development of the science curriculum has been based on Piaget's ideas of the development of understanding, but teachers recognise that this development is not directly related to age. Intervening can change the way in which pupils look at their own thinking. This gives what are called 'higher order skills' with which they can tackle the ordinary curriculum and look at ideas. Researchers have found that these pupils can get better results, particularly in the secondary school.

If you are interested in the details of Piaget's work and can cope with the jargon, the appendix of *Children's minds* (Donaldson 1984: 129–46) is useful. This book, which constructively criticised his work, was first published in 1978, before other theories came to the fore, particularly those connecting language and thought development and recognising the importance of the context of learning.

Language and background: social constructivism

Chomsky, an American linguist, wrote in the 1950s of the connection between language and thought. He believed that language development was special and not explained as part of general knowledge acquisition. Language and communication is needed in literacy and numeracy as a vehicle for development. Bernstein argued that the differences in children from different backgrounds were due to the differing ways different groups of people used language – that people of a lower class or income group had a restricted vocabulary and grammar structure and could be inhibiting the mental development of their children. There are still arguments about which comes first, the restricted code of language or the mental capacity to use language. There are powerful non-verbal ways of communicating, such as a hand gesture or a smile. Body language can create discomfort or raise expectations. We should also recognise that changes of background, language or culture can create barriers to learning. And it is important not to talk down to children, thinking you are using the appropriate language for their age or stage of development. You must recognise that they need to increase their vocabulary, and can take part in quite sophisticated conversations and arguments, given the opportunity. Listen, observe and discuss any findings with your class teacher.

The social environment

Vygotsky, working in the 1970s and 1980s, believed that the tools or symbols of language enable people to act outside as well as within their environment, broadening their horizons, and this gives added possibilities to their development. While studying children's development he, like Piaget, felt we should be considering potential, not what has already occurred. Development, he said, lagged behind learning. He also thought that others could assist us in achieving our potential more effectively by working with us than if we worked alone. Social interaction is part of learning. He described higher mental functions as 'internalised social relationships', and said you could see this in the influence of parents on learning to talk.

We learn a lot from each other and our surroundings in ways that do not use words. Offices and hotels can give 'messages' about the kind of places they are from the décor of their reception areas and the body language of their receptionists. Schools have a 'hidden curriculum'; we receive motivation and encouragement in our learning from other people.

Discussion and interaction between peers, teachers and pupils, adults and children, adults themselves are crucial to enhancing learning.

Vygotsky particularly developed the concept of a 'zone of proximal development' (ZPD) and emphasised the importance of guidance or collaboration in learning. If we can see the potential learning of pupils we can put in place stepping stones or 'scaffolding' to bring them to the next stage of development – a clear role for a perceptive TA. As the pupils develop 'mastery', external guidance or scaffolding can be reduced. The important thing for the pupil is that the TAs provide the scaffolding, not build the complete tower. Bruner (1966) also used the idea of scaffolding, but added that we can help this process by searching out the patterns and putting the right pieces in place at the right time. As with language, it is important to use the appropriate equipment for the developmental levels of the pupils with whom you work. By inventing codes and rules, seeking out the regularity and predictability of patterns in knowledge or skills, the teacher–pupil interaction can be speeded up. Bruner emphasised the importance of culture and social interaction but he also acknowledged the constraints of our genetic make-up.

Socio-culturalism

This theory advances the previous one another stage, recognising that it is useful to have more knowledgeable others within the group who are learning together – not to guide them to the 'correct' way but being able to look at different solutions to a problem. It is about bringing a different perspective to a discussion. The importance of interdisciplinary dialogue is recognised much more now in, say, faculties of universities or hospital departments. Building a house needs aesthetic considerations as well as engineering ones. Art and science are not distinct entities although useful separate disciplines. Those using art media such as pottery glazes need a knowledge of chemistry; an oil slick on a puddle can be a thing of beauty. The ECM agenda is a good example of the need of those trained in different disciplines to bring their own, distinct and various expertises together to make life better for children growing up in our country.

The cyclical nature of learning

One way of looking at the learning process is that of a cycle of activity, like Figure 5.4, first proposed by Kolb.

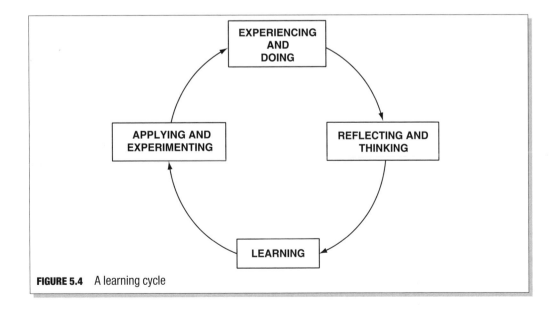

FIGURE 5.4 A learning cycle

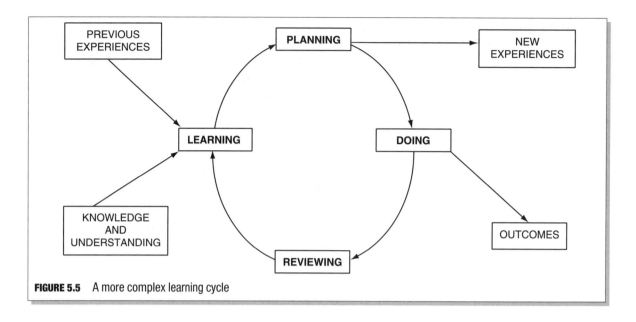

FIGURE 5.5 A more complex learning cycle

Learning is not as straightforward as these cycles try to depict; it will be spiral because of the effect of maturation, interventions and the social context of the learning, which will influence how it is repeated. Figure 5.5 begins to show the kinds of influences which can affect the simple process. You could try adding more ideas to this as you observe learning.

Outcomes of learning

As the learning process is so difficult to see and assess, the emphasis has been put on the outcomes of learning – the results of assignments, tests and examinations. We count the number of right answers to our questions and believe this relates to how much the pupil knows. Such is the number-crunching facility of computers, and the related ability of communicating the numeric results in written and electronic forms, that a whole industry of league tables and target setting has grown up around the results of such tests. The arguments about selection are always interesting, whether it is for a place in a school, university or football team or for a job. Are the results of competitive examinations or tests reliable indicators of potential? Many other kinds of test have been devised, such as assessing competence by watching, or psychometric tests designed to find out hidden thoughts, but still the humble interview, talking face to face with the candidate, has a place. A teacher's assessment of pupils will include things such as attitude to learning and progress made over time as well as test results.

The input/output model talks of learning outcomes, as though they were some kind of product. One of the readings from the Primary National Strategy CD, *Intuitive and deliberate learning*, has a list of a whole range of outcomes.

Some varied outcomes of learning:

- physical adaptations and habituation
- perceptual learning
- imitated sequences of actions
- learned sequences of skilled movements
- changes in attitudes or values
- discovering a new strategy
- understanding of concepts

- remembering of facts

- learning of a rule

- increased conscious awareness of our own thinking, learning, etc.

(DfES 2004b:1)

Unfortunately, this emphasis on outcomes has resulted in publicity and even rewards. People move to live in the catchment areas of schools with high places in the league tables, resulting in more pupils going to those schools and thus more funding for them. Within some schools it has resulted in a disproportionate amount of time being spent on revision and rote fact learning and inappropriate booster classes. There are good things to come out of the publicity. It has increased the debate about the purpose of education; it has made some 'coasting schools' recognise that their pupils could do better, and some inner-city schools realise that other similar schools enable their pupils to achieve higher standards. Do talk with your mentor or class teacher about their feelings about these matters, recognising the very real tensions that all schools and teachers are under.

Another thing to bear in mind is that we learn by making mistakes, not just by being able to produce right answers. All pupils like to see a page of sums with ticks, yet this can indicate they are not being stretched enough by the questions. Many pupils, when asked to guess or estimate a quantity, will feel good if they are right or near in their guess, and even alter their incorrect guess to match the correct quantity, rather than recognise the process of estimating is the important learning point, not the answer.

Some outcomes of learning that are very difficult to quantify are in the areas of creativity and problem solving. With the emphasis on easily accessible outcomes and formal examinations such as the GCSE and 'A' level, the creative arts and vocational skills have had to struggle for recognition. It is this debate which underlies the apparent muddle that 14 to 19 years education sometimes seems to have become. It must be difficult to be a student or pupil within that age group, or a parent of such a person, but the proposals for diplomas, the popularity of the baccalaureate in some schools and the recognition of vocational qualifications will mean more pupils have their talents and potential recognised.

The significance of theories

It is important that you consider not just what you are learning but how you learn, and to continue that process for the pupils with whom you work. The kind of learning you want in the classroom should influence the kind of instruction, activity and responses that you plan for. Behaviourist approaches may be needed for some skills learning but will constrain creativity or divergent thinking. Constructivist or developmental approaches can be useful in organising hierarchical aspects of subjects like mathematics or science and understanding the stages that learning may need to go through. The need for language, interaction and dialogue in developing ideas and communicating them must mean having lessons that are not pure 'delivery' mode. Not all students will be at the same stage of learning or think at the same time. There is value in mixed ability groups as well as the setting of pupils. There is more about observing pupils, planning work for them and helping with assessment in Chapter 11.

Once you get away from the idea that intelligence is a fixed inherited characteristic and the Victorian idea that everyone had their place in society to which they were born, you realise the role of education is to enhance potential, enrich and enable children's minds to develop as widely as possible, to understand their own ways of learning and recognise that learning never stops. Various people have developed specific programmes to help the processes. While each have their successes and their uses, no one method will serve to help all children or support all subjects.

The nursery pioneers of the early part of the twentieth century, people like Issacs and Montessori, had a great influence on defining the role of play in learning. Piaget's work on development of conceptual understanding through handling materials and artefacts has been taken on through the work of Adey and Shayer, particularly in science (Adey and Shayer 1994). They developed various thinking skills programmes with their students which enabled higher test results to be obtained in the subject and their ideas have been used in other areas. De Bono developed his divergent thinking programmes but they tend to be a bit idiosyncratic.

Bloom's taxonomy (Bloom, Krathwohl and Masia 1956) is often used instinctively if not directly when considering which kind of thinking and thus teaching is needed. If higher order thinking is needed which will be more demanding, more time and dialogue will be needed. If it is a series of facts, 'pure' knowledge base – for example tables or spellings – then a repetitive, drill approach will suffice. Bloom suggests knowledge acquisition is at the bottom of his list, which is:

■ knowledge;

■ comprehension – or understanding;

■ application – or using the knowledge;

■ analysis – being able to organise the knowledge;

■ synthesis – being able to put different bits of knowledge together from various sources and make sense of them;

■ evaluation – being able to make judgements based on criteria, not opinion.

Metacognition

This is the study of our ways of thinking about thinking itself. Just like trying to define thinking, defining thinking about thinking is as complex. However, you can ask your pupils to reflect on why and how they are going to do something rather than just telling them 'this is how you do it' [18K18]. Just as I am encouraging you to be a reflective learner in Chapter 2, you can encourage your charges to do the same. Some generalised questions, whatever the context of the lesson, could include:

■ What did you think at the beginning?

■ What do you think now?

■ How did you find that out?

■ What strategies did you use?

■ How has your thinking changed/developed?

■ How is your thinking about this different or similar to someone else's?

■ Why do you think your ideas are different?

■ What has influenced your thinking (doing something; listening to someone; explaining to someone; reflecting on something)?

(McGregor 2007:218)

Obviously you wouldn't ask them all every time, it would depend on the lesson. For instance in mathematics at Key Stage 2, children are taught various methods of calculation. They could easily debate which they understand best and why. McGregor also suggests that students can be encouraged to evaluate their own progress by asking questions like:

- What am I doing here?

- Is it getting me anywhere?

- Am I doing the best possible?

- What else could I be doing instead?

(McGregor 2007):218

Thinking skills are defined in the NC to complement 'key skills' which the authors believe are needed by all developing children and young people. It distinguishes between information processing, reasoning, enquiry, creative thinking and evaluation. It sees these attributes as being embedded in the NC but does not indicate where or how or whether they should be taught independently or concurrently. They need to permeate everything you do. A recent report into learning skills and the development of learning capabilities suggests there should be:

- explicit strategies built into everyday tasks for pupils;

- better dialogue between the learners and the adults with both sides willing to talk about what is going on;

- group interactions which encourage talking about how we learn;

- helpful feedback about progress linked directly to what is going on;

- teachers with a good understanding of subject matter;

- a focus of learning on how to succeed through effort rather than ability where the learner can choose an appropriate strategy.

(Higgins, Baumfield and Hall 2007)

One of the most useful things for anyone to do is to make connections. So much of learning appears to come in discrete packages, universities have faculties, schools their departments, the NC its subjects. It is necessary to recognise the differences and organise knowledge but it is in making the links that things begin to make sense and form patterns in our minds that have meaning for us. It is these patterns that enable us to remember things – remembering where you found a bit of knowledge rather than trying to remember all the facts. Using a dictionary for spelling for instance or which website had the information on flights are examples. Another link is between a fact and its use. Learning tables or spellings on their own could be meaningless and useless, but being able to calculate how much three packets of something will cost is useful. Knowing the difference between pair and pare and pear can be funny. Meaning adds interest, and often motivation.

One thing is clear. While you can teach in as talented and understanding a way as possible, you cannot do the learning for another person or child [18K15]. There is more about independent learning in the next chapter. Your role is to do yourselves out of a job; the role of the school and education is to enable the pupil to learn for themselves and know both themselves and where to go for help, how to access information and skills tuition [18.2P1–7]. Your role is to facilitate this process so you need to understand as much as you can about how the process works, how each individual can be helped and motivated to learn for themselves [18.1P4, 5; 19.2P1]. This is now referred to as 'personalised learning'. There is a lot of information about this with practical suggestions and references to further reading materials in the strategies publications and resource packs on the DCSF Standards website. It suggests there are five main components to be considered:

- assessment for learning

- effective teaching and learning

- curriculum entitlement and choice
- organising the school
- beyond the classroom.

Attitudes to learning can make all the difference as to whether pupils are prepared to put in their own effort. The report on teaching and learning called *20:20 vision* talks about pupils taking ownership of their learning and suggests that this is cyclical:

'developing the skills and attitudes to become better learners (**Learning how to learn**)'

leads to

'pupils establishing the habit of talking about learning and teaching and how to improve it (**Pupil voice**)'

which feeds into working with teachers

'coming to a shared understanding of learning goals and how to achieve them (**Assessment for learning**)'

which of course helps learners **Learning how to learn**.   (DfES 2006a:20)

The website materials suggest that the essential features of personalised learning for teachers and support staff could be:

- They will have high expectations of every learner, giving them confidence and skills to succeed.
- They will have access and be able to interpret data on each pupil to inform teaching and learning, incorporating more fine-tuned assessment and lesson planning.
- They will be in a stronger position to share and exchange information about best practice among their colleagues in different schools and through external networks, resulting in opportunities to develop a wide repertoire of teaching strategies.
- They will participate in high quality professional development, working with other teachers to develop their skills in understanding the learning needs of their pupils and how best to address those needs and engage them.
- They will be able to depend more routinely on the support of non-teaching staff and other adults from outside the school to provide an holistic, tailored educational provision for all their pupils.

(http://www.standards.dfes.gov.uk/personalised learning/about/:1,2)

You can remove barriers to learning or give your pupils strategies to overcome barriers for themselves. STL 50 is a unit which formalised this supportive process in what is called mentoring. While the unit is designed for those of you who have a formal 'learning mentor' role it is worth looking at to see the kinds of activities suggested. In normal class work you will not be writing down the details in the way you are expected to by this standard. The routines give some helpful guidance.

More and more teachers are setting their pupils short-term targets which they feel are achievable and you may well be part of this process. If you are allowed or even encouraged to mark books you do need to understand the kind of language that is helpful to support learning – challenging without being frightening, having appropriately high expectations without being daunting and the ways in which your intervention – or not – will facilitate their achievement. 50K6 wants a candidate to know: 'how to assist children and young people's decision making in ways that promote the child/young person's autonomy; factors and pressures which impact on children and young people's ability to make informed decisions; the range of relevant sources of information which can be accessed to support and assist children and young people and factors which may affect ability to access information'. Knowing how we think learning takes place is a foundation on which to build your knowledge and understanding of individual children.

Questions to ask yourself

Look again at the factors which have affected a recent learning experience of your own.

- Why did you start it?
- What did you need to help you – books, an instructor, discussion with other people, time on your own, the right tools or machine, practice?
- What facts did you learn? What skills?
- How has your understanding of the matter increased?
- What mistakes did you make?
- What went wrong? Why?
- What went well? Why?
- Did a certificate at the end help?
- Did other people's views matter?
- Can you still improve?
- Could you do it again?

Now consider a recent topic you have been following with a pupil or group of pupils.

- Can you answer the same questions about their learning?
- Can they answer the questions?
- Do you or the pupils need to make any changes in the way you work together?
- Can you help your pupils understand their own learning styles better?

Some further reading

Bruner, J. S. (1966) *Towards a theory of instruction*.

Donaldson, M. (1984) *Children's minds*.

Dryden, G. and Vos, J. (1994) *The learning revolution*.

Lee, V. (1990) *Children's learning in school* (especially Part 1, Learning theories).

McGregor, D. (2007) *Developing thinking developing learning: A guide to thinking skills in education*.

Pollard, A. (2002) *Reflective teaching: Effective and evidence-informed professional practice* (especially Chapter 7).

Smith, A. (1996) *Accelerated learning in the classroom*.

Wood, D. (1998) *How children think and learn* (especially Chapters 1 and 2).

For books on play and early years development, anything by Tina Bruce, Janet Moyles or Marion Dowling will be firmly based in theory and experience as well as being easy to read and accessible.

Understanding other aspects of pupils' development

THE EDUCATION REFORM ACT (ERA) of 1988, which brought in the National Curriculum (NC), set it in the context of spiritual, moral and cultural development as well as the physical and mental development which appears to be emphasised by the NC itself. It required 'that all maintained schools provide a balanced and broadly based curriculum' that:

- promotes the spiritual, moral, cultural, mental and physical development of pupils and the school and of society;

- prepares pupils at the school for the opportunities, responsibilities and experiences of adult life.

(DfEE 1999a, 1999b:12)

These aims are repeated along with the statement of values in Curriculum 2008 – the revision of the NC for those working with Key Stages 3 and 4, the 11- to 16-year-olds (QCA 2008). It is well worth getting hold of a copy of the NC and reading the introduction and the section on values. These sections are rarely referred to in discussions of what is to be taught yet they are the principles on which we base all that we do. This chapter is more about the development of pupils. There are further strategies for supporting children in the next chapter and more about the curriculum in Chapter 12.

It is this area of development that is strong in the ECM agenda. Some people see these aspects of learning as the softer side of teaching, but it is clear that while schools are not there just to make children happy or to provide a safe place to put the children while the parents go to work, unsafe and uncomfortable surroundings do not facilitate learning. The emphasis on curriculum delivery and testing has not helped schools pay attention to how best to support the learners in the more pastoral ways. The new Ofsted framework used since 2005 is based on the five ECM outcomes:

1   **Being healthy:** enjoying good mental and physical health and living a healthy lifestyle.

2   **Staying safe:** being protected from harm and neglect.

3   **Enjoying and achieving:** getting the most out of life and developing the skills of adulthood.

4   **Making a positive contribution:** being involved with the community and society and not engaging in anti-social or offending behaviour.

5   **Economic well-being:** not being prevented by economic disadvantage from achieving their full potential in life.

All the items which inspectors should evaluate are related to one or more of these outcomes. For instance under *Achievement and standards* which will be evaluated is listed the 'emotional development of learners' and related to item ECM1 as is 'the care, advice guidance and other support provided to safeguard welfare, promote personal development and achieve high standards'.

STL 41 is a standard for those of you who are supporting pupils with particular developmental needs with emotional or social problems, but part of growing up is about all of us learning to cope with our emotions and taking our place in the world. This is not a smooth ride for any of us and nor should it be. A child who is brought up totally protected from problems as their parents or carers see them will have emotional and social problems of a different kind. We learn to cope with ourselves and others by being with them. In working with children or young people with particular needs it is well to remember we all have these needs or have had them, and all children growing up will have them in differing amounts at different times. STL 41 is appropriate for those of you who are supporting those whose needs are seriously affecting their ability to learn or to conform to certain expected behaviour patterns over a period of time [45K9]. Your empathy, listening and observation skills will be of great help in any situation. Your respect for others, maintaining a positive outlook and looking for things to praise will enable you to be a role model for the pupils in your care.

Emotional development

Sometimes computers are held up to be analogous with the brain function. Certainly, there are definite similarities, and many things the computer can do better than a single brain, such as multiple calculations. But computers cannot feel in the way humans do, and this characteristic, that of having emotions, is a major difference [18K13].

If you think back to a learning experience you have had as an adult like the process suggested at the end of the last chapter, you will recognise that however bright you are and however good the supporting environment, including the teacher, if you are preoccupied by other problems, bored or insecure, your feelings get in the way. Maslow in 1954 identified a hierarchy of needs that we have to satisfy in order to learn. First we need physical security but after that we need psychological security. In order to fulfil our potential we also need love and a sense of identity and belonging, which, plus a sense of mutual respect and self-esteem, will help us take risks to make the most of new experiences, what he called self actualisation. Later, in the second edition (Maslow 1970), he added two more levels: the desire to have knowledge and understanding and an aesthetic need.

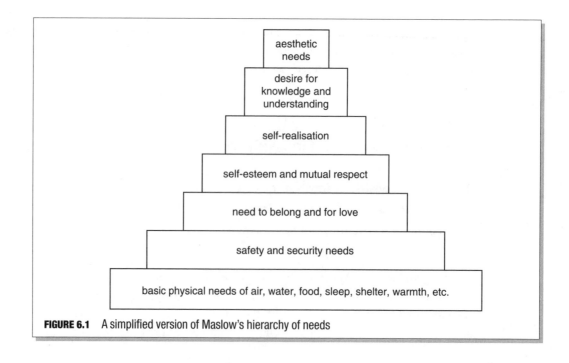

FIGURE 6.1 A simplified version of Maslow's hierarchy of needs

Emotional development and condition affects learning at a very basic level. This is sometimes called the affective domain of our brains. Part of growing up is to become able to put some of our emotions on hold when having to do other things. Younger children are less able to control their emotions and teenagers' hormones play havoc with their control systems. TAs can be of great help to the learning situation by providing an understanding ear to pupils in distress. Just a brief note of warning about dealing with confidences, please make sure you read the child protection section of the next chapter.

A relatively new concept that has been proposed is that of 'emotional intelligence'. This follows the ideas about multiple intelligences of Gardner, but really indicates that our emotional state is part and parcel of the way we think and act. Goleman, who has developed this idea, suggests combining the interpersonal and intrapersonal intelligences of Gardner to form emotional intelligence, and which can then be expanded into five domains:

1 knowing ones's emotions

2 managing emotions

3 motivating oneself

4 recognising emotions in others

5 handling relationships (Goleman 1996).

He looks at social competence and incompetence – the abilities that underpin popularity, leadership and interpersonal effectiveness and recently has developed his ideas further into what he calls 'social intelligence'. He also believes, thankfully, that we can develop good habits and improve upon our capabilities in these areas and remedy any lapses. STL 45 refers to 'emotional competence'.

Some people describe these ideas as 'touchy-feely mumbo jumbo', but the DfES took them seriously. They have launched a pilot programme called 'Social, emotional and behavioural skills' (Sebs) to look at practice in 1,250 school in 25 LEAs (Hastings 2004). From this has come the project materials widely used in primary schools and being introduced to secondary schools, the SEAL project (Social and emotional aspects of learning). Any school which is involved in a Healthy schools project will have already come across many of the ideas anyway: the importance of feelings like anger or depression in how one learns, of the relevance of considering self-esteem and so on [45K5].

Consider someone you know who seems popular and gets on well with different kinds of people.

■ Do they show their own emotions?

■ Do they talk about their own feelings?

■ Watch their body language as well as their speech patterns.

■ Listen to their tone of voice.

■ Are they consistent in their actions and speech regardless of others or do they change depending on their audience?

■ Are they able to listen as well as talk?

Goleman offers a caution. He points out that people who are very good at connecting with other people smoothly, reading their reactions and feelings, can lead and organise and handle disputes, are performers or actors. This can turn a person into saying one thing and meaning another, creating an impression, without being true to oneself. So, the intrapersonal intelligence, the ability to understand one's own needs and feelings has to go alongside, to balance the social skills with a personal integrity. Intrapersonal skills are about knowing oneself. You will find the importance of maintaining self-esteem for pupils often referred to in books on teaching and behaviour management, but we also have this need.

You have strengths to offer and have achieved positive things. You have interesting ideas and experiences to share. But, you have to recognise that not everyone will like you and you are not an endless resource for others. Some of your thoughts and beliefs will be different from those of other people. You do not have to go along with everything anyone else says, your personal integrity matters. It is a question of where you draw the line between making a stand, compromising or changing what you do and say. Only you can establish this. You need to know who you are and what you stand for, your own personal identity. This does not prevent you from being a full member of school teams, learning from or working with colleagues. Each group or team within the school will have its own identity, depending partly on the purpose of the group and partly on the individuals within that group. It is also important that you uphold the ethos of the school and what it stands for, play your part in the whole-school team.

Motivation

This is one of the greatest influences on learning. The will to achieve can overcome many physical and social handicaps. When one becomes bored, or other interests take over, it is difficult to concentrate or persevere. Even easier tasks become a chore. Setting up a home of one's own can make do-it-yourself experts of even the most impractical people. Learning to read for some is a matter of accessing information about football, keeping a pet or using a computer. One of the skills TAs develop is finding out what interests a reluctant pupil and building upon that: finding the book about football, or advertisements for guinea pig food or an internet guide. Another skill is being able to repeat a task but change it slightly to create interest, while retaining the learning objective. Keep a note of changes you make and share them with the teacher; these make a useful assessment tool for them. Some people say that motivation is an intrinsic quality, we cannot motivate others, we can only build on our knowledge of what motivates them. TAs can certainly do this [18.2P2, 4].

Self-confidence and self-esteem

This was sometimes overlooked in the past. We all have stories of the teacher who was demeaning of our efforts. Sometimes the put-down can motivate a person to achieve despite the comments, but even then the memory stays of the sense of discomfort. Failure or even perceived failure can prevent us all from trying a second time [18.2P3]. An interesting and readable couple of books are *How children fail* (Holt 1964) and *How children learn* (Holt 1967), where he emphasises the impact of feelings on our capacity to learn, and the blow to our progress that failure or even apparent failure can be. These are old, and probably out of print, but can be found in most educational libraries. They were very influential when published in getting teachers to recognise their role in demotivating children and young people in school. Fox (2001:19–31) devotes a whole chapter to the importance of self-esteem, with many ideas on how an assistant can encourage this. Another useful book for those who work in primary schools is *Feeling good* (Whetton and Cansell 1993) and of course the SEAL materials.

Small children normally come to recognise their own identity in their first year; they understand that there are other people, some who love them particularly and others who are on the periphery of their lives. These early relationships are crucial in helping the child form a concept of themselves – a self-image. They know they are valued and develop the self-confidence to walk and talk, which later on gives them the self-confidence to accept challenges. Adults who have good self-images will be a good role model for children. Confident, encouraging parents and teachers (even though they may be acting) will support younger learners.

Sometimes adults underestimate or overestimate a child's emotional maturity. Small children can be very sensitive to atmosphere and recognise when adults are very distressed, yet nobody talks to them about what might have happened in the family circumstances to cause the distress. Conversely, an adult can sometimes assume that the child can cope with difficult happenings without problems. The increased recognition of the need for pupils to talk to someone after traumatic events has meant an increased emphasis on the work of counsellors. Children often regress in terms of physical development when they are under emotional stress: toddlers can revert to soiling, primary age children can become bed wetters, and children who were apparently more detached show the need for more comforting and cuddles. Some children may stop eating properly or talking. It may be a reason for children staying away from school – refer to the statements in STL 51 on attendance. Elective mutes are children who appear not to be able to speak yet clearly understand all that is spoken, and have no physical disability preventing them. They can talk but choose not to in particular circumstances, such as with people they do not know.

You need to think about what causes emotional distress, things such as changed circumstances or instability at home, changing boundaries, people or places. Pupils with SEN or EAL may find it more difficult to understand what is happening and therefore find it more difficult to adjust to such changes. Drama and play activities can be a very powerful way of enabling children and young people to explore and express their own feelings and those of others. The way in which role play materials and props are provided in early years' settings can help provide a variety of scenes for the pre-school child – from domestic situations to shops, hotels, hospitals and holiday destinations. Observing children at play in these circumstances can give clues as to their joys and worries but do beware, you can misinterpret their behaviour. Scary television programmes may be being acted out, not an imminent family break-up, or it may be an active imagination at work! Opportunities for creative and exploratory drama seems to have died in many primary schools: performances still take place but often under direct production guidance from adults. Opportunities for enhancing such play in lunch breaks with props takes a bit of organising but can be done. The knowledge statements in STL 45 (promoting well-being and resilience) give many pointers toward strategies which can help vulnerable pupils: the importance of trust, openness and honesty, being non-judgemental, demonstrating empathy and yet recognising your own feelings.

A popular formal way of exploring feeling is the use of 'Circle time' developed by Jenny Mosley (Mosley 1993). A leader guides the group to contribute only their own comments, to listen and not respond to the comments of other members of the circle. An object of some kind is circulated and its holder is the speaker. Members of the circle are free not to speak when the object comes to them. Again, there should be a health warning. To undertake this process with the serious intent of exploring feelings and not just a glorified 'news time' is a skilled activity requiring training as children can reveal areas which need counselling. Increasingly the need and opportunities for proper counselling is being recognised in schools and many of you may be involved with it [18K17].

Small children without words to express their feelings will show their distress or temper in tantrums and their joy or excitement by running around. By the time they are of school age, able to voice their feelings and to understand circumstances, tantrums are usually under control. Communication is important as a means of self-expression and developing self-esteem. By seven or eight years of age they have a concept of the passage of time and the excitement of anticipation of things such as parties and holidays becomes more manageable. By ten and eleven they are competent to deal with more complex situations without panicking, such as finding themselves lost in a shopping centre or falling off their bicycle in a strange place.

The body's hormones – the chemical messengers – can disrupt emotional stability in puberty, creating frustrations, mood swings, even tantrums again. An apparently stable child becomes a stranger at times, yet this is the time when crucial life choices have to be made and the main external examinations are held. It is important that you recognise such changes for what they are, and know how to manage them. Do seek help if you feel an emotional outburst calls for intervention, and tell someone what has happened even if you have dealt with it appropriately. It may happen again, and parents might need to be told. Emotional distress may not just be signalled by tantrums. Moody or withdrawn behaviour can signify that something is wrong. Some cases of the teenage eating disorders of anorexia (not eating enough) and bulimia (eating but then inducing vomiting to stop the food being digested) may be due to emotions being unbalanced. As you will be closer to some of the pupils than many of the teachers are, you will notice such changes and you will be able to alert them to a possible problem. STL 46.3 is particularly about helping young people when they are distressed and 46K7 is about understanding why self-esteem and self-worth are important at this age.

Adults, too, have problems in this area, particularly, it seems, if you are in the caring professions. If you are a social worker or a doctor or working in schools, there will be times when you are 'at work' and times when you are with your family or doing other things. You never have enough time to do all that you want to do, so you experience a sense of failure. This can colour your way of dealing with the next problem – 'I can't do it' may be the thought. Feeling good about what you can do is a necessary part of the job. In teaching you cannot 'win them all' and this has to be faced, but you can do some things well. TAs have suffered quite significantly from lack of self-confidence in the past, because of your comparative invisibility in the school system and your low pay. Where you are valued by the school and your colleagues, and they make you know this, you feel good about the job. It is a job with great job satisfaction – a reason most TAs give for remaining. You are doing a most worthwhile thing – remind yourself about this when you feel low. Then consider how the pupils you work with feel – probably singled out for their lack of achieving what the others in the class can do. Be an active listener, don't feel you have to 'do' anything; understanding the problem is half way to solving it [45K10, 13].

Communicating feelings can help, letting the pupils express themselves in words, spoken or written, or drawings or even music or some kind of supervised physical activity. Giving them time for this may enable them to control what would otherwise be an uncontrolled and possibly dangerous outburst and to maintain their self-esteem [18.2P5]. Let the pupil talk; sometimes getting them to keep a diary will help them to express their needs and ideas. The importance of being able to listen is a thread running through all the pastoral units, as is making sure that anything you do is within the school guidelines for dealing with emotional problems.

Often smaller children can draw their feelings rather than write. They can make lists or flowcharts which can be positive or negative. If they are negative, try to get them to work also on the opposite:

- what I did wrong – what went well today;
- what I hate about school – what I like about school;
- what makes me sad – what makes me happy.

Older pupils may be able to think of positive things about other people, e.g. 'What I like about Miss Smith, Jane or Ahmed'. Some pupils may need some help with describing words, so you could make a collection of these in case you need them.

The main theme is to look for strengths in the pupil – what they can do, not what they cannot – and build on them, and to provide the pupils with a positive role model in yourself. Appropriate praise is important, phrases like 'well tried' rather than 'well done' if the work is still not up to the standard it should be. Encourage pupils to look for the positive in situations, in adults and in their peers. Discourage them from 'putting down' their fellow pupils, particularly when they resort to stereotypes such as 'he can't play in the team, he's too young', 'she's stupid, she's just a girl', 'he's thick because he's in a wheelchair' or 'black people smell'. Remember, 'there are many kinds of abilities and one challenge for teachers is to enrich their pupils' lives by identifying, developing and celebrating the diverse attributes of each child' (Pollard 2002:151).

When pupils are more able to cope with expressing their feelings, you can move on to more constructive ideas to help them prepare for such feelings and deal with them. Use the language of choice – 'you can either accept a situation and move on or make yourself even more miserable', 'I can help you with your reading/writing if you put in your bit of effort'. Make sure they have telephone numbers of friends or even helplines. In the end, you cannot live the pupils' lives for them; you can only give them the tools and strategies to make the best of what they have got. If you are particularly involved in this area of support, STL 45 may be a standard for you. It is all about developing well-being and resilience. Even if you are not specialising as a counsellor or similar, it and some other standards are well worth reading for the kind of skill and knowledge which are useful in this area. Words like trust, openness and honesty are used to describe those who can help pupils [45K6, 7, 11, 12].

Talk to the person in your school who is responsible for PSHE (personal, social and health education) about what strategies they use, and whether they have any books you can read or any simple tips for dealing with pupils about whom you may be concerned. Always tell the class teacher what you are doing and keep them informed of your progress (or lack of it). The non-statutory guidelines for PSHE available on the NC online website give suggestions for the knowledge, skills and understanding that should be taught at each key stage to enable children and young people to develop healthily in mind and body. The guidelines are in four sections, the first being 'developing confidence and responsibility and making the most of their abilities'. The website also links to resources to support teaching in this area. The third one is about 'developing safer, healthier lifestyles', the conventional medical understanding of being healthy.

Social development

Some schools are particularly good at what they call 'life skills', enabling all their pupils to cope with the challenges that life outside school might bring. These may just be about doing basic things such as shopping, handling money, contacting emergency services or cooking, but most programmes will include dealing with relationships, becoming independent from the family home and living with oneself as a person. Some of the discussion about the development of good relationships in Chapter 3 is relevant to this aspect of development [45K4]. The second section of the PSHE guidelines is all about 'preparing to play an active role as citizens' and the fourth is 'developing good relationships and respecting differences between people'. Children need to develop good relationships with those around them, or life will become unbearable for them [18K6]. Children learn about relationships from watching and imitating people around them. The bonding between parents and babies is considered crucial and mothers are encouraged to hold new-born babies from the word 'go'. Fathers are encouraged to be present at the baby's birth.

If you do not work with very young children, it is very interesting to spend time in a nursery or playgroup just watching the children in the role-play areas. Children will act out what they have seen at home or sometimes on television screens. They will cook and look after other children if that is what happens in their home, or shout at the other children and send one out for a takeaway if that is what they are used to. You need to be careful when interpreting role-play, as sometimes children act out their fears as well as reality, so always discuss what you see with the staff in the group. Father figures or male role models in the home are still considered significant whether the children are male or female, even in this era of successful one-parent families. Educationalists are concerned that schools, particularly primary schools, are becoming increasingly female domains. Toys such as teddy bears and for the very young even a piece of blanket can become a surrogate friend. Many of us have had imaginary friends when little. Bowlby was a significant influence on childcare strategies in early childhood, believing that the mother – or mother figure – was the significant central person in a baby's life. However, while there is a lot of truth in this, it is not only relationships with parents that are important, but also having grandparents, carers, brothers and sisters. It is the quality of the care and of people that determines their significance and influence. Many babies attend day nurseries successfully from a very early age, but a key worker is usually assigned to them in these stages to ensure that the right sort of bonding and relationships develop. The idea of having a key worker is spreading into mainstream schools and hospitals.

By about three years of age, the toddler is able to leave their mother or influential carer or the close caring of a day nursery for a while and this has become the general entry age for playgroups and nursery schools. Here, children are encouraged to play with other children whom they will only see in those surroundings. By five they are happy to spend the day at school sharing the teacher with up to thirty other children, although if you work in these classes you will understand the importance of the settling routines. You may have seen the way in which some children still find it difficult to adjust to not being able to demand the teacher's attention without waiting their turn. During the primary years children develop firm friendships, occasionally forming small gangs or clubs for different activities. They join organisations such as Brownies or judo clubs, and can operate in teams, collaborating and sharing. All the time, they try out their boundaries, and experiment with situations. They see what happens when they do things that are not allowed, and can have several ways of operating depending on differing circumstances. They also influence how other children and adults behave to them by the way they behave. Often parents will say to teachers, when their child's behaviour at school is described on an open evening, 'But he's not like that at home' or 'She's never done that before'.

Transitions

When children change schools, either because their family has moved house or because they are of the age for the next kind of school, they have to re-form friendships and teacher–pupil relationships, as well as find their way about a strange building and adjust to different timetables and subjects. All sorts of things affect a child's ability to settle in a new environment [45K2]. Generally, an unsettled child will be fearful and tearful, but such feelings could show themselves in angry or even aggressive behaviour as the pupil is cross at being put in this strange situation. STL 49 is purely about supporting children and young people during transitions in their lives. It is well worth looking at this standard, particularly the knowledge and understanding section, to see if it prompts you to situations which may be affecting the pupils you are working with. The other useful source of prompts is in the Common Core of skills (DfES 2005a) where *Supporting transitions* is seen as one of six important areas that all those working with children should be able to do, know and understand. Making effective links with other professionals is one of the key areas here in order to exchange information, preferably ahead of a transition, in order to smooth out the effects. Plymouth City Authority has a team of specially trained TAs who work in what they call the PIE team (Plymouth Inclusive Education). The team completes a simple pen picture of the child which can be used by all staff who come into contact with the child so that there can be some continuity without each person having to delve into family histories afresh. Figure 6.2 gives their rationale and Figure 6.3 gives the form they use with prompt headings.

The *New arrivals excellence programme guidance* (DCSF 2007b) identifies the needs of both primary and secondary pupils who come into school as a result of international migration, a phenomenon which has increased dramatically with the enlargement of the European Union. The guidance also contains some key resources which you might find useful. Another group of children who are very vulnerable are looked-after children, previously called foster children, or children 'in care'. It is known that the success rate in school learning measures for this group of children is very low, and they are missing that crucial block in the hierarchy pyramid of a sense of belonging to a particular family. There is an excellent booklet, again produced by the government, which, although designed for governors, is very helpful in describing both the problems and what schools can do about them (DfES 2006b). In addition to all the usual school records, looked-after children must have a Personal Education Plan (PEP). These cover academic achievement targets but also personal and behavioural targets and identify who will be responsible for carrying out the plan. They have to be reviewed regularly and should be helpful at times of transition for the child.

A4 Pen-picture

The A4 Pen-picture:

1. Includes a photo and personal details of the young person

2. Gives name and contact details for the school based staff member

3. Provides brief general information on a disorder

   - The information is directly related to how the disorder impacts on the particular young person

   - Situations and/or events which may heighten or lessen sensory responses, stress or frustration are identified

   - Strengths and interests are highlighted

   - General recommendations and simple specific strategies are recorded

The point...?

The A4 Pen-picture is a colourful user-friendly document which quickly and simply conveys:

   - Personal and confidential information about the young person

   - Basic information about a disorder

The document is designed to be used by all staff who come into contact with the young person. It has proved useful in disseminating information quickly to large numbers of staff particularly during transition times: staff coming into contact with the young person for the first time; or those who may have sporadic or minimal yet significant input e.g. supply staff, lunch time supervisors. The details contained in the document have been compiled by staff following observations of the young person and the contents have been agreed upon by family/carers and staff who know the young person well.

FIGURE 6.2   Plymouth LA rationale for a pen picture

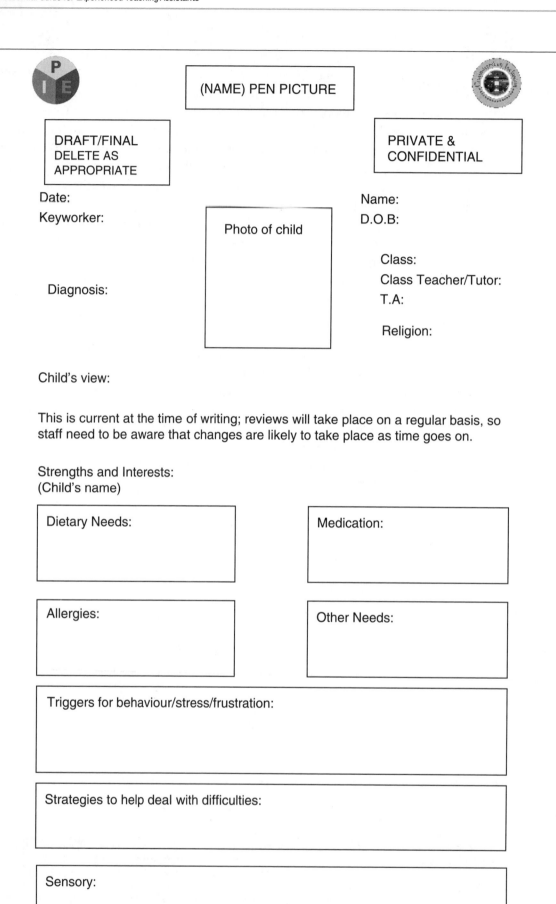

FIGURE 6.3 The Plymouth Inclusive Education transitions team pen picture form

Current areas of concern:

Socialisation:

Communication:

General recommendations for Staff:

In agreement with:

Parent/Carer..

Class teacher ....

Pupil/Student ....   Date: ....

FIGURE 6.3 Continued

Pupils with learning problems or a disability or with little ability to communicate, either because of their home language being different or through speech problems, have a higher risk of unease with new situations, as they find it more difficult to understand what is happening. But beware of misinterpreting the reasons for difficult behaviour; always talk matters through with the teacher if you have concerns, and respond as he or she directs. It is important that you are aware of the pupils' need to form relationships as well as just get on with the task in hand. You cannot make people get on with each other but you can help them see the point of doing so. The language of choice is helpful: 'Shall we do something together or can you do it on your own?' Children choose whom they want to be with and do things with; social relationships are a two-way process.

As children get older, they become much more influenced by the children around them, particularly so in the teenage years, when peer pressure can induce long-lasting changes in lifestyle and attitude. Strong friendships formed in the late teens, in the last few years at school, at college or university, or in a first job tend to be friendships for life [9.1.i]. Hopefully by the time the pupils reach this stage they can both recognise and control their own behaviour to fit in with the society in which they live.

While you may have your ideas of what is antisocial behaviour, you must determine the school's policy for what is acceptable in the various situations. Classrooms, playground, lunch hall, laboratories, toilet areas will all have their limits of acceptability. Different cultures will have their own rules or customs of behaviour towards others, and even their own ways of being abusive. Not only will different languages have different words which are considered offensive, but gestures which are ordinary to some are obscene to others. Even within our own culture things change. For instance, it would have been wholly unacceptable in my own childhood to have received an invitation or a posted present and not to reply with thanks in writing, but now the use of telephone and e-mail mean that such a practice is much rarer.

More can be found about dealing with antisocial behaviour in the section on behaviour management in the next chapter. The principles of positive strategies, reinforcing and rewarding the good and providing choice and sanctions for the less acceptable hold good.

Cultural development

It can be seen from much of the above that language and culture are going to influence social and emotional development as well as intellectual development. The power of being able to express feelings in discussion, or even confession, and being able to share ideas is enormous. The way in which different cultures have differing methods of child care – whether boys and girls are educated together, or whether girls are educated at all – clearly makes a difference to other development. The kind of clothing, food, art and music which surround a child from the early years will influence development and growth; they are part of the environmental influences on inherited characteristics mentioned in the previous chapter. The rituals and customs of daily life or religious festivals become part of our lives but also influence the kind of person we grow up to be. You must guard against forming stereotypical assumptions that, because of a person's gender or apparent ethnic origin, they will behave in a certain way or hold certain opinions.

Your main objective when working with pupils whose cultural background, dialect or home language is different from your own is to appreciate the additional richness that they bring to school life. It is about reinforcing their self-image. Their knowledge and understanding of ways different from yours, their food, clothing, art, music and traditions add a diversity and interest. Multilingual pupils have a skill that many of us do not have. There will be school policies about such celebration of cultural diversity, about how various different religious festivals might be observed, how dress codes might be modified and where additional resources might be found.

One group of children who sometimes get left out of these discussions are the gypsy, Roma and traveller children. They do not have language problems but they do have mobility ones. These may lead to social insecurity as relationships and friendships are not easy to form when the children are moving on frequently. They also have cultural differences which may set them apart form the other children in a school. The DCSF guidance is helpful (DCSF 2008) and there is further guidance to support those of you who may be working with such children in their early years on the Save the Children website. 'At school and pupil level, children who are confident about their personal and community identity are so much better placed to be happy and successful learners. The importance of the notion of self-worth is well known as a major determinant of learning success' (DCSF 2008:para 2.3). The teachernet website has information on resources to help schools foster better relations between communities. Ofsted has a duty to inspect schools' performance against the duty to encourage community cohesion from September 2008 onwards.

Variations in family values and practices may make pupils' responses to school work differ. For instance, it may be traditional within a family or group that females never answer before males have had their turn, or that it is not done to contradict a teacher. Thus a pupil may be reluctant to challenge ideas or comments. Homes where books are rare and conversation is limited may encourage children to feel that all books are pointless and words are not helpful to express feelings. Beware of having stereotyped images of various cultures and jumping to conclusions when you see particular forms of dress or hear particular languages or dialects [3K21]. For some pupils the motivation to learn from the printed word is minimal and problems may be resolved by violence rather than open discussion. Understanding the background from which its pupils come obviously helps the school, and it may be your role to act as an intermediary between the parents or carers, as you know them from where you live in the vicinity of the school, and the teachers [19K17].

There has been quite a lot of discussion recently in the media as to the meaning of 'Britishness' and whether this should be taught in schools. Citizenship in its wider meaning is part of the NC for secondary schools. It is part of the PSHE agenda where it is entitled 'developing good relationships and respecting differences between people'. STL 47 is a very useful one for this area – 'enabling young people to be active citizens'. It is very much about enabling young people to communicate, negotiate, articulate and identify their own skills and points of influence. It is about finding the issues that are important to young people in the communities where they live but also about understanding how people interact. In order to undertake this standard you have to help young people actively negotiate and make presentations of their points of view. It means you need to understand how communities work. STL 48 goes further, where the young people are enabled to plan and take action to tackle problems. While these units were designed for youth workers rather than those working in schools, with the emphasis on extended schools and many secondary schools being involved with Duke of Edinburgh awards, Prince's Trust projects or fundraising for charities, it is likely that those of you working in secondary schools may be involved with these kinds of activities.

Spiritual and moral development

These aspects of development are often ignored. Moral development appears to come about as part of social and cultural development. Even small children, where boundaries are clear, whether they are strict or lenient, know when they are doing 'wrong'. It seems to be natural to challenge boundaries, and if these are flexible or ever-moving, the children may experience problems. The child knows they have overstepped the boundary by the reaction of the one setting the boundary. Too great a reaction can result in rebellion.

Spiritual development is not confined to the development of religious belief or participation in the practice of a particular faith. Young children experience wonder and joy, they accept mystery, they are curious, creative and imaginative, and suppression of such feelings in infancy or the early years of school can inhibit their expression for many years to come. Eight- to ten-year-olds begin to seek the meaning of things, want a purpose for doing things, and even for their own existence, and are beginning to recognise their own and others' identities as people. They get a very strong sense of injustice, and often start small action groups to raise money for worthy causes, or argue strongly for fairness in a game. It is at this age they will start asking abstract questions about beliefs, such as 'Do you believe in a life after death?' Primary age children can face death in others, in their pets and even in themselves, as terminally ill children do. They can appreciate straight but sensitive talking from adults, although many adults will feel that they need help in talking with children about such matters. Children begin to sort out legends and myths from factual evidence; for instance, recognising the myth behind the tradition of 'Father Christmas' delivering presents.

Many teenagers will fight shy of discussing their deep feelings about spiritual matters; peer pressure and fashion may dictate that such things are cissy. Yet most of them will be trying out their own beliefs in practice, and will still feel strongly about the beauty of the world around them or the expression of joy or sadness in poetry, music, art or drama. They can get emotionally involved with the more extreme versions of religious belief or practice, as their instinct for trying new ways and rebellion comes to the fore, but most young people come through such experiences. They develop a greater understanding of the variety of human nature, the reality of the consequences of their actions, their place in the world and their interdependence with their family and the community around them. You can be an active listener at all these stages of development but, as in all such matters, ensure you know what the school policy is before you contribute too much of your own beliefs. You may be working in a faith school, or where some parents hold firm views such as those of Jehovah's Witnesses. It is not your place to uphold or change any particular belief.

Schools need to help children and young people retain 'a capacity for reflection, curiosity, and a sense of awe and wonder as well as an ability to discuss beliefs and understand how they contribute to individual and group identity' (Ofsted 1993: 15) in the world about them, as well as encouraging the sense of fair play. A few moments spent in looking at some new flowers growing in the school grounds, or pointing out a rainbow formed by the edge of bevelled glass in the sunshine, the growth of the class pet, or the colours of a visiting bird or butterfly can all help spiritual growth. The intensity of the curriculum and the constraints of a timetable have tended to squeeze out not only thinking time but also reflecting time [18K17]. This is not part of religious worship, although of course it can be, but is part of feeding an aspect of life that can so easily be lost. For some, poetry or music may trigger such a moment, and it is always worth trying to include something that has moved you when planning work. Different people are moved by different things, but you never know when such moments might happen.

The school will be inspected on 'learners' spiritual, moral, social, and cultural development' which are related to the ECM agenda outcomes 3 Enjoying and achieving and 4 Making a positive contribution (Ofsted 2007b:19). When evaluating learners' spiritual, moral, social and cultural development inspectors should consider:

- learners' response to spiritual and moral issues, such as their attitudes to bullying and their effective discussion in lessons;

- the quality of learners' social development as expressed through their relationships with their peers and with adults;

- learners' understanding of Britain as a diverse society and their readiness to engage with others from a different cultural background;

- the extent to which they embrace the shared values of the community and contribute to its cohesiveness . . .

When evaluating how well learners enjoy their education, inspectors should consider:

- their attitudes and behaviour in lessons including their attendance, punctuality and enjoyment of learning, completion of tasks and engagement in independent work . . .

When evaluating how well learners contribute to the community, inspectors should consider:

- how far learners are developing appropriate ways of relating to each other and to adults;
- how far learners participate in decision-making or consultation within the school community and with the outside community;
- the development of learners' understanding of citizenship;
- how far learners share a sense of belonging to one community and build positive relationships with people of different backgrounds.

(Ofsted 2007a:12,13)

The schedule also gives a definition of what 'good personal development and wellbeing looks like':

> ... Young children are learning to understand their feelings. All learners enjoy school a good deal, as demonstrated by their considerate behaviour, positive attitudes and regular attendance. They feel safe, are safety conscious without being fearful, and they adopt healthy lifestyles. They develop a commitment to racial equality. They make good overall progress in developing the personal qualities that will enable them to contribute effectively to the community and eventually to transfer to working roles.

(Ofsted 2007a:14)

Inspectors also look at how TAs are deployed to support the effectiveness of teaching and learning in meeting the needs of a full range of learners. Good care, guidance and support for learners is described as being 'seen in the high level of commitment of staff to encouraging enjoyment and achievement and in promoting learners' health and safety. There are effective strategies for promoting learners' social and economic wellbeing...' (Ofsted 2007a:19).

The individual and independence

While in a school, pupils have to conform to certain rules and boundaries, so that they are safe and their activity is purposeful, but they are all individuals, and will grow into separate adults responsible not only for their own lives, but probably for those of their children or colleagues at work or fellow members of a team. Any of you who are parents or managers will understand the dilemmas that face adults working in schools. You always have to maintain a balance between encouraging or allowing individual wishes against the needs of the family or organisation or your perception of the future. Where there is mutual respect for the role and needs of the other members, such a balance is easier. Even very small children will show their personality in many ways. Your personality will affect the way you work with both the adults and the pupils in your school and it is worth spending time reflecting on facets of your own personality and the kind of contribution you will make to the life of the school.

Pollard (2002) has quite a powerful section on knowing oneself as a teacher (pp. 90–6), and an equally useful section on understanding individual children (pp. 96–108). In completing the first few sections of your personal/professional portfolio you will have identified many of the contributions you can make in terms of experience and qualifications, but it is also useful to reflect on your own personality. As with your self-review of your job, your self-analysis is something that is ongoing throughout your life. Knowing yourself as a person and a learner helps you have an insight into the ways of pupils, to establish a rapport with them and empathise with their efforts to learn. For many managers, the personality of a TA is a strong contributor to acceptability for the job.

Chapter 3, on relationships, had some discussion on the importance of rights and responsibilities of individuals, and the need for respect and voice. One of the problems you will encounter is that it is very likely that you have been appointed to help those who need assistance, and this very assistance labels the pupils as being disadvantaged in some way. It is a fine balance, and a continually changing one, between helping appropriately and enabling the pupils to achieve more of their potential and feel a sense of their own achievement [18.2P1]. Somehow, the pupil has to maintain their own self-esteem and self-confidence and become increasingly independent of you [18.1P3, 4]. It is important that pupils do not become dependent on their helpers whatever the nature of the SEN. This can have two effects: first, the pupil does not try for themselves, and will not be able to repeat the exercise without you being present; and second, the situation could label the pupil in the eyes of the rest of the class [18K15].

Discuss with the teacher the sort of strategies they use and would like you to use to promote independence, to encourage and support pupils, to enable them to make their own decisions. It is about getting pupils organised into a system so that they can operate without you; for example, with ICT equipment. It is also about helping pupils with SEN to learn and operate with minimum support. It is about showing them how to do a task but not doing it for them, working alongside on a separate sheet of paper but ensuring they do not copy your work directly. If they ask for a spelling get them to try first, sound out the word, and praise them for how close they have got; or send them to a dictionary or show them how to use the spellchecker on their word processor; do not just give them the spelling of the word. Watch out for those 'zones of proximal development' where you can put in 'scaffolding' to support the crucial next step.

Tell pupils to remember what the teacher said on a previous occasion, to jog their memory; do not let them rely on yours. Sometimes aids to independence cost money, but schools have ways and means of getting assistance for those with SEN. Items such as laptops, for

PHOTOGRAPH 6.1 Encouraging independence with support

PHOTOGRAPH 6.2   Encouraging independence by allowing experimentation

those with a physical impairment which makes writing difficult, mean that a pupil can write independently of a scribe. Even simple tools such as left-handed scissors can mean the difference between the pupil doing it for themselves and you having to do it for them. Sometimes it is a question of time, to allow for a slower way of doing things or a thought process. Remember, praise for trying is as important as praise for succeeding, if not more so. Part of all children's growth and development into adulthood is the increasing acceptance of responsibility for their own actions and their own learning [18.2P2, 3, 6; 45K3]. Children cannot be protected from all bullying or conflict as they grow up but have to be helped with strategies for dealing with difficult circumstances without escalating the problem [20K26].

This and the previous chapter have looked at the many facets of the learning process. Sometimes the theories and ideas seem in conflict:

- inherited characteristics versus the influence of the environment;
- maturity versus accelerating learning;
- stages in development versus intuitive jumps of reasoning;
- the biological function of the brain, the computer-type action of the brain, versus the more ephemeral things such as emotions and spirituality;
- the importance of social and cultural context versus 'scientifically proven' facts;
- valuing diversity versus the need for school conformity;
- collaborative learning versus independent learning;
- intervention versus natural development;
- rights of the child versus the responsibilities of the adults;
- rights of the child versus their responsibilities.

All these go to make up a complex process of development which results in a person being like the facets of a well-cut gemstone. Different surfaces catch the light at different times and turns of the stone. Different stones need different cutting techniques to bring out their particular brightness. It is part of your job to be alert to the nature of the learning, personality and context of the pupil you are working with; listen to them, watch them at work and encourage them to talk about their own feelings and learning [45K8, 9]. You can then assist the teacher in utilising the best learning strategy for each one and planning for their future development [18K8].

Questions to ask yourself

- If you are now part of the way through reading this book or through your course, have your feelings about learning changed since you started?

- Do your feelings or beliefs influence how you behave?

- Are you clear about the ethos and values which your school stands for and your role within them?

- Is there any conflict between your belief systems and that promoted by the school? What can you do about this?

- What do you do when pupils ask you about your feelings or beliefs?

- Do you know about the cultural backgrounds and sensitivities of the families whose children come to your school?

- What does the religious education policy for your school contain? Or the policy for collective worship?

- To whom can you go in the school to discuss any problems which may arise when dealing with pupils?

- To whom can you go to discuss any personal learning problems that you may have?

Some further reading

The introduction and appendices to DfEE(1999a) *The National Curriculum: Handbook for primary teachers in England; Key Stages 1 and 2* or DfEE (1999b) *The National Curriculum: Handbook for secondary teachers in England; Key Stages 3 and 4*, or find the sections on 'Aims' and 'Values' from the www.curriculumonline.gov.uk website.

Holt, J. (1964) *How children fail.*

Holt, J. (1967) *How children learn.*

Hook, P. and Vass, A. (2000a) *Confident classroom leadership* (especially Chapter 2).

Hook, P. and Vass, A. (2000b) *Creating winning classrooms* (especially Chapters 2 and 3).

Lovey, J. (2002) *Supporting Special Educational Needs in secondary school classrooms* (especially Chapter 3).

Ofsted (2007a) *Using the evaluation schedule: Guidance for the inspection of schools.*

Ofsted (2007b) *Every Child Matters: Framework for the inspection of schools in England from September 2005.*

Pollard, A. (2002) *Reflective teaching: Effective and evidence-informed professional practice* (especially Chapter 5).

SCAA (1996) *Education for adult life: The spiritual and moral development of young people* (Discussion papers: No. 6).

Whetton, N. and Cansell, P. (1993) *Feeling good: Raising self-esteem in the primary school classroom.*

Useful websites

www.dcfs.gov.uk

www.teachernet.gov.uk

www.savethechildren.org.uk

Care and support of pupils to enhance development and learning

MUCH OF THIS CHAPTER is similar to the Level 2 book *The essential guide for competent teaching assistants* (Watkinson 2008a) as STL 3 is a compulsory unit for both Level 2 and Level 3. It is included for those of you who have not read the other book. All staff should be able to cope with health and safety issues and should know and understand the aspects of child protection dealt with in this chapter.

Physical health

It was pointed out in Chapter 2 that you need to take care of your own health, but you also need to be alert to changes in your pupils. Chapter 4 pointed you at the school policies which should be in place for all health, hygiene and medical matters and these will be updated in the light of guidance following the publication of the ECM agenda. You must make sure you have a copy of all the relevant ones and that you have read them, understand them and follow the guidelines set out in them. Chapters 5 and 6 described the norms of development given the optimal environment. Sick children or adults will not work well, and may be infectious to other pupils. If you see anything that concerns you, always tell the class teacher. Sometimes children come to school with minor ailments, such as a heavy cold, and you need to be able to deal with these. It is sometimes useful, particularly with small children in winter, to equip yourself with a box of tissues or a soft toilet roll to deal with runny noses. Children do not need to be off school for a cold, but you can help prevent its spread to others. Dispose of the used materials properly. A polythene bag with you could contain the used material which could then go to an incinerator or adult toilet. Ask for advice on procedures like this.

Always reassure ill pupils, and comfort unhappy ones, and recognise that '. . . no school should have a policy of "no physical contact" . . .' (DCSF 2007c:5). However, recent years have seen school staff worried about what is appropriate in order not to be falsely accused of child abuse. Touch may be appropriate during PE, first aid procedures, if a pupil is in distress or being congratulated, but for some pupils touching may be unwelcome because they are sensitive or for cultural reasons. Differences in gender between adult and child could be significant and even 'innocent and well intentioned physical contact can be misconstrued' (DCSF 2007c:15). So a useful rule of thumb with a child who needs comforting is to do it verbally and in an appropriate manner unless they seek physical comfort from you. A returned hug in a public place from a small child missing a parent is one thing, but the same action in a quiet corner can be misinterpreted [3.2P4].

Younger children or those with a disability may need more physical support than older ones and are less likely to be able to tell you what is wrong if they are miserable. Be sure to read the section on child protection below. You may need to summon help. Some schools have a simple card communication system where staff have access to the cards which are sent in an emergency to the office. Depending on the colour of the card, the office personnel alert the appropriate support. It could be red for a fight, green for illness and yellow for an accident, for instance. Enquire whether you are able to use such a system in your school. It may be important to help pupils not directly involved in an incident, who can suffer shock particularly if the incident is severe. This is the kind of role you can play if you have to summon expert help: you will be able to support the onlookers. This may just be in the form of reassurance or may involve removing them from the incident site.

You need to be able to recognise if a pupil you are working with is just 'under the weather' or is really feeling ill. The important thing is to get to know the pupils with whom you are working closely, what is their normal range of behaviour and appearance, then you will recognise significant changes should they occur. As you are likely to be working more closely with the pupils than any other member of staff, you may be the first to notice.

The sort of things you may notice are:

- changes in facial colour – becoming very red or pale, becoming very hot or cold, becoming clammy or shivering – fever usually means some kind of infection;
- changes in behaviour, like not wanting to go out at break-time when they usually want to be first out;
- general distress;
- reduced concentration, which can even be to the point of falling asleep at their desk;
- scratching more than usual – ask about the school policy regarding head lice – you should not examine a head unless it is appropriate in your school – or this could be an allergic reaction;
- complaining of pain which persists, including headaches and stomach pain, particularly if they are not easily distracted from mentioning it;
- rashes – these can develop rapidly and may be associated with fever in the case of infection or could be an allergic reaction;
- coughing and sneezing excessively;
- diarrhoea or vomiting – these you will have to deal with as emergencies [3.2P5, 6; K14, 15].

You should not try to diagnose from these conditions, although always note any unusual circumstances that you see or that the pupil mentions. They may talk of strange-tasting food, or parties, circumstances changing at home, visitors to home or recent holidays. Your role is to recognise the changes and report them appropriately, unless there is an emergency to deal with. You will soon recognise the difference between the pupils who want a brief spell in the sick room or a bit more attention, and the threat of 'I am going to be sick' which needs immediate action. Make sure you know where or to whom to send sick pupils, and to whom to report the symptoms you have noticed. You may even need to summon help rather than leave a sick pupil.

Remember too, changes in mental and emotional state can also occur, particularly if something traumatic or dramatic has happened at home which can show itself in unhappiness, mood swings, lack of concentration and attention-seeking or withdrawal from activities. Some cultures and religions have different ways of dealing with illness, so if in doubt, ask. The age of the pupil will affect how well they can tell you what is wrong; once you know the pupil well you will be able to tell how reliable any information from them might be and the circumstances of the incident. Some pupils can fake illness if they do not like sports or if the weather is inclement. There may be changes in patterns of behaviour. A small child who has always come to chat stands alone, or a teenager usually friendly is moody or withdrawn, or a usually quiet but confident pupil follows you around. It could be just growing up, the hormones of puberty taking over, or it could signify something more significant. Either way, you need mentally to register the changes, keep an eye on the pupil over a period of time and if really concerned talk to the pupil's teacher or tutor. Such changes could signify problems at home, even abuse of some kind, self-inflicted substance abuse, or bullying within or outside the school. If the pupil will talk to you, follow the guidelines set out below regarding child protection – never promise confidentiality, always tell someone of the conversation and make a simple record of it.

Many TAs are appointed to help a child with special learning or physical needs. You must ensure you know the full extent of your role and responsibilities with any pupil, and all the appropriate ways to support them, and whether there are particular changes or signs peculiar to them of which you should be aware [3K4]. For instance, sometimes pupils are on particular medication which has certain specified effects, or they may need to be given that medication at a particular time. You should familiarise yourself with any particular needs of pupils with whom you may come into contact. If these details are not readily available in the staffroom, check with your line manager. Also, there may be pupils with whom you are not directly coming into contact, but who have specific conditions of which you should be aware. Most schools now ensure all staff know of pupils with allergies such as peanut or bee sting allergy, or the existence of pupils with diabetes, epilepsy or other disorders. These conditions could have crises with which you may need to deal appropriately. Each individual will have their own medication or procedures for dealing with any incidents.

One condition that has become more common is asthma; approximately one pupil in four will have some kind of allergic or asthmatic condition, some much worse than others, some just manifesting as hay fever in the summer or a sensitivity to certain drugs. You should check at some early point whether you will be working with pupils who suffer from asthma, where they keep their inhalers and how they are used. Usually schools have information from the Asthma Association which you can read. The NICE website (National Institute for Health and Clinical Excellence) has published guidance on school-based interventions regarding alcohol, obesity, social and emotional wellbeing and atopic eczema.

- Ask your line manager for the four most common ailments of pupils within the school.
- See what more you can find out about these ailments.
- Find out whether these ailments are treated the same way in all countries.
- Does your school have any pupils from the countries where customs are different?
- Find out more about any conditions that apply to pupils you are working with closely.
- Does the school have any written guidelines in any of these areas?
- Do you have a copy?

Whatever the problem, make sure you know where and when to seek help, what kind of written records are needed and to whom you should report any concerns, including whether you contact parents directly or notify someone else to do this [2.2P7; 2.3P5; 2K3, 4].

Health education

The school will also have a policy to do with health education of the pupils. It is usually located in PSHE education. This will cover areas such as sex education, how to help pupils with personal hygiene, diet and exercise, as well as emotional and mental health. It will deal with self-esteem, its importance and how to promote it, bullying and coping with it, whether the school has access to people with counselling skills. While you will not necessarily be directly responsible for teaching pupils in any of these areas, your relationships with them are very important in enabling them to grow into mature, self-confident adults. A healthy school is not only hygienic and safe physically but is a welcoming and secure place with good relationships between all who work there. Your example to the pupils is important. You can show by the way you talk to colleagues or pupils, by your tone of voice, what can be expected. You give an example in the way you listen, or are prepared to follow up problems, to get help. Even remembering names shows that you care and are prepared to bother about others. The way in which you show respect engenders respect in others [3.4P6]. If you are willing to assist with preparation of resources for teachers or get someone a cup of tea when they are fed up or overstretched, it shows you can think about them and do something practical to assist. If all staff had such an attitude, the school would be a good place to work and pupils would soon recognise it as a good place to learn.

It is highly likely that you will be asked questions by pupils, as they get to know you and you work in close proximity to a small group or to individuals. Note that primary schools only have to have a sex education policy. That policy does not have to ensure sex education is done by the school; it may indicate that it should be done at home. It is really helpful if you are able to talk with children and young people about health issues informally and possibly individually, to talk about how their bodies work in a matter-of-fact way provided you are sure you are working within school policies and the information you are giving is correct [3.3P6, K20]. Ask for help from a senior member of staff if in any doubt.

Find out

- Whether you should listen to the exploits of the teenagers without comment, such as:
  - smoking on the school premises?
  - substance abuse?
  - getting drunk at the weekend?
  - declaring their sexual habits or preferences or that they are pregnant?
- What do you do if you are told of incidents of bullying, or disastrous friendships?
- Whether you can talk about HIV and AIDS if they ask the questions?
- What should you do if they show you pornography?
- Whether you should comment on a pupil's diet or exercise level to them even if they seem excessively thin or obese?
- Whom you tell if they are so upset about something that it is affecting the way they behave?
- Simple ways to boost pupils' self-esteem.

The SEAL programme offers seven themes, one for each year of primary school. It is a whole-school approach, to help children develop skills of self-awareness, managing feelings, motivation, empathy and social skills. The seven themes are:

- new beginnings
- getting on and falling out
- say no to bullying
- going for goals!

- good to be me
- relationships
- changes.

The secondary pack has a full programme of four themes for Year 7. More information, including some material for parents, can be found on the website www.standards.dfes.gov.uk/primary/publications/banda/seal

---

Some suggestions for raising self-esteem

- Talk to everyone the same way, regardless of gender, race or background.
- Address pupils by their preferred name.
- Use positive comments: 'thank you for walking', 'well done for being quiet', including written comments if you can: 'well read today', 'I liked the story'.
- Use praise appropriately, not indiscriminately.
- Treat boys and girls equally, whether for tasks or treats or even lining up.
- Provide a good role model in gender, culture and disability, both in reality and when finding examples in teaching materials such as books and magazines.
- Use rewards, praise and congratulation systems for work, including showing it to other staff.
- Catch them being good or working hard and tell them.
- Set small achievable targets and congratulate them on achieving them.
- Have reward systems for behaviour – telling the teachers about the good as well as the troublesome.
- Value work by ensuring it is taken care of, and presented well, both by you and by the pupil.
- Encourage independence appropriate to age and maturity.
- Enable and encourage peer tutoring.
- Use humour carefully.
- Encourage children to value their own performance.
- Listen to the views of pupils and act on them where possible.
- Avoid being patronising or sarcastic as pupils recognise both.

Can you add to this?

(Watkinson 2002:38)

Settling pupils

One area where you are likely to be involved is with pupils who are very new to the school. This is particularly likely if you are working with children in the early years' class, sometimes called the reception class, or with Year 7s in a secondary school (Year 5s or 9s if your area has a middle-school system). The importance of helping with transitions is discussed in the previous chapter. The school is likely to have well-thought-out procedures, some of which will have taken place before you meet the pupils. The teachers may have visited the pupils' previous school or playgroup, or even their homes, and pupils are most likely to have had at least one visit to the school before their first 'real' day. You may have visits and documentation from a transitions team as in Plymouth [20K8]. You need to find out what these procedures are and may even accompany members of the teaching staff on their visits.

Remember

- how you felt when you started school;
- how you felt when you transferred schools;
- how you felt when you started this new job;
- how you felt if you went to a new school if you moved house as a child;
- what helped you to settle;
- who helped you to settle;
- how long did it take;
- so – what can you do to help newcomers to your school?

As a TA, you can be invaluable in settling pupils in. It may be an idea to negotiate with the teachers for you just to be available for this task at the beginning of a new school year. In this way the pupils will get down to the school work much more quickly and satisfactorily. It may even be important to change your timetable for a couple of weeks to spend more time at the beginnings and ends of days ensuring the new ones know where they are going and get there happily. The teacher may ask you to liaise directly with the parents and stagger entry and exit times for the new pupils. In this way an easier transition can take place, especially if a larger number are starting together. Changing classrooms or teachers can unsettle pupils. A constant change of teacher when supply teachers are standing in for a teacher on sick leave can also be a problem. In these situations you may be the one constant person in their school lives. Do ensure you talk to the class teacher if you continue to notice signs of distress after a week or so, or to a more senior teacher if the class teacher's absence is the problem. Talk any problems through with the class teacher.

Strategies that may help to settle pupils

- Be warm and welcoming.
- Learn to recognise distressed pupils.
- Learn their names as soon as possible.
- Make sure they know the name of their class teacher or tutor and encourage the other pupils with you to befriend and help the newcomer.
- Make sure they know where they are going round the building, where their next classroom is, where their cloakroom and the toilets are and to whom they can go if they are worried.
- Smile at them when you see them in the building but are not directly working with them.
- Allow them to talk about their previous school or playschool.
- Allow them to work a little more slowly at first.
- Have patience, listen and possibly talk about your own experiences if appropriate.
- Keep to classroom routines and where possible to the layout.
- Make sure you know whether they have special educational needs or speak a different language.
- Try wording your sentences more simply if that is a problem.
- Try to learn a few words of their language, as they begin to learn our words – their words for mum and dad, for home and toilet, bag, book and table would do for a start.
- Carry the tissue box with you in case of tears.
- Ensure you tell their class teacher or tutor if they have problems after the first week.

Child protection

It is essential to know about this, although it is a sensitive area. Some of you may have had close personal involvement with family or friends where problems have arisen, or feel that these matters are better not dealt with until an incident arises. You will all have been checked by the police through the Criminal Records Bureau (CRB) before you took up post. However, there are things that, as a member of staff likely to come into close physical and pastoral contact with pupils, you must be aware of. All schools will have written policies in this area and make sure all staff are trained together at least every three years, but it does not always happen. If it does not happen in your school, then suggest it. If you are at all uneasy in this area ask for help and training [3.3P1]. Standards 45 and 46 are for those of you who may have particular responsibilities in this area.

There are legal and organisational requirements and implications for you when you work with other people's children. The Children Acts apply to schools as well as to the general population. The school policy should lay out clear guidelines for all staff on what to do if there is a suspicion of abuse and on how to prevent allegations against staff themselves. The latest guidance from the government is clear and available to anyone. *Safeguarding children and safer recruitment in education* gives references to all the guidance and websites from which further information can be obtained (DfES 2006) [3K25]. There should be a designated senior person (DSP) who has lead responsibility for dealing with child protection issues. Their name should be known by all staff; they are trained in what to do and where to go if help is needed. In a primary school this is usually the headteacher. There is clear guidance in the induction training of the DCSF provided by LAs so try to make sure that you are able to go on the courses.

Abuse is 'when a child is hurt or harmed by another person in a way that causes significant harm to that child and which may well have an effect on the child's development or well-being' (TDA 2006a,b:2.18). This must be compared with that which could reasonably be expected of a similar child, but the judgement and responsibility for care does not lie with the school but with Children's Social Care.

There are two main areas of sensitivity, one in recognising the signs of abuse and the other in behaving appropriately as a member of staff. Keep yourself aware of any proposals which could affect you or your work. All staff should all be aware of the possible signs of abuse, and these are not always physical. It can also be emotional abuse, neglect and sexual abuse. While some of these signs can be listed, they must be considered only indicators. All sorts of personal or family events can cause changes in behaviour. Social factors can increase a child's vulnerability to abuse, but it is not restricted to certain kinds of people or behaviour [3K18].

The important thing is to tell someone senior to yourself of your concern, as patterns may emerge when several people's evidence is collated, or several different signs appear on or with the same pupil [3.3P2]. Different local authorities will issue slightly different guidance, giving local arrangements for training, case conferences and support systems. For instance the Southend, Thurrock and Essex (SET) guidance gives a useful list of signs and symptoms of abuse in a small handbook which all schools have and makes available considerable multi-service guidance on a special website www.escb.co.uk

Some of the lists below come from the SET guidance.

Child abuse and neglect may:

- come about through inflicting harm or failure to prevent harm;
- come about in a family, institution or community setting;

- be found in all social groups, regardless of culture, social class or financial position;
- be perpetrated by those known to the family or more rarely a stranger;
- be perpetrated by adult/s or other child/ren.

The presence of factors described under recognition IS NOT proof that abuse has occurred, but they:

- must be regarded as indicators
- justify discussion
- may require consultation and/or referral.

In practice the categories overlap and an abused child frequently suffers more than a single type of abuse [3K17a and b].

Physical abuse may involve hitting, shaking, throwing, poisoning, burning or scalding, drowning, suffocating or otherwise causing physical harm to a child.

Physical harm may also be caused when a parent or carer fakes the symptoms of, or deliberately causes ill health to, a child whom they are looking after.

Possible indicators:

- explanation inconsistent with injury;
- several different explanations;
- unexplained delay in seeking treatment;
- parents/carers uninterested or undisturbed by injury;
- parents absent without good reason when child presented for treatment;
- repeated presentation of minor injuries;
- family used different doctors, hospital emergency departments other health provisions;
- reluctance to give information or discuss previous injuries.

Possible signs:

- bruising
- bite marks
- burns and scalds
- fractures
- scars.

Emotional abuse is caused by persistent or severe emotional ill-treatment or rejection such as to cause an actual or likely adverse effect on the emotional and behavioural development of a child under the age of 18 years. It is difficult to recognise and may need observations over time. There may be:

- parent/carer and child relationship factors
- child presentation concerns
- parent/carer related issues.

Sexual abuse is the actual or likely sexual exploitation of a child or adolescent under the age of 18 years by any person. This would include any form of sexual activity to which the child cannot give true consent either by law or because of ignorance, dependence, developmental immaturity or fear.

Possible indicators:

- boys and girls scared to talk;
- full account must be taken of cultural sensitivities of any individual child or family;
- difficult to recognise unless disclosure;
- behavioural indicators;
- physical indicators.

Persistent or severe neglect of children under the age of 18 years involves persistent failure to meet a child's basic physical and/or psychological needs or the failure to protect a child from physical harm or danger.

Recognising neglect:

- child related indicator;
- indicators in the care provided.

Golden rules (TDA 2006a,b:2.20)

- It is not the responsibility of education staff to interview pupils. If a pupil makes a disclosure of abuse they should listen carefully to what the pupil has to say, but should not question them in a way that puts words in their mouth.
- It is important to make accurate notes about what has been heard, seen or told.
- Interviewing pupils should be left to the police and social care staff, who have the necessary training to carry out this role effectively. Inappropriate interviewing may jeopardise the chances of a successful prosecution at a later date.
- Concerns should always be made known quickly to the DSP, or in their absence to another senior member of staff.
- Concerns should not be discussed with parents/carers until advice on how to proceed has been obtained from the DSP.
- A pupil must not be promised confidentiality about any information on abuse they may choose to disclose. The member of support staff must explain that they may need to pass on information to other professionals to help keep the pupil or other children safe.

[3.3P3]

Staff are vulnerable to false accusations:

- when alone with pupils;
- when providing intimate care;
- if restraint is needed;
- when taking action if concerned about the action of a colleague;
- when talking to parents or carers – care about confidentiality.

Do not use any list as being definitive: you need proper training from the trained Child Protection Officers or whoever does it in your area. All children can have bruises from accidents or playing roughly. It is the type of bruise and where it is on the body that can be important. Do not be obsessive or inquisitive, but just be vigilant, for instance when children change for PE or are talking informally.

Revealing

A child may reveal to you what has happened to them. You are particularly well placed for children to feel secure with you. You will work in small groups or with individual pupils for periods of time and build up friendly relations. No school staff are trained to deal with children or families in detail in child protection matters but you all have a responsibility to recognise and report to people who are. You should not question a child in these circumstances as you may ask leading questions. You should never promise not to tell anyone. Listen carefully, sensitively, caringly, inwardly note what they say and then tell the named designated member of staff as soon as possible. Make a short written record afterwards, date it and give it to this named member of staff. It is that person's responsibility to deal with it by informing Social Services or the police, who do have trained personnel for helping the children and their families and any matters that arise [3.3P4, 5].

It is difficult, because you make assumptions or have memories which could prevent you from listening properly, but it is a responsibility that you take on when working in a school. If you have any doubts about what you have heard or seen, and these incidents are rarely clear cut, discuss what you have seen or heard with the class teacher, your teacher mentor, the designated teacher or the head. If you are involved further, be guided by the designated senior person in the school. These people will understand about case conferences, child protection registers, and agencies which can support vulnerable children and their families. Of course, you maintain confidentiality with the staff concerned, in all these proceedings.

The other area where you can be involved in these issues is when you are dealing with children in intimate situations. Again this often happens when TAs have been appointed to deal with pupils with physical disabilities, or very young children who have toileting accidents. Usually the parents know what the policy is as well, whether school staff can clean children up after toilet accidents or change underclothes. TAs are sometimes asked to work in pairs when these events occur. Always comfort unhappy children, but do it in public, not privately. Pupils need sometimes to see school as a haven, a place of safety and security which they may not otherwise have, but do not put yourself into a situation that could lead to unjustified accusation. Always be aware of, and respond to, troubled children, but recognise how to do this appropriately. Do not single them out for attention; it is better for them to come to you.

Contact

Another aspect of this can be when dealing with difficult pupils. Again, you may have been appointed just for this purpose. The proper procedures cannot be taught to you in a book. Touching pupils inappropriately, let alone restraining pupils, can get you into difficulties with parents and even with the law. The pupils concerned are usually particularly volatile, liable to act up, or react unnecessarily to being told how to behave. So do make sure you know the school policy on restraint, and if possible get appropriate training in this area. You should not be in a difficult position with a pupil swearing in your face, being aggressive or dangerous to others in your early days in the school. Make sure you talk quickly to your line manager and sort out who does what. Most LAs have people who will be specialists in this area who can help.

In all these health and safety issues it is vital that you know the policies and procedures that exist for your school. Some of these may be based on national guidance. They may seem irksome but they are written to protect the pupils and to protect you. Ensure you know about what liaison there is with parents over various incidents, what records the school requires to be kept and maintain confidentiality appropriately at all times.

Behaviour management

Behaviour management is not something you turn on when there is a problem. It is something that goes on all the time. You and your colleagues must present role models of behaviour which enable the pupils to see how adults behave towards each other [3.4P1; 19.1P2; 19K4]. It is not something you switch on as you enter a classroom, but something you use all the time you are in the building or environs. Some would say it doesn't stop there, that if you live in the locality, pupils will see and know how you conduct your whole life. This is why many teachers choose to live away from their schools, as they then feel they are not being observed all the time, going to the supermarket, the leisure centre or the pub.

All schools have policies and procedures which all staff must follow, the important factor being consistency of approach whatever the incident [3.4P1, 4; 3K21; 19.1P1; 19K1, 2]. Some of the policies that do not directly give guidance about behaviour management are also important in this area. For instance, if you withdraw a pupil from class because he or she is behaving badly, you are depriving him or her of that part of the curriculum but sometimes it has to be done; restraining a pupil could be construed as child abuse; dealing with bullying may be in a separate policy. You must know the limits of your authority, when and to whom you refer incidents outside that authority, your particular role within the school and the roles of others [19K3]. If you are newish to the school go through them with a mentor or line manager to identify your role and appropriate strategies. As you become more experienced you may see situations or learn of strategies which could be introduced into your school. Make sure you feed back your views to any reviews of the system or any in-house training sessions for discussion and that you know when these take place [19.1P9, 10; 19.2P9; 19K14]. You may be asked to participate in specific reviews, collecting data and observing certain pupils. Always remember the proper procedures for doing this kind of thing, including confidentiality in dealing with sensitive data [19K24].

Rogers has some useful things to say about discipline and behaviour; decisive discipline is marked by these characteristics:

- a focus on the due rights of all;
- an assertive stance (assertion is distinguished from aggression and hostility on the one hand, and passivity or capitulating to student demands on the other. Essentially, assertion communicates one's own need and due rights without trampling on the other parties' rights);
- refusal to rely on power or role-status to gain respect;
- speaking and acting respectfully even when frustrated or angry;
- choosing to respond to discipline incidents (from prior reflection and planning) rather than reacting to incidents as they arise;
- preparing for discipline as rigorously as for any aspect of the curriculum.

(Rogers 1991:43)

When actually disciplining, a decisive approach engages the student by:

- establishing eye contact;
- speaking clearly with appropriate firmness;
- speaking briefly, addressing primary behaviour and ignoring as much of the secondary behaviour as possible;
- distinguishing between the child and his or her behaviour;

- expecting compliance rather than demanding or merely hoping for it;
- re-establishing working relationships as soon as possible.

[19.1P4]

You must quickly learn what is acceptable behaviour in the various areas of the school and what is not, how to identify pupils in difficulties and what is normal [19.2P4]. Negative behaviour may be verbally or physically abusive or offensive. Racial or sexist actions or language should not be tolerated. Bullying needs to be recognised and dealt with. Try to spot signs of potential conflict – it is more easily dealt with in the early stages – then monitor developments. You must also recognise that sometimes circumstances change, both for pupils and for the school, and be alert to these changes. Changing rooms or buildings or going from inside the school to the playground or sports field can alter behaviour. In order to learn all this, you will need to understand the limits of normal behaviour and have copies of the policies and procedures for your school on dealing with what, for the school, is inappropriate behaviour [3.4P5].

Behaviour patterns develop as do other aspects of physical and mental development [19K6]. Emotional and social development also take place, so expectations of behaviour will vary with the age of the pupils. Physical changes such as those experienced by pupils going through puberty can alter their behaviour radically, as any parent of a child of this age will know. Peer pressure can make an otherwise well-behaved child do something out of character, such as play truant or cheek a teacher. In some cultures, certain behaviour is acceptable for boys but not for girls. This can sometimes be seen in early years' settings where rough play might be acceptable for boys, but girls will be admonished for similar behaviour. We all have assumptions of what is appropriate, depending on our own upbringing. For instance, many people still have the idea that young people with severe learning problems do not have sexual urges; they do, and can fall in love just like more able youngsters. The paraplegic athletes have challenged our ideas of physical capacity in recent years. What is age-appropriate in an infant school pupil may be considered inappropriate in a secondary school pupil, yet some secondary pupils may behave in an infantile way, when expressing their feelings or emotions in coping with a problem. While you will aim to respond to the older pupil hoping they will respond in a more mature way, in responding to their behaviour rather than to them personally you may need to modify your actions. You need to observe carefully and make allowances for the pupil according to his/her level of development and be able to recognise uncharacteristic behaviour. You need to report this and your actions to the relevant teacher and find out more about the pupil [19K15–17].

It is important to recognise that behaviour management takes place all the time, not just when things go wrong. Thanking, smiling, praising appropriately, all contribute to positive attitudes in relationships. Encouragement is very important for all children, and for adults too [3.4P2; 19.1P3]. Think back to that personal learning experience suggested earlier, and your own relationships. How much easier it is to work with people who recognise your effort, even if the actual achievement is small. Many of those with learning problems have poor self-esteem and this can be a real drawback when learning, although low self-esteem can affect a pupil of any ability. Let them know when they are doing well and show them how close they are to getting the desired outcome [19.2P3]. Ask the teacher whether you can write on pupils' work and what kind of comment is acceptable. Specific remarks are much more useful: 'completed quickly' and 'clearer handwriting' say more than 'well done'. Be careful not to do too much for them (no matter how much they wheedle). One of the real problems is that children with poor learning skills can develop a kind of learnt helplessness.

Being pleasant whenever possible means that when you have to correct inappropriate behaviour it has more effect. Role model how you wish children to behave; modulate your voice; walk, don't run; be punctual and polite. Keep calm (whatever you are feeling inside), listen and be consistent. Respect breeds respect [3K23; 19.2P7; 19K7]. We all need boundaries, so rules are developed. We all have rights, but we also have responsibilities. This includes access to school facilities, equipment and materials for staff and pupils, and developing responsibility in pupils. The aim is to make pupils take responsibility for their own behaviour [19.2P5]. The behaviour management training of the TDA's induction package for TAs (TDA 2006a:4.6; 2006b:3.6) talks of the 4Rs approach: Rules, Routines, Rights and Responsibilities, leading to choices which have consequences.

Rewards and choices

Your school may have a systematic reward system, with stickers and certificates for achievements. If so, you will need to know whether you can operate this and what for, and, if not, how you can best bring achievements to the attention of someone who can do the rewarding [3K22; 19K8]. Similarly, there may be sanctions which you can use, such as giving a pupil 'time out' for misbehaving in the playground, or ensuring a particular item gets mentioned in a home dialogue or report book [19K10]. Usually you are there on the spot to see to the immediate situation, but a more senior member of staff will carry out a punishment such as detention or informing parents. If the situation occurs in the classroom in a lesson, you need to know what to refer to the teacher and what you can deal with [19K12]. Once you know the ways of the school, you are in a strong position to say to a pupil who might argue with you, 'You have a choice – you can do what you know is right or . . .' whatever the consequence is for that misbehaviour in your school [19.2P6].

Using the language of choice:

- helps pupils take responsibility for their behaviour;
- enables adults to redirect pupils to more positive behaviours;

PHOTOGRAPH 7.1   Using stickers as part of a reward system

■ enables pupils' behaviour to be managed without them taking it personally;

■ allows for improvement.

(TDA 2006a:4.14; TDA, 2006b:3.14)

Deal with matters immediately you see inappropriate behaviour [19.1P5, 6]. The secret is to be assertive without being aggressive or confrontational and to ensure that you are separating any inappropriate behaviour from the pupil. This enables the pupil to save face and maintain their self-esteem, which is probably low. Keep the focus on the primary behaviour, the thing that drew your attention in the first place, and actively try to build up your relationship with the pupil concerned.

Separate the inappropriate behaviour from the pupil:

■ make the behaviour unacceptable, not the pupil;

■ making the behaviour wrong allows for changing to better behaviour;

■ linking poor behaviour to a pupil's identity or personality inhibits positive change;

■ linking good behaviour to a pupil's identity builds self-esteem.

(TDA 2006a:4.14; TDA, 2006b:3.14)

Always follow up on things that count: if you have said you will refer the matter to someone else, or you will talk to the pupil again the next day, then be sure you do it. Always seek help if you need it [19.1P7, 8]. Try not to get yourself into a situation where you are alone with very challenging pupils. If you see a potential problem situation, make someone else aware and attempt to defuse it. Such a situation can occur with an individual if there is a shortage of equipment or a challenging piece of work; or with a group, for instance, in a slow lunch queue. Typical positive strategies include appropriate praise and encouragement. Pupils who are motivated and interested are less likely to misbehave. Do not touch or restrain a pupil in a conflict situation unless you have been specially taught the procedure for your school.

Many schools are developing school-wide, long-term strategies to support pupils:

■ consulting with pupils about their needs, wishes and what works;

■ training older pupils to work with younger ones as buddies;

■ talking with pupils themselves about the strategies and how they can help themselves [19.2P2, 8; 19K20, 23];

■ using school councils to listen to problems;

■ employing specialised staff such as counsellors or learning mentors or specially trained TAs;

■ working with the external specialists over a period of time rather than in one-off situations.

Counselling is a skill. Before you embark on any in-depth work of this kind with pupils, do take advice and, if possible, training to ensure you know what you are doing. Most authorities have groups of experts and often use talented TAs as part of that team.

You need to find out [19K9; 20K9, 24, 25]

what is appropriate for:

■ classrooms (different teachers' classrooms will vary slightly)

■ other areas of the school (laboratories or technical areas will have different rules or codes of practice)

- outside the school premises
- individuals
- groups
- whole classes

what are:

- the rules
- the rewards and sanctions that can be applied
  - by you
  - by others

what strategies are available for you to use in managing inappropriate behaviour:

- time-out places
- sources of help and referral at different times of the day
- report forms or notes
- withdrawal of privileges

how you:

- report incidents
- develop your skills of behaviour management
- seek advice [19K13].

Behaviour problems

It is possible that you have been appointed to assist in the support of a pupil who has special problems with conforming to the expected behaviour patterns of the school, thus disrupting the work of other pupils and not learning well themselves [19K18]. STL 37 is particularly designed for you if this is so and there is a little more about supporting such pupils in the next chapter. But, whatever the reason for your appointment, and at whatever level you are studying or working, you must become part of the whole school's system for behaviour management [19K5]. While all of you need to know about your own general situation, as detailed in STL 19, a mandatory unit at Level 3; STL 41 contains more specific details for those of you undertaking special support. You must be aware that this optional unit demands a high level of skill and understanding in order to deal with some of the problems associated with behaviour management.

An example of good behaviour management

An infant school in a very poor social area, where few children received pre-school education apart from the school nursery class, had had low expectations of behaviour and academic standards in the past. Over a number of years, the new head established a positive behaviour management regime which enabled the whole school to become a happy learning establishment. It took time to establish the ethos and train all sectors of the staff to understand the detailed approach. Each teacher and their own TA became a small team, and the teaching staff had away-days, sometimes incorporating team-building exercises. Over several years teaching staff went to summer schools in their own time to undertake specific training in positive techniques which were incorporated into their classroom practice with their TAs. This even included practice sessions, with agreed prompt phrases pinned inside cupboard doors. Later, as classroom support staff became converted to the particular way of dealing with all the children, office, caretaking and midday staff were trained. Money was put into resource organisation such as shelves, labelled boxes, sufficient quality tools, materials and equipment to enable children to organise themselves and take responsibility for their own learning. Playground equipment and activities were organised; joint curriculum planning reflected the whole-school ethos. Even the youngest pupils had to plan some of their own work, and all children helped in cleaning up. Children were thanked for walking; assemblies were quiet, disciplined affairs. Parents became aware of the calm and even started to emulate the staff's attitudes and phrases while on the school site. Test results began to climb as the philosophy of high expectations permeated the formal curriculum.

Bullying

This is a particular concern of many pupils and parents. No school is without its bullies and the nature of bullying is that it will take place away from adult sight, so may be hard to detect. 'Bullying is forcing others to do, act and feel the very things a bully would never want done to him. Bullying is not accidental, it is learned.' Schools have policies for dealing with bullying issues, as there need to be 'clear, school-wide consequences' (Rogers 1994: 101). There is a legal requirement for a discipline policy which includes an anti-bullying one. There should be strategies not only for dealing with the bully, but also for helping the victim, both in the short term and in the long term, to become more assertive. It is likely that pupils will debate the issue in class and strategies such as circle time are available to help. These are probably run by the teachers, but you may be asked to undertake training in this area to run such sessions as well as participate in discussions.

There are two new areas of bullying that are of current concern, linked under the title cyber bullying. Children and young people with access to chatrooms on the internet are publishing photos or accounts of their 'friends' for a laugh. It can be extremely hurtful and in one or two tragic incidents the bullied child has taken their own life, believing themselves worthless. The ubiquitous carrying of mobile phones, with or without cameras, had resulted in text messages designed to hurt. A resource pack to help with this problem, produced by Childnet International for the DCFS, can be found on www. denizen.org.uk.

Conflict resolution

Relationships do not always go well. Sometimes there is a competitive element which gets out of hand and becomes conflict [19K21]. You need to be able to recognise when the competitive element is constructive to the relationship and also understand some of the principles of conflict resolution. This will help you both in enabling pupils' relationships to be positive and in your work with colleagues. Competition often enhances team spirit in a group of people; for instance, sporting teams in training need to have a purpose: leagues, cups and matches of all kinds create a rationale for developing the team. But, as football hooliganism shows only too clearly, it can get out of hand. Patriotism can become ethnic cleansing. House points in schools can spur pupils on to greater effort, but can also create for some a sense of being at the bottom of the pile. Where there are winners, there are always losers, and it is a skill to lose gracefully. Conflict is usually the result of some other incident or issue intruding into the relationship, causing the participants to get out of control. When people are stressed or unsupported they get aggressive for less reason than normal. This can be caused by low morale, an ambiguity over the allocation of roles, or timing of events. Factors that prevent good relationships, such as poor communication, over-assertive colleagues, lack of sensitivity to feelings, misunderstandings and distrust, create the climate for conflict. Physical tiredness or emotional exhaustion from the job or home circumstances, illness, anxiety or a sense of personal inadequacy can all contribute. Continually dealing with pupils or parents who are challenging or have difficulties can drain you and make you less able to cope with situations you would normally take in your stride. These are things to look out for in yourself, to try to prevent or understand, and to make allowances for in your colleagues. Conflict resolution is about trying to unravel the causes of the breakdown in normal relationships and then attempting to deal with the causes as swiftly, safely and considerately as possible.

If you are placed in a situation where you are the mediator, you may need to seek the help of a trained counsellor. Many conflicts can be helped by enabling the participants to explain their point of view separately to a mediator, and then feeding both points of view back to both parties to help them see what is going wrong. Looking for some jointly acceptable resolution together is then needed. Simple versions of this will work even with small children, who, given time and understanding, should be able to make more constructive relationships. Time-out places in playgrounds provide a thinking time for pupils as well as taking the heat out of the situation for the others using the space.

Some basic principles of conflict resolution are given by Rogers (1991):

1 Address the situation – the problem, not the people involved.

2 Avoid put-downs and criticism of the person – getting uptight yourself will not help, explain if it happens.

3 Acknowledge the emotional climate – recognise feelings and state them, including your own; respect is important.

4 Keep the heat down and avoid a power struggle – try to remain calm, assertive without being aggressive.

5 Call in a third party – get help.

6 Follow up conflict situations – use trained mediators if necessary; look towards future situations and their resolution.

Pupil conflict resolution

It is important that you are well-versed in the school policies for behaviour management and child protection, the limits of acceptable behaviour for your school, the reward and sanctions systems for your school and your limitations in being able to enforce any of them. It is also important that you get special advice and training in this area to protect yourself.

Be on the lookout for potential situations such as two pupils getting together whom you know are trouble when they are together. Windy days make little ones restless; parties or matches taking place in the locality may create excitement, or the arrival in town of a popular group or film. A new face in the class or playground may change the dynamics, or September can bring a new year group who are finding their feet by upsetting established ways of working. You should be able to recognise signs of anxiety and distress. Changes in personality can be cause for concern: do watch out for possible bullying, although it tends to take place away from adult eyes. Recognise that there could be problems due to a breakdown in relationships between you and the pupils. Do tell a teacher of your concerns and if necessary make a private note of time and place and concern.

In a playground situation, you may find you are able to interact with a group of pupils and help them deal with disagreements, or give individuals an opportunity to tell you of their problems or anxieties. You may see pupils reacting to other pupils in an aggressive way, a potential situation for a fight; facial expressions give away a lot. Swearing, tantrums and emotional outbursts, irritating and annoying mannerisms can all be indicators of possible trouble spots. Have some strategies for diverting or diffusing potential situations, such as sending a participant on an errand, engaging them in conversation, or offering to start a game or activity. Keep calm, reassure, give time out for each to think things through, and an opportunity for rethinking. Again, you should be a good listener, hear all sides and offer choices, not solutions. This allows potential situations to be defused without anyone losing face. Use those protocols mentioned above; remember the language of choice, reminding pupils of their rights and responsibilities.

Rogers (1991) also talks of stages in conflict, both in the classroom and in the playground:

1 Antecedent conditions: environmental factors;

2 Parties feeling or recognising the situation;

3 A conflict situation: arguing, yelling, screaming, fighting, etc;

4 Resolution: communication, mediation, withdrawal and intervention;

5 Aftermath: maintained hostility, revenge or genuine resolution – needs discussed, negotiated and resolved.

Do not use physical restraint unless you have been specifically trained in this area. Ensure you read your school's and the government guidance in this area if you consider you may be involved (DCSF 2007c). You should always know where to get help, whether during a situation or afterwards, both for yourself and for the participants. You must also recognise your own emotions when dealing with these kinds of situation. You may well get angry and frustrated. Do discuss how you feel with a mentor in the school, don't just bottle it up till you get home and then take it out on your own children or partner. Go through what you did with your mentor, and whether it could have been handled differently and whether anything could have been done to prevent the situation developing [19K11].

Questions to ask yourself

- What health problems do I have? Do these affect my performance at school?

- Should I discuss these with anyone in the school? Will that be difficult?

- What can I bring from my own experience to any discussion which is part of the school health education programme? Is this important?

- Do I know the expectations of behaviour for my school and what to do in any circumstances? (Try out some 'what if' situations in your mind and the actions you hope you would take.)

- To whom do I turn in a difficult situation?

- Can you remember situations when you were at school which were demeaning or unfair?

- Could you deal with those situations differently as a member of staff?

- Are there situations in your current post which make you feel uncomfortable?

- What can you do about them?

Essential reading

Your school's policies for health and safety, child protection and behaviour management

DCSF (2007c) *The use of force to control or restrain pupils (Non-statutory guidance).*

Some further reading

Any of the books by Bill Rogers are readable and practical, for example *I get by with a little help* (2006a) and the 2nd edition of *Classroom behaviour: A practical guide to effective behaviour management and colleague support* (2006b).

There are some very useful contributions about understanding behaviour during school break-time in Blatchford, P. and Sharp, S (1994) *Breaktime and the school*: 13–76.

Baginsky, M. (2000) *Child protection and education*.

Fox, G. (2001) *Supporting children with behaviour difficulties*.

Hook, P. and Vass, A. (2000a) *Confident classroom leadership*.

TDA (2006) *Behaviour management module: Induction training for teaching assistants*.

Useful websites

www.publications.doh.gov.uk/safeguardingchildren

www.teachernet.gov.uk/childprotection

www.nspcc.org.uk – for child protection advice

www.denizen.org.uk – for the cyber bully advice

www.nice.org.uk – for health advice

8

Supporting pupils with individual needs

Equal opportunities and individual needs

ONE OF THE DIFFICULTIES of teaching, maybe the main one, is that we are all different and all pupils are different. The expression 'delivering' the curriculum is largely inappropriate when you think of the learners who are 'receiving' the curriculum. Teaching pupils in classes depends on there being more similarities than differences and provides a cost-effective and efficient way of assisting learning, particularly when imparting information is required. Learning also has a social context; groups and classes provide the way to do this. The size of the group or class will depend on the age and nature of the pupils, the subject being taught and sometimes the size of room available. Students in university can be taught in a lecture hall of 500, seminars of 15 and tutorials of two people. Assemblies can similarly have several hundred present. Classes with their own class teacher can be small, even four to six in special units or special schools, more often 12 to 30, some as high as 36. Groups can range from two to eight or so. All pre-school provision has to have a ratio of at least one adult to 13 children [3K11].

Schools in the United Kingdom usually organise their classes in year groups. With the demands of the NC, annual assessments, the suggestions of nationally published schemes of work and the national strategy suggestions, fewer and fewer mixed-age groups are now found. In rural areas or in primary schools with definite catchment areas, however, where it is more obvious that children are not born in neat groups of 30 a year, mixed-age groups have to exist in order to fund the staff. Other countries are more flexible in some ways. If a pupil 'fails' to make the grade one year, they stay on and go through that year's work again, so the teacher is more likely to have a mixed-age similar-ability class than a teacher is in the United Kingdom. Secondary schools, and more frequently primary schools, have recognised that teaching a 'mixed-ability' class is not as easy as taking classes where pupils have similar ability. In the middle of the twentieth century, in the state system, when there were selective grammar schools and secondary modern schools streaming was widespread. Pupils were in classes and schools supposedly suitable for their perceived ability. Primary classrooms were organised hierarchically on ability with the 'bright' children at the back of the set of desks and the slower ones at the front. Special schools were those where children went who were deemed unable to cope with ordinary or 'mainstream' schools, and some children never went to school at all.

Research found that this kind of extreme segregation labelled pupils, and many pupils lived up to the predictions that others had made on their behalf. The system meant that pupils who were late developers, or 'handicapped', or even just lacking in self-esteem or self-confidence, never got the opportunities offered to others. Much talent and potential was missed. The comprehensive system of schools, totally mixed-ability classes, and the increasing integration of those with special needs into mainstream school were moves to try to redress the balance and be more in keeping with the increased emphasis on equal opportunities for all. Yet, organisation or reorganisation of systems was not enough to enable all children to progress according to their ability and needs. Teaching tended to aim at the middle of the ability range and those with higher or lower abilities were neglected. It was hoped that those with higher abilities would be able to fend for themselves, but those with physical or learning problems needed support, hence the emphasis on what is now called SEN.

The Warnock report of 1978 led to the 1981 Education Act. This highlighted these needs for the first time and proposed a system of identification and funded support (DES 1978). This was the beginning of the 'statementing procedure' and the definition of special funding into schools for assistants to support those identified – the beginning of learning support assistants as distinct from general ancillary or welfare assistants. In 1988, this time by what became known as the Education Reform Act (ERA), it became statutory that all children had an entitlement to a National Curriculum whatever their ability or disability. Equal opportunities legislation had also influenced schools' policies and procedures.

Until the Warnock report those with learning difficulties or disabilities that impeded their access to teaching in a mainstream school were described as educationally 'handicapped'. Special schools had their own specialist staff and different curriculum from mainstream schools. The two kinds of school co-existed in most education authorities: mainstream schools, which the majority attended, and special schools, which catered for a minority of pupils with learning difficulties or physical and sensory disabilities. Since then this picture has been changing gradually. Although special schools continue to provide for a section of the school population, an increasing number of pupils with significant learning difficulties or physical and sensory disabilities are being educated in mainstream schools. This is often described as inclusion.

Integration and inclusion

Until 1990 the term 'inclusion' had not been in common use in education. 'Integration' was more commonly used to express the alternative to education that segregated a section of children from the mainstream. Segregation was seen to be undesirable for social reasons as well as for educational reasons. If one group is segregated from the rest of society there is a tendency for them to become second class or low priority even if that was not the original intention. SEN had become low status within the education system and the poor quality of education in many special schools went unnoticed. Dessent (1987:14) summed up the general picture at that time with 'There are no votes in children with special educational needs'.

The contemporary picture has changed. The integration of increasing numbers of pupils with special educational needs into mainstream schools and classrooms is insufficient if it means simply placing them in situations with learners who do not have SEN and providing another TA or LSA to support them. A deeper level of integration is needed. This is expressed as 'inclusion' or 'belonging'. The inclusive classroom is not one where, for example, the child with Down's Syndrome sits with a TA engaged in learning tasks that bear no relationship to the curriculum followed by the rest of the class. Inclusive classrooms should be communities that accommodate and value every member. Thus one of the teacher's primary goals is to make sure that all children are able to participate as fully as possible in the routines and rituals of the classroom culture. While inclusive education of children with special educational needs is now an objective of public policy in the United Kingdom, it remains the subject of debate. Some authorities have closed all their special schools while others recognise that this is not only impractical for those with profound disabilities, it is also unsuitable and unfair. Special schools can be included in the local community or schools can be repositories of specialist knowledge and expertise, as can specialist teachers of units within mainstream schools. Change brings with it uncertainty and anxiety. It may also require an adjustment of values and a reframing of formerly held beliefs. The appointments of TAs in a school may be part of a strategy to increase the inclusive nature of a school. If so, your contribution to the strategy

PHOTOGRAPH 8.1   Individual work can take place within a group so that the pupil is included

PHOTOGRAPH 8.2   A classroom TA supports all who need it, not labelling a particular child

will be enhanced by an understanding of the theory of inclusive education. You should have seen, if not actually have, copies of your school's policies on inclusion and admissions, equal opportunities, SEN and behaviour [18K7; 20K3, 4].

Participation in the routines and rituals of the classroom culture includes sharing in the curriculum and learning experiences of the class. It includes working collaboratively with the teacher and other children and learning from them as well as with them. Learning in school is a social activity and it is important that the pupil with SEN is fully engaged in the social dimension of learning in the classroom and in the social life of the school as a whole [18K6]. If the school is trying to support fully the theory of inclusion, you will be there, not to take the child aside while the teacher enables the other children to move on, but to work with the teacher to intervene sensitively where support is required to enable the child to engage in learning as an equal participant with his or her peers [18K15; 20.1P4]. There is a whole section of the standards [Group B] for those TAs who are specifically appointed for helping those with individual needs, contained in which are 12 various standards for helping children and young people with various needs, but these standards must be seen in the context of the whole school and the whole range of differences of human beings.

It is not only pupils who need to feel included. The most effective TAs are those who perceive themselves to be an integral and recognised part of the whole-school team and approach their role as such, hence the emphasis in this book and the standards on relationships and teamwork [STL 21]. Included TAs will not underestimate the value of their contribution to the ethos of the school: 'Where the assistants feel as included as these, the likelihood is that pupils they support will also feel they are fully included in the classroom and school learning environment' (Balshaw and Farrell 2002:140).

Gifted and talented

The increased use of testing and the published league tables have highlighted discrepancies in the higher-ability range, hence the increased emphasis on specialist schools and the pinpointing of the gifted and talented (G & T) in school and the recognition in the standards of their work [STL 34]. Many schools, including primary schools, 'set' pupils as a way of organising them in ability groups for some subjects, e.g. English, Maths and Science, but retain the mixed social grouping of ordinary classes for all the other subjects. Some gifted and able children are now offered special classes or activities particularly designed to stretch their ability as discussed in the previous chapter. You may be working with the more able children who need encouragement or adult support for an activity. Traditionally, however, your role has been to support those who are less able.

G & T has been a neglected area for schools until recently. Much emphasis, support and money has gone into supporting the less able and those with disabilities, largely thinking the more able can get on with things anyway. If anything, this group have been left more to their own devices than the more average pupils. They were seen as quicker to learn and so capable of doing the necessary without extra resources or support. However, it is clear that in some schools this has meant children coasting, and not reaching their potential. Children from deprived backgrounds where there is no history of further or higher education may be just as bright but not have any incentive or encouragement to progress further, or the strategies to get information for themselves or realise what sorts of opportunities there might be. Able and particularly the gifted and especially talented children should be identified and their needs recognised. They do not have SEN in the general understanding of that term but they do have particular needs. The government believes the top 5 to 10 per cent in every school should be so identified, but clearly there is going to be a variation from year to year and from school to school.

The definition is not just about identifying those with a high academic potential, often called a high IQ. Children can be talented or gifted in a sport, in drama, music, the performing or graphic arts or in doing practical things in general. Often these children can have low self-esteem if they are not shining in academic subjects as these are so much emphasised in schools. Some of these children have emotional or social problems because they think so differently from their peers, and need special help in dealing with these problems. An imbalance between their area of giftedness and their emotional or chronological age can lead to frustration, emotional disturbance and poor behaviour. They can become bullied as 'swots', and they can easily become bored if neglected. You are in a good position to spot such talent and bring it to the attention of a class teacher. You are also able to question and challenge such children when they are working and perhaps find extra resources for them. Supporting such children is not just about pushing them on through the curriculum, enabling them to sit GCSEs early or whatever, but is about extending and broadening their experiences and making effective use of their talents.

As with any special need, you can find out more from relevant websites and help support pupils and their families, with ideas about extra-curricular opportunities like clubs or societies which specialise in the area in which your pupil seems to have a gift. The government website for 'young gifted and talented' is www.ygt.dcsf.gov.uk.

Special educational needs

Pupils are no longer described as educationally handicapped but rather as having special educational needs. Many TAs are employed specifically to assist one or more pupils with SEN. All of you will come across pupils with SEN in your work in mainstream classrooms. The Education Act 1996, which revised the original Act, contained a clear expectation that pupils with SEN will be included in mainstream schools. The Act requires education services to do everything possible to provide a mainstream place for a pupil with special educational needs if their parents/carers want it. Schools cannot refuse to admit a pupil on the grounds that they cannot cater for their special educational needs. Even if you have not been employed specifically to support such pupils and are working as a classroom or subject support TA in a mainstream school, an understanding of SEN is necessary to the effectiveness of your role. It will also help you understand that the principles of support for pupils with SEN are not significantly different from those applied to supporting pupils generally.

The concept of special educational needs

The formal definition can be found in the Education Act 1996, which is cited in *Special Educational Needs code of practice* (DfES 2001:6):

Children have special educational needs if they have a learning difficulty which calls for special educational provision to be made for them. Children have a learning difficulty if they:

(a) have a significantly greater difficulty in learning than the majority of children of the same age; or

(b) have a disability which prevents or hinders them from making use of educational facilities of a kind generally provided for children of the same age in schools within the area of the local education authority;

(c) are under compulsory school age and fall within the definition at (a) or (b) above or would so do if special educational provision was not made for them.

Children must not be regarded as having a learning difficulty solely because the language or form of language of their home is different from the language in which they will be taught. Special educational provision means:

(a) for children of two or over, educational provision which is additional to, or otherwise different from, the educational provision made generally for children of their age in schools maintained by the LEA, other than special schools, in the area;

(b) for children under two, educational provision of any kind.

The Code (p. 7) goes on to define disability:

A child is disabled if he is blind, deaf or dumb or suffers from a mental disorder of any kind or is substantially and permanently handicapped by illness, injury or congenital deformity or such other disability as may be prescribed.

(Section 17 (11), Children Act 1989)

A person has a disability for the purposes of this Act if he has a physical or mental impairment which has a substantial and long-term adverse effect on his ability to carry out normal day-to-day activities.

(Section 1 (1), Disability Discrimination Act 1995)

The term special educational needs was intended to facilitate a move away from determining a pupil's education by reference to a handicap or label towards educating them according to their individual needs. It shifts the focus from deficiencies in the pupil to deficiencies in the resources and environment in which they are to be educated. It moves the emphasis from the medical model of viewing disability as something that can be cured to a social model where it is society that needs to change and that disabled people or children have rights and choices. As an example, it is not because of their physical limitations that a physically disabled child with no learning difficulties may have special educational needs but rather because they may need resources to overcome barriers to accessing normal class teaching that their physical disability causes. A child with a learning difficulty has special educational needs only if that difficulty is greater than the norm and resources that are not normally available are needed to overcome their difficulties. The statutory definition of special educational needs is a relative one. A child with special needs in one context or environment may not be considered to have special educational needs in another. The presence of a special need depends upon the interaction of deficiencies within the pupil with deficiencies of the environment. This relativistic notion of special educational needs has been described as follows: 'The problems of the handicap are the result of the interaction between the nature of their deficiencies and the nature of their environment. The needs of the handicapped are therefore seen to be relative both to the deficiencies "within" the child and to the deficiencies of the environment' (Weddell 1983:100).

The task of meeting the pupil's SEN in the classroom therefore requires not only an understanding of what the child's strengths and weaknesses are but also an assessment of the learning situation and what adaptations to it are needed to enable the pupil to learn effectively. There will be circumstances in which your role is an integral part of making the learning environment more 'user-friendly' to the pupil with difficulties. Your time and skilled support is a resource that augments the work of the teacher in a number of ways and increases the chance that a pupil with SEN will be successfully integrated in the class. For example, you can meet a pupil's need for more frequent adult–pupil contact to cope with set tasks or problems. You, therefore, add not only to the resource of available adult time in the classroom, but also to the quality of teaching and learning. Unfortunately SEN defining has become as labelling as the old 'handicapped' system in many cases. TA support should not be reinforcing this labelling.

It is frequently said that a school with good provision for pupils with SEN will be a school that makes good provision for all its pupils. Such a maxim recognises that special educational needs exist along a continuum from children who need a very small amount of support in their learning to those who require a considerable degree of help. The pupil who is on the register of pupils with SEN might sometimes differ in only a small degree from other pupils in a class. The division between SEN and the general needs of pupils in a class can therefore be an arbitrary one. While much of your attention will be focused on the needs of a particular child or group, the effective TA will make themselves aware of the needs of the whole class and offer support at a range of levels. The experienced assistant will be proactive in identifying where this support is needed at any one time. By being proactive with other members of the class, you will enable the teacher to work with the pupil(s) with SEN. This means that the pupil(s) do not become over-reliant on one adult's support and they practise social skills with their peers and the teacher. Social skills are often inhibited in pupils with SEN due to the constant attention of a TA; the pupil with SEN needs to work independently even if for some children this is for the briefest of moments.

Statements of special educational need and the Individual Education Plan

As indicated earlier, a pupil may have a statement of special educational need because they have a learning difficulty that is significantly greater than that of other pupils, or they have a disability that impedes their access to the curriculum and requires resources that are not generally available. An allocation of support time may be provided for in the statement together with clear information on the type of provision that is required. Your primary task may be to give that support so that the provision can be put in place.

A well-written statement of special educational need should give a clear description of the pupil's strengths and weaknesses. It should indicate the areas of weakness that are interfering with the child's progress, or the disabilities that impede the child's access to the normal curriculum. It should specify a set of aims and objectives for the child's education provision. If the LA is fully committed to the principle of inclusive education, one aim should be to give the pupil full access to a broad and balanced curriculum appropriate to their age. Some objectives will be very specific and measurable; for example, to achieve a reading age of x years in y time. Others may be less exact but nevertheless observable; for example, Oliver's listening skills will improve.

Such objectives should be part of the Individual Education Plan (IEP) that follows the statement. The plan will specify usually three or four short-term targets towards the achievement of objectives set out in the statement. For example, a short-term target might be: By the next review Olivia will be able to recognise the ten most frequently used words by sight. The IEP will outline proposed resources and strategies for meeting such targets, and provision including how TAs are to be deployed. It should also describe arrangements for assessing and reviewing the pupil's progress and achievement of the targets. The SENCO will have responsibility for the preparation and management of an IEP. However, in secondary schools 'delivery of the IEP will be the responsibility of subject teachers'. (DfES 2001: para 6 : 67) and in primary schools delivery of the IEP is the responsibility of the class teacher. Your role is to support the implementation of the requirements of the Statement and the IEP.

You may find that you are part of a team of TAs, especially in secondary schools, which works with a child across the curriculum depending upon how the TAs are deployed, i.e. using the TAs' SEN experience and skills together with their curriculum strengths. Regardless of whether you are the only TA working with a pupils with SEN or are part of a team, you will be monitoring the pupil regularly and be making observations about the pupil's response to his/her IEP. You will, therefore, be required to make notes on a daily/lesson-by-lesson basis so that you can keep the SENCO informed of the pupil's progress towards the objectives in the IEP.

You will need several things if you are to be successful in monitoring the effectiveness of the IEP. Obviously, you need to know what the IEP is and keep its objectives in mind at all times. Where your role is to assist with the delivery of an individual learning programme you should feel well briefed by the SENCO and the class teacher on how the programme fits in with IEP objectives. You should also be told whether the pupil is on medication and how this might affect their performance and behaviour. Many SENCOs now hold regular meetings for the TAs, not only to brief them on individual pupils but also to keep them up to date with ideas, resources and moves the school may be making to increase inclusion or organise the work of all the TAs. You should be able to report back progress and problems to the SENCO, suggest what works and what is not working and contribute to the general discussion. When you are supporting a child in the general class lesson you must be aware of the overall aim of the lesson. You should intervene to support the pupil sensitively and at the minimum level required. As has been said already, be proactive within the class as your task is not to follow the pupil and stick by them regardless, sometimes referred to as the 'Velcro' approach. Some TAs describe their work as 'doing myself out of a job'. It can be tempting for the school to retain the provision to keep the funding that supports it but this should not happen.

If an important part of your role is to facilitate inclusivity in the classroom, it should be perceived by all pupils to be a normal part of what goes on there. Offering support at the minimum level required, rather than seeming to impose it on the pupil, is more likely to promote independent learning and develop self-confidence and self-esteem. The willingness to take risks and make mistakes is important for effective learning. Encouragement in the face of difficult tasks is more likely to promote the child's learning than protection from difficulty, provided that the tasks are achievable. When supporting a pupil in the subject lesson you should have in mind objectives in the IEP relating to the improvement of basic skills as well as the pupil's need for help with the content of the lesson or subject-related tasks. The subject lesson can be seen as providing a context for learning or practising basic literacy or numeracy skills as well as for acquiring subject knowledge and related skills. It is worth remembering, at this point, that the pupil's teachers are 'responsible for working with the pupil on a daily basis and for planning and delivering an individualised programme' (DfES 2001 para 6:53), i.e. delivering the IEP and differentiation. Therefore, liaison between yourself and the teacher is crucial regarding how the pupil is achieving the tasks and the degree to which you are supporting the child in accessing and completing activities.

If you find that the pupil is unable to work independently, despite your support, then this suggests that the task needs to be differentiated more and the teacher needs to know that this is the case. The optimum level of TA support (i.e. avoiding the 'velcroed' TA) will depend, of course, on the needs of the child which may change from task to task. Teachers should plan for the role of the TA within a lesson and enable themselves to work with the pupil so that they can make their own observations as to how a pupil is doing. There should then be a conversation between yourself and the teacher so the teacher's planning for the next lesson is informed and includes your input. The goal should be for support to be minimal and appropriate and you should be able to make suggestions considering your knowledge of the pupil and his/her strengths and needs.

School Action, School Action Plus and beyond

Not all pupils with learning difficulties have statements of special educational need. The current *Special Educational Needs code of practice* (DfES 2001) requires schools to identify pupils with learning difficulties and to decide whether action needs to be taken which is in addition to or different from the normal provision for pupils in the school. This provision forms part of a graduated approach. 'School Action: when a class or subject teacher identify that a pupil has special educational needs they provide interventions that are additional to or different from those provided as part of the school's usual differentiated curriculum offer and strategies. An IEP will usually be devised' (DfES 2001:206).

If upon review after a suitable period of time the pupil continues to have significant difficulties resulting in lack of progress in the curriculum, the school might seek expert advice from an advisory teacher or an educational psychologist. Such advice will be incorporated in School Action Plus: 'School Action Plus: when the class or subject teacher and the SENCO are provided with advice or support from outside specialists, so that alternative interventions, additional or different strategies to those provided for the pupil through School Action can be put in place. The SENCO usually takes the lead although day-to-day provision continues to be the responsibility of class or subject teacher. A new IEP will usually be devised' (DfES 2001:206). It is only when the school has taken all relevant steps available to it and a pupil is still not making the progress expected of them that the Local Authority would usually consider starting a statutory assessment of their learning difficulties. The assessment might lead to a statement of special educational needs, or a note in lieu of a statement if the assessment indicates that continued support at the Action Plus stage is appropriate.

The Code requires the parents/carers to be involved at every stage of the process of preparing and reviewing a School Action. The pupil's views must also be taken into account. If you have established a good working relationship with the pupils whom you are supporting, you can make a significant contribution to the process of pupil and parent/carer involvement. Systematic recording of the pupil's approach to learning, their motivation and attitude to support, is as important to the evaluation of the School Action as measurement of their progress in a particular skill, such as reading. The Code of Practice requires schools to involve pupils in decision making by ensuring that the pupil understands the purpose of support and is actively involved in monitoring and developing their learning targets. The nature of your role often enables you to get closer to the pupils to whom you are assigned than a teacher can. As a consequence pupils often feel more confident or encouraged to express their view to you and it is not unusual for the TA to be given the task of helping the pupil to record their contribution to a review.

You may also have contact with parents/carers, either at reviews or informally at other times. In general, you should keep in mind when working with parents/carers that your role is a supportive one. The ability to listen is an important skill in the process of building a supportive relationship. When talking with parents/carers you should be aware of how to respond if issues arise that are outside your responsibility or beyond the scope of your role. You should know whom to turn to for advice and to whom to direct the parent/carer, usually the SENCO. It is always worth letting the SENCO know about any conversations with parents/carers that are more than just comments about the weather.

Current developments about Individual Education Plans and SEN provision

There are developments for SEN provision to be 'mapped' in each school, e.g. across year groups, type of need and level or 'wave' of intervention. As a result, the National Audit Commission is developing an SEN Provision Mapping Toolkit in consultation with schools and local authorities. You will need to find out how your school is responding to these developments, since it may mean that, as pupils' targets are set by the class/subject teacher following the development of target setting for all students, only students with Statements of SEN and those on School Action Plus have the traditional IEP. Provision for students on School Action together with the details required in an IEP, as outlined above, apart from their targets, may be in a different document and presented in a different format. However, reviews for all students with SEN will still take place, with the focus for reviews depending upon the level of need of the pupil.

The four areas of special educational needs

While it has been a long-established principle that labelling children with SEN is undesirable, in practice it has proved difficult to avoid describing categories of pupils with SEN. One viewpoint is that labels or categories are needed for purely administrative purposes. Standard 38 is for any TA who is supporting children with a disability or SEN regardless of the particular concern. Determining the number of pupils in each category helps with the rational distribution of finite resources. On the downside, even the new categories may facilitate the exclusion of some groups of pupils. The current *Special Educational Needs code of practice* describes four areas of need:

■ communication and interaction;

■ cognition (understanding and reasoning) and learning;

■ behaviour, emotional and social development;

■ sensory and/or physical.

It would not be difficult for you to identify which category of pupils is most likely to be at risk of exclusion. However, you will undoubtedly meet many pupils whose special needs do not fit readily in any single category. Indeed, the Code of Practice recognises that the SEN are interrelated 'although there are specific needs that usually relate directly to particular types of impairment' (DfES 2001:85). The Code refers to some learning difficulties in descriptions of more than one category (e.g. dyslexia). While the focus of an assistant's support may be presumed to be upon a particular type of 'impairment' or learning difficulty, in reality your support for any individual is likely to demand understanding and skill in dealing with any combination of the four areas of need. It is well known that pupils with SEN often have multiple needs. For example, many pupils with learning difficulties have accompanying problems of behaviour, poor social skills or low self-esteem. The majority of pupils who are singled out on account of primary behavioural or emotional problems also underachieve in basic literacy and number skills. To be effective, you need to recognise that the support you give is not necessarily confined to a specific category of need but that such support may be the context for contributing to the promotion of the child's wider development. For example, if you are assigned to help a child with their reading difficulty, you will need to develop a relationship of trust with them and work on building their self-esteem and confidence before they can make progress with reading. If you are working towards the NOS in any of the four areas of need or with a pupil with any particular need, you will need more information than this book can provide. Some further reading is suggested at the end of the chapter and SENCOs will guide your study and suggest possible courses or contacts for you.

Communication and interaction [39]

The description of this area of special needs in the Code of Practice covers a wide spectrum of difficulties. The Code acknowledges that most children with SEN have strengths and difficulties in one, some or all of the areas of speech, language and communication. Access to and progress within the curriculum depend upon the ability to understand and communicate through language. By definition, therefore, the child with learning difficulties will have more weaknesses than strengths in their language development. The purpose of intervention and support is usually two-fold:

■ facilitating access to the curriculum by helping the child overcome barriers to effective communication in the classroom;

■ the development of specific skills.

In the first instance you might be in the classroom to ensure that the child has understood instructions, has the support needed to read texts, or is able to express themselves effectively in written tasks. In the second instance, your support might focus on developing specific handwriting and spelling skills, or reading fluency and comprehension. In more complex cases where, for example, the pupil has a severe speech and language delay or a hearing impairment, your role might be to focus on broader language and communication skills. It might focus on the development of expressive skills, such as the ability to talk clearly and fluently in age-appropriate sentences; or on the development of receptive skills, such as the ability to listen and to act upon instructions of increasing complexity.

Children with severe developmental language delay might benefit from learning a sign language. Signing is often employed in special nursery classes. An assistant working in such a class should be prepared to learn and use sign language with the children, just as in other situations they would expect to interact with children and model proper forms of speech and language. Sign language is not intended to be a long-term substitute for speech in children with developmental delay. However, it is a means by which central processes upon which language development depends can operate. A child who is able to communicate by signing has the basis for later communication by speech. Signing may be the long-term means of communication for profoundly deaf children and for some partially hearing children. Historically, signing has been a subject of dispute among educators of the deaf and partially hearing. The Code lists what a pupil with communication and interaction difficulties might require to meet their special needs (DfES 2001: 86, para 7: 56). However, if you are helping the pupil in one or more of those areas, you need to be aware that the pupil's needs will often extend beyond the limits of help in articulation, acquiring, comprehending and using language, or any other of the requirements listed.

Language is important to the development of thought and self-regulated behaviour. It is the medium by which we relate to and interact with others and as such is important to social development. The child with limited or delayed language skills may therefore be expected to show immature or poorly developed social behaviour. Young children with delayed speech and language skills are likely to be more impulsive and lacking in concentration than expected for their age. Pupils with dyspraxia and those with characteristics within the autistic spectrum have problems of social communication and understanding that are directly caused by deficits in their understanding of the practical effects of language in social situations. They have difficulty in understanding another's point of view. The child with dyspraxia often appears to be rude and provocative in their manner towards other people and this can frequently lead to problems. Supporting a child or young person described as having problems of communication and interaction may therefore demand a high level of professional tolerance on the part of the assistant, as well as good skills of behaviour management.

The standards refer to Alternative and Augmentative Communication (AAC). This is just a term used to describe the different methods that can be used to help people with disabilities communicate with each other. It may include manual signing, writing, lip reading and the use of various electronic aids sometimes referred to as inclusive technology.

English as an additional language

The Code makes special mention of children whose first language is not English. Some children may first come to school lacking competence in English not because they have special educational needs but simply because English has not been the preferred language in their home culture and community. The Code states that lack of competence in such circumstances must not be equated with learning difficulties as understood in the Code. In other words, while the child needs assistance to develop fluency in English to access the curriculum in school, it should not be assumed that they have a learning difficulty. Chapter 9 is about supporting EAL pupils.

On the other hand, where a child is making slow progress, it should not be assumed that it is because of their language status. Careful assessment is important in such cases. It should include consideration of their background, and their fluency in their first language as reported by parents/carers. It should also include observation of their performance in a range of situations in school. The observations of an experienced assistant can be a significant contribution to the assessment. How much use the child makes of their own language, how actively they try to make themselves understood in play or group activity with other children, and the skills and competencies they show in activities such as drawing, construction or number can all be indicators of the child's learning capacity. You could report on how quickly the child appears to pick up and use words and phrases from other children. Indeed, the learning of language can be viewed as a social activity, and an assistant does as much for developing a child's English language skills by setting up situations for active social learning as by direct instruction. At the same time, you should take cultural factors into account when observing a child's behaviour in different situations. The social norms that are accepted in nursery class learning might be significantly different from a child's home experience and difficult for the child to interpret and understand. Assumptions about the child's learning abilities cannot be based solely on apparent differences from the norm in the child's social behaviour in the classroom or small group. You and the teacher should always carefully and critically examine the content of the curriculum, and the nature of the learning situation for young children who are at the early stages of learning English, before looking for 'within child' special educational needs to explain a child's progress.

Cognition and learning [40]

The Code of Practice says that children who demonstrate features of moderate, severe or profound learning difficulties, or specific difficulties such as dyspraxia or dyslexia, require specific programmes to aid progress in cognition and learning. Children with physical or sensory impairments may also need help in this area, as will children with conditions on the autistic spectrum.

The overlap between difficulties of cognition (or knowing) and learning and those of communication and language is considerable. Many items on the lists of their requirements in the Code of Practice apply to the needs of both groups. However, the special emphasis given to cognition and learning is an attempt to distinguish between pupils who have an underlying potential for effective learning and those whose general ability is below average and who are likely to progress relatively slowly.

These are children who need time to take in and grasp ideas. They do not learn as quickly as the average child and need a slower pace of teaching. They need more repetition and practice to learn basic skills. They do not have good memories. Working memory in particular is essential for learning. It is the ability to take in information, hold it in the memory in the short term while organising it mentally. Take a mental arithmetic problem such as 'Jean had four sweets; she ate one and gave one to Sally. How many did she have left?' To solve it the child has to take in several pieces of information and keep them in mind while using them in two number operations. To solve the problem therefore requires an efficient working memory. So does the ability to follow instructions and solve problems in any area of the curriculum. Cognition also refers to the child's level of awareness and understanding of the world around them. It involves being able to see relationships, similarities and differences in things and to solve problems. The type of support that a classroom assistant will be asked to give a child will depend upon the child's age and severity of need. For children with the most profound learning difficulties it may involve helping to stimulate their senses of sight and touch and helping them develop their ability to respond and interact with their environment. Support for the pupil with moderate learning difficulties might involve breaking down problems or classroom tasks into manageable steps, checking the child's understanding of the content of the lesson and what is required, and helping with reading, spelling and recording. The intensity of involvement will depend on the severity of the child's difficulties and the degree to which you judge the child to be able to cope independently at any stage.

Behavioural, emotional and social development (BESD) [37 and 41]

Pupils with emotional and behavioural difficulties may also have general or specific learning difficulties or they may be pupils with normal or good potential. However, it is their emotional and behavioural difficulties that are the main barrier to their learning and access to the curriculum. Sometimes a child's challenging behaviour is a feature of a complex learning or developmental disorder. Some autistic children, for example, have extreme characteristics of challenging behaviour. In other cases a pupil's emotional and behavioural problems in school are symptomatic of traumas and difficulties in the home or social environment outside the school. A primary aim of intervention for a child with these difficulties will be to reduce or eliminate the incidence of behaviours that are interfering with the child's ability to learn and to replace them with more appropriate patterns of behaviour.

This book can only give you the essentials, and you must get both training and more specialised information for dealing with specific situations and specific pupils [19.2P10; 19K22]. For general use you will find Fox (2001) helpful. Senior members of staff will always be available for you if a situation becomes more than you should deal with, either to refer matters to at the time or later for advice. Schools also have access to specialist teams and psychologists to whom you may be able to talk. There will be courses available both within the school INSET (in-school education and training) programme and externally delivered.

Interventions should include a behaviour plan (which is similar to an IEP) that is known to the child's teachers and to you. As with an IEP, it should contain clear targets. Clear targets mean that teachers, teaching assistant(s), parents/carers and the pupil know exactly what is being focused upon. For example, 'John will become less disruptive in class' is a 'fuzzy' or unclear target. A 'fuzzy' is a description of performance that is unclear or ambiguous. It is better to describe problem behaviour in clear, observable terms. Precisely what does John do? He may 'frequently leave his seat without asking permission' or 'shout across the classroom'. These are descriptions of 'disruptive' behaviour that give a clear idea of precisely which behaviour is to be reduced if John is to be less disruptive. Thinking of behaviour in this way will help you by clarifying what you can focus on in your support role. It is also important to observe the circumstances in which inappropriate or undesirable behaviour occurs and to ask what changes can prevent the behaviour happening in the first place. This is like putting a gate at the top of the stairs to protect a child from falling. A child who constantly interferes and disrupts others in their class may have less opportunity if they have their own ruler and rubber and do not have to reach across or leave their seat to 'borrow' one from another child. If you are being observant and react in such small ways you can sometimes pre-empt behaviour which otherwise might escalate into major disruption. Government guidance for those helping in this field has recently been issued as a reminder (DCSF 2008) pending a review of the Children and Adolescent Mental Health Services announced in the Children's Plan. It is available on the teachernet website.

First and foremost, you must be able to stand back from any situation and deal with it objectively. This is not always easy but it helps if you have an understanding of what motivates the child to behave in a particular way. The origins may be in their upbringing or disturbing experiences at home. The purpose of all behaviour is to satisfy a need. Undesirable or problem behaviour of children in school or at home frequently occurs to satisfy the child's need for one or more of the following:

- attention
- affection
- protection
- power.

Thinking of behaviour in such terms offers clues as to how to respond appropriately to it. For example, frequent reprimands may reward rather than punish the child who is desperate for attention and may increase their attention seeking. The child who needs to dominate and exert power over adults does so by refusing to respond to reasonable requests, provoking conflict and anger in adults. Recognising this possibility enables the adult to maintain control by anticipating potential conflict and avoiding confrontation. Confrontation and conflict often arise in response to secondary behaviours rather than primary behaviours. For example:

> TEACHER: Jane, put your mobile away, please (primary behaviour).
> *Jane puts mobile away but scowls at teacher and mutters something under her breath.*
> TEACHER: Don't look at me in that way and don't be so rude (secondary behaviour).
> JANE: No I wasn't. Why pick on me? I wasn't the only one.
> TEACHER: Calm down or you will have to leave the room.

Jane is now in danger of being excluded from class not because she was playing with her mobile but because of her secondary behaviour. It is frequently better to ignore secondary behaviours if the child has responded to your attempt to deal with the initial behaviour. The questions of respect and responding to reasonable requests do not have to be ignored but in cases like Jane's they can be addressed later. You will undoubtedly be faced with many similar situations or observe them in pupil–teacher confrontations. If you are aware that a child is behaving inappropriately, you should try to respond in the least intrusive or confrontational manner. Depending on the circumstance, a non-verbal message such as a look, a shake of the head or a gesture might be enough. This keeps the message personal and private between the pupil and you. If it is necessary to speak to the child it is always easier to direct them to what they should be doing than to what they should not. Offer simple choices, and establish that they are responsible for the consequences of their behaviour. Reminding the pupil of a class rule may be sufficient. A casual statement or question can be enough to redirect a pupil's attention to a task. For example, asking the distractible child where they have got up to, or what they are going to write next, can be more effective than drawing attention to the distractible behaviour. Another strategy is to engage with the pupils near the child with behavioural needs first and support them to work on task briefly or praise them for their work before giving your attention to the pupil in question. This reinforces positive role models as well as using inclusive working approaches.

Sensory and/or physical needs [42]

The Code of Practice refers to a 'wide spectrum of sensory, multi-sensory and physical difficulties' (DfES 2001: 88) affecting children's ability to profit from the curriculum at school. Special educational provision is usually available to children with the most severe difficulties from an early age. It is possible therefore to find the expertise of TAs deployed in all phases of education from nursery classes to secondary schools.

Your role could be wide-ranging in some contexts, especially at the early years stage or where the individual child's needs are complex. For example, pupils with complex needs require support for their physical management and welfare as well as help in learning tasks. You will need to be aware of the nature of the child's disabilities and how they affect their learning. For example, it is not enough to know that a child is visually impaired and conclude that they will respond to large print. Visual impairment takes different forms and each affects the child's access to print in a different way. If you are aware of the particular form of impairment, you can adjust your approach to helping that child accordingly. Similarly, a child with a hearing impairment is not hearing 'normally' just because they are wearing an aid. The fact that a child has partial hearing does not mean that their language development will be that of a child with normal hearing. You will need special advice and training if you are to use equipment designed to support pupils with many of these needs, such as hearing aids, computer-assisted devices, hoists and other supports.

Whatever the impairment, if you are aware of its potential effects on the child's overall functioning, you will be better able to help them in the classroom. The fact that you work under the direction of the teacher does not stop you observing the pupil's response to the task or materials and asking questions: can he/she see this properly? is it in the right place, at the right angle, in the right light? has he heard all the parts of the question? is this too difficult or too easy for her? You also need to be aware of the effects of any medication on the pupil's functioning at any time. Some children will be on drugs that suppress their activity levels and responses to stimulation. They may appear at times to be fractious or just plain tired as a result. Your demands for them to take part in activities will need to be adapted accordingly. The school day of children with significant physical and/or neurological disabilities can often be interrupted for therapeutic or medical treatments. Again, you must be sensitive to the mood and motivation of the pupil on return to the classroom and adapt your work accordingly. Support for the child in the classroom and wider school will in some circumstances require you to help with physical aspects of the child's needs. At the simplest level this could mean helping to transfer the child from a wheelchair to a special standing frame. You should receive some guidance and training before taking on tasks where correct physical management of the child is necessary, both for the welfare of the child and for your safety. You must not hesitate to ask physiotherapists or experienced teachers for guidance on how to lift the child or use any specialist equipment.

While some children are likely to require care throughout their lives, the development of maximum independence and self-sufficiency should remain a key objective of any long-term plan for them. You should be sensitive to the pupil's age and developmental needs when offering support. Some children seek independence, and disabled young students can become resentful of over-intrusive efforts to help them. Remember, if you are aware that a teenaged student with physical disabilities is likely to have the same emotional needs for independence as your own teenaged child at home, you will manage them with the same sensitivity and respect. You might also recognise 'learned dependence' in another pupil, in which case your role will be to draw back from giving the child assistance in areas where they are able to cope independently. Here the task might be to encourage the child to take the next step on the path to self-sufficiency rather than giving way to your natural impulse to help. Increasing independence may also form part of the IEP.

The glossary of terms at the beginning of STL 13 (Level 2) is a very useful summary of principles. The carer aims to:

- maximise the potential and independence of the individual;
- respect the rights, wishes, feelings of the individual in order to meet their needs and take account of their choices;
- where necessary or possible, act as interpreter and advocate for the individual;
- act within the law;

- treat the individual equally with their peers and not discriminate against them;
- treat them with dignity, respecting privacy;
- protect the individual from danger and harm;
- enable access to information about themselves;
- communicate with them in their preferred method and language.

Self-esteem is even more important for children or young people who have any disability, so talking with them, telling them what you are going to do, asking their advice on the preferred way of doing things is really important. They need to feel they are in charge of what is going on. Remember what it is like when somebody cares for you when you are unwell. It is tempting to feel sorry for yourself and even pretend to be worse than you are to get sympathy. So there is the balance here between doing the right thing for an individual and getting them to help themselves.

Motor education

A detailed explanation of the principles and practice of motor education is beyond the scope of this chapter. However, a summary of what motor education is will enable you to decide whether you want or need to pursue the subject in more detail. 'Motor education' is a term that includes teaching methods for the physically disabled and neurologically impaired based upon the principles of Conductive Education pioneered at the Peto Institute in Hungary. The method is based upon the theory that physical and some cognitive difficulties, caused by damaged or disorganised nerve pathways in children with congenital conditions such as cerebral palsy, can be reduced through a systematic programme of physical and sensory exercises. The theory suggests that the sensory experiences produced by systematic physical activities develop or activate new neural pathways and enable the child to develop functions that they previously lacked. For example, normal development involves the gradual integration of senses and the development of structures in the brain that enable the child to respond to their environment in a meaningful way. Thus an infant learns to integrate sight and arm movement to reach and explore an object. They become increasingly aware of the relationship of body parts and learn to use them in a coordinated way to stand and walk. The neurologically impaired child is prevented from developing in this way spontaneously. They therefore need systematic help. Initially they need someone to move their limbs for them so that the relevant sensory messages can establish new pathways in the nervous system that eventually allow the child to move autonomously in a purposeful, coordinated way. If you are a TA working in a special school or unit, you could be involved in programmes of this kind.

Questions to ask yourself

- Do you know where the most recent copy of the Code of Practice is in the school?
- Do you have and have you read and understood the school SEN policy?
- Have you seen the IEP format for the school?
- Have you seen the IEPs of the pupils with whom you work closely?
- Have you discussed the content with the SENCO?
- Are there any national associations supporting the pupils with SEN with whom you work closely and their families? Can you make contact with them?

Essential reading

DfEE (1998a) *Excellence for all children: Meeting Special Educational Needs.*

DfEE (1998b) *Meeting Special Educational Needs: A programme for action.*

(DfES 2001) *Special Educational Needs code of practice.*

Some further reading

The TDA TA induction materials for inclusion, Section 6 in the TA files.

DCSF (2008c) *The education of children and young people with behavioural, emotional and social difficulties as a special educational need.*

Any of the national strategy materials designed for supporting aspects of SEN.

Balshaw, M. and Farrell, P. (2002) *Teaching assistants: Practical strategies for effective classroom support.*

Booth, T. (2002) *Index for inclusion: Developing learning and participation in schools.*

East, V. and Evans, L. (2006) *At a glance: A quick guide to children's special needs.*

Lovey, J. (2002) *Supporting Special Educational Needs in secondary school classrooms.*

Spooner, W. (2006) *The SEN Handbook for trainee teachers, NQTs and teaching assistants.*

Thomas, G., Walker, D. and Webb, J. (1998) *The making of the inclusive school.*

The David Fulton Publishers and Routledge lists for SEN with specific titles, e.g. Dyslexia, Dyspraxia, Aspergers, etc.

Useful websites

www.dcsf.gov.uk

www.teachernet.gov.uk

www.nasen.org.uk – the National Association for SEN

www.ygt.dcsf.gov.uk – for advice about young gifted and talented

Supporting bilingual and multilingual pupils [35, 36]

English as an additional language

IN SCHOOLS throughout England and Wales, you will come across pupils who have EAL. They make up about 13 per cent of the total school population and have origins all over the world, from Colombia to Afghanistan and from Sri Lanka to Lithuania. Pupils with EAL tend to be found in schools in urban areas such as London and Birmingham, and some boroughs, such as Tower Hamlets and Hackney, have more than 50 per cent of pupils with EAL. Schools in rural areas, however, often have EAL pupils too and local authorities such as Devon and Norfolk provide support to these pupils. They bring a cultural and linguistic richness to schools and are sometimes our highest achievers. EAL pupils are referred to in most DCSF and Ofsted publications and EAL can be quite a high profile aspect of Ofsted inspections.

It is useful to be clear about some terminology used concerning EAL pupils. You may have come across the term ESL or English as a second language. This was dropped some years ago because many EAL pupils speak more than two languages. For example, a child from Kenya may speak Swahili and Panjabi and be learning English as a third language. The term EFL (English as a foreign language) should not be used as this usually refers either to students learning English in countries where English is not the mother-tongue, or to students coming to Britain to study English for short periods of time. The term 'bilingual' is often defined as living in two languages or having access to two languages but not necessarily being fluent in them.

Who are our EAL pupils?

EAL pupils come from a diverse range of backgrounds throughout the world. Not all, however, are born overseas and indeed many have been born here to families whose first language is not English. These pupils may enter school not speaking English as they have grown up in communities in Britain where English is not the first language. Their television programmes may also not be in English, so little English may be used in the family home.

Of course, not all EAL pupils are beginners in English. Local authorities usually have their own system for grading pupils from beginners to fully fluent bilingual pupils. Some use stages of language learning with between four and seven levels, while others have moved over to additional National Curriculum step levels as recommended by the QCA. You can find out about these through the EAL teacher in your school or through your local authority. It is currently thought that it takes children between five and seven years to achieve full fluency in English, although there can be considerable variation depending on the pupil. Remember, full fluency in terms of schooling does not just mean being able to use conversational English but to have knowledge of academic language and the literacy and oracy skills that go with this.

EAL pupils are not a homogenous group of learners and can be put into three general groups:

1   Some children come into school with little or no spoken English but with strong literacy skills in another language, particularly if they are older. They may have received a good education in their home country and already be competent in many National Curriculum subject areas. These pupils are sometimes referred to as 'elite bilinguals' and often come from middle-class homes where there are considerable expectations and knowledge of the education system. These children may come from families who have chosen to travel abroad for business, academic or diplomatic reasons or may be from educated refugee families, forced to flee their home country.

2   A further group of children are those who enter school with limited spoken English and little or no reading or writing skills in their first language. The child's home language may have low status in wider society yet there will be strong pressure from the local community to maintain the first language and culture. The family may value education highly but not understand what is specifically needed to support a child's academic learning. These pupils are sometimes termed as coming from 'linguistic minorities'.

3   Some children come from homes where another language is spoken by one parent and the child grows up with two languages in a bilingual family. Quite often the language of the host country (English) will predominate as the child gets older.

When working with EAL pupils, it is important to find out as much as you can about their backgrounds to inform your expectations. For example, if you are working with an 11-year-old child who is at an early stage of writing development, this may be because the child has had a disrupted education because of war or lack of access to schooling rather than having a special educational need. Other children may have had an excellent education in their home country and may be very good, for example, at maths – you may find the work you have been given to do with them is not at the right level and needs to be more challenging. Do give the teacher you work with any information you gain about problems and progress and also any background information about the pupils.

As well as policies, the school may well have protocols on finding out information about pupils and it is important to follow these. There may be an EAL or Ethnic Minority Achievement (EMA) teacher or department in your school, or the class teacher themselves may know a lot about the pupils concerned. The school office should hold much useful information in the pupil files on the languages children speak, their previous educational experience and their ethnicity and religion. Remember that some of the information may be confidential, so check either with the office or with a senior member of staff that it is all right for you to see this.

Factors affecting pupils' learning of English

Apart from the aspects of a child's background which may affect progress in learning English to do with class, social background and educational experience, and the quality of teaching and support children receive, there are some other factors. These include:

Age

It is often assumed that it is easier for younger children to learn languages than for older children. This is not necessarily the case. Some children who arrive at nursery school speaking little English can find it quite a stressful situation and can take some time to start learning English. On the other hand, older secondary age children may well already have considerable language skills in their first language, which they do not have to relearn when learning English. These skills can be transferred to English and this partly explains how some EAL pupils can achieve high GCSE grades within two or three years of arriving at a school in this country.

Immersion

It is often assumed, too, that the best way of learning English is to be thrown in at the deep end: to be immersed in it totally. It seems logical that if the language is all around you, you must learn and learn quickly. However, many high-achieving children, for example from Chinese or Indian backgrounds, speak more than two languages regularly. They may speak English at school in lessons, speak Chinese and English at home with their parents, and watch some Chinese television. There is no evidence of a correlation between time spent in an English-speaking environment and learning English. Indeed the evidence suggests that it is critical to have a well-developed first language and that this is a key factor in learning English. Furthermore, in lessons, if you can provide a quick translation of a key word, this can help understanding of a concept and support a child's learning.

Character and emotional factors

Inevitably, a child's character is important in determining success in language learning. Children who are more outgoing and who are prepared to take risks tend to be better language learners. Shy, quieter and less adventurous children may be less successful. Emotional issues may also inhibit a child learning. If a child is unhappy because of experiences she/he has been through, is worried about friends and relatives left behind in another country or has not settled well into the school, inevitably this will get in the way of effective learning.

A safe and welcoming environment

It is important that all children feel safe and supported within their school. Because some EAL pupils have little English and some may be obviously different from other children in terms of skin colour, hairstyle or dress, they may be picked on, bullied or isolated from other children. You need to be aware of this and work with the school to follow the advice offered below on supporting children new to the school. Ensure you know the school procedures for dealing with bullying and racist incidents. Children who are bullied may suffer low self-esteem and their attendance at school may also suffer.

Teaching styles

Children who arrive in school from overseas may have had a very different experience of schooling. Some may have gone to schools with a similar education system to ours but others may be used to what might be termed a more 'traditional' system. There might have been a lot of learning by rote, little expectation that the pupil should contribute to lessons and very little pair or group work. Children may take a little while to adjust to a different system.

Beginner EAL and bilingual children

Don't panic! You will find that in some schools panic will set in when a child arrives who speaks little or no English. How do we communicate with him/her? Will he/she understand anything? In other, usually inner-city, schools, staff see this as par for the course and indeed in some nurseries the vast majority of children have little English when they arrive.

At the admission interview which should normally occur with the parent or carer, important information should be found out by the school about the child. You may have been involved in the admission procedure or, if not, you should then find out as much as you can. Hopefully an interpreter will have attended the interview to support both the parent/carer and the school (this may have been you if you are bilingual yourself). Good admissions practice will usually mean that the child will not start school immediately, so you and other members of staff can be ready for the child's arrival.

How do you prepare? It is important that you try to communicate as clearly as possible whatever you do [20K15]. If you know what language the child speaks it may be possible for you to learn a little bit of that language, such as greetings or 'What is your name?' You may assist the class or form teacher to identify a buddy or buddies to look after the pupil when he/she starts. This may include someone who speaks the child's language – this can obviously help the child settle in fairly quickly, although sometimes the buddy child may not want to do this – be sensitive to this. Often the best buddies are the children you know will be supportive and friendly. You could find out some information about the country the child has come from and, with the class teacher, conduct a short input on this with the class or form. This could include looking at how to help someone in school if they don't speak English and how it might feel to be in that position.

If you speak the child's language and are familiar with the culture, you could prepare some school and classroom signs in the child's language or even (with the class teacher's permission) teach the other children some greetings in the new language. You could talk to the class teacher/s and to the class about the new child's country and culture and any key differences to do with religion or food. You could even find some posters for a display about the country the child has come from.

Having everything prepared for when the child arrives is also very important. In primary schools this will mean, for example, ensuring there is a place to sit, books ready and tray labelled. In secondary schools, it may mean having exercise and textbooks available and a school diary. Make sure you know how to pronounce the child's name correctly and you know the child's first or calling name. Children have been known to go through school being called by the wrong name or having been given an 'English' name instead. If you have been asked to support the child, it can be very useful to establish who the home contact is – and, in primary settings, to establish contact with the person who brings the child to school. As with all the strategies you use, talk to the class teacher about this.

When the child starts school

This can be quite a daunting experience for some children. Try to imagine how it might feel. Spend a minute or two thinking about this and make some notes about what might be different and how you might feel.

You enter an institution in a strange country, where no one or few people can speak your language and you can't speak theirs. You have no friends, people may be a different colour to you and look different, you don't know the rules (written and unwritten) of the school and you don't know what to expect in lessons.

It may be that you didn't even want to come here – it was your parents' decision or you had to leave! You may be missing your home and your friends. Because of this, it is important that the school is as welcoming as possible. The teaching assistant should:

- be prepared (see above);
- show the pupil around the school – where the toilets are, dinner hall, etc.;
- introduce the child to his/her buddy and make sure the child is looked after at break and lunchtimes;
- introduce him/her to a supportive child, perhaps an older child, who also speaks his/her language;
- establish a home contact;
- smile and be friendly and relaxed;
- talk to the child normally (don't be slow and halting) and use clear, simple language.

In lessons, the child may not say anything at all to start with, even if they do know some English. This is quite normal and is often known as the 'silent period' – the child will be listening and learning but not necessarily speaking. This can continue for some time – perhaps for a couple of weeks or even up to six months. Monitor this but do not worry too much. If a child is outgoing, they are much more likely to start talking earlier – character obviously plays a role.

You may be asked to work with a newly arrived pupil in induction sessions separate from the rest of the class for the first half term to term. These may be every day for half-an-hour to an hour, although this varies considerably from school to school. Work should be set for you to do by the class teacher or EAL teacher. It is important that you liaise with these staff on an ongoing basis about the lessons and the progress pupils make. If you do speak the child's first language, this can be the ideal time to talk to the child in this language about how school is going and to establish rapport. This can be a great relief for some children who may be struggling to communicate and succeed in school.

Supporting the child in the classroom

You will need to talk to the class teacher about the best ways you can support the EAL child in lessons; further guidance may be provided by EAL staff. There is some very helpful further reading listed at the end of this chapter. Being prepared is essential. One very important strategy is to use visual aids to explain ideas and concepts which are vital in the early stages. For example, a child may know a lot about volcanoes because there are volcanoes 'back home' or because she/he has studied them in school. If the lesson has no visual aids or the introduction is just 'talked' or in plain text, the child is not likely to learn much from the lesson. It is essential for you and the class teacher to discuss what is needed before the lesson to make it accessible.

There is a danger that in the first part or introduction to a lesson, the early stage learner of English may gain little from the teacher's explanation, unless it includes the use of relevant visual aids. Whispering to the pupil to try to help in the introduction, even in the child's first language, can be very distracting for the rest of the class. If you have spoken to the class teacher beforehand, you may be able to identify some appropriate visual aids. If the lesson is the literacy hour, you could discuss with the class teacher the possibility of your using a different text at a more appropriate language level outside the classroom for the first half hour, if the school has an appropriate space – a corridor is not normally appropriate. The class teacher should plan this with you – the text needs to be age-appropriate.

There is a wide range of activities that can be used with EAL pupils when they are following up a teacher's introduction to the lesson and these will inevitably vary according to the aims of the lesson. Some examples are matching vocabulary or sentences to pictures, matching definitions to explanations, retelling stories or doing an experiment using picture prompts, and gap-fill activities. Your role here would be to support pupils in understanding but, of course, not to do the activities for them! It is also important not to avoid key vocabulary items. For example, words such as 'transparent' and 'translucent' may seem difficult but are actually quite easily taught if items which have these qualities are brought into the lesson.

You will need to be aware that sometimes things that we assume that 'everybody knows' are not known by some EAL pupils. This is because we often make cultural assumptions about the curriculum and the prior knowledge pupils bring with them to the school. A topic such as 'Going on Holiday' or 'Going to the Seaside' may be alien to some cultures, as would some fairy tales and nursery rhymes; or in higher-level texts there may be literary or historical references that the pupil does not understand. As you gain more experience, you will be able to identify these before the lesson. During the lesson it may mean that you will have to explain the topic or item, or alternatively it may be appropriate that a different task is set.

In some schools, you will be a very important language model for EAL pupils, particularly when working in small groups. This does not mean that you should speak in slow, halting language or, if the pupils don't seem to understand, speak louder. You should speak at a normal pace initially to pupils and then slow down or focus on key words as necessary. There may be specific language or vocabulary targets for the lesson which should help you focus. If you ask a child a question, allow a little more time for the pupil to respond. The child may need more time to process the question.

This chapter is only a start in understanding the needs of children learning EAL. You may well want to attend further training or read more if you are going to undertake a qualification in this area or specialise in it. It can be very useful to put yourself in the child's position or reflect on your own experiences and perhaps frustrations when travelling or living abroad and what would have helped you. A useful activity you can do is to compare two EAL pupils, one who is succeeding and achieving well in school and one who is not doing as well. Find out as much as you can about these two pupils and try to work out why this is the case.

And finally, remember that EAL pupils should not be judged as having special needs just because they are learning English. The Code of Practice on SEN makes this very clear. You should normally have high expectations of EAL pupils. If you are concerned about their learning, discuss this with the teacher or SENCO. It is usually a tremendously rewarding experience working with EAL pupils, seeing the progress they make, and it is a privilege to play a part in this.

Questions to ask yourself

- What do you know about the countries which the pupils with whom you work come from? Where can you find out more?

- Do these pupils have other educational needs as well as language problems?

- Do you know to whom on the staff and the LA you can go to get further information about support for the pupils' EAL needs?

Essential reading

Gibbons, P. (1991) *Learning to learn in a second language*.

Some further reading

DCSF (2007b) *New arrivals excellence programme guidance*.

DCSF (2007d) *Supporting children learning English as an additional language: Guidance for practitioners in the Early Years Foundation Stage*.

Hall, D. (2002) *Assessing the needs of bilingual learners: Living in two languages*.

Hounslow (2007a): *EAL at KS1: Framework for Early Years*.

Hounslow (2007b): *KS2 Beginners scheme of work*.

Lambeth (2004) *Admissions and induction good practice for mid-term or non-routine admissions*.

Richmond-upon-Thames (2008) *Don't panic: Meeting the needs of new arrivals*.

Useful website

www.naldic.org.uk – The National Association of Language Development in the Curriculum – a professional body for those working with pupils with EAL.

Supporting teachers in and out of the classroom

Roles and responsibilities

THERE ARE CLEAR REGULATIONS which are part of the 2002 Education Act that, however senior you are as a TA, whatever happens in the classroom in terms of teaching and learning is the responsibility of the teacher.

> Other persons who may carry out specified work
>
> 10.–(1) This paragraph applies in the case of a person who is not a qualified teacher . . .
>
> (2) Such a person may carry out work specified in regulation 6 (q.v. below) only if the following conditions are satisfied–
>
> (a) he carries out the work specified in regulation 6 in order to assist or support the work of a qualified teacher or a nominated teacher in the school;
>
> (b) he is subject to the direction and supervision of such a qualified teacher or nominated teacher in accordance with arrangements made by the headteacher of the school; and
>
> (c) the head teacher is satisfied that he has the skills; expertise and experience required to carry out the work specified in regulation 6.
>
> (DfES 2003c:10)

> Specified work
>
> 6.–(1) Each of the following activities is specified work for the purposes of these Regulations–
>
> (a) planning and preparing lessons and courses for pupils;
>
> (b) delivering lessons to pupils;
>
> (c) assessing the development, progress and attainment of pupils; and
>
> (d) reporting on the development, progress and attainment of pupils.
>
> (DfES 2003c:3)

TAs teach but do not take the responsibility for the direction and organisation of the learning. What this means virtually has to be re-established for each teacher and TA partnership. One teacher is happy for you to change direction when working with a pupil because things are not going well, another will want you to ask him or her first. On the whole, TAs have proved a sensitive group of staff, intuitively watching each teacher and 'feeling their way' as to the limits and boundaries for each classroom. As job descriptions become more common and detailed, misunderstanding should become rarer. However, what seems to happen now is that managers negotiate a job description, but each teacher is not aware of the exact purpose of the TA in a lesson. The more you and the teacher can find time to make these implicit understandings explicit, the better you will work together.

Remember, teachers have not often in the past been trained to work with additional adults in the classroom, nor have managers realised the importance of relationships and communication to the effective working of TAs. Make sure you read Chapters 3 and 4 on relationships and partnerships with teachers alongside this chapter [18K1]. The knowledge performance criteria for STL 23 are well worth reading as they cover the whole range of things you should know if you are working in a classroom. It is still not uncommon in a secondary school to have three TAs turning up to some teacher's lessons where the teacher does not have any idea why they have come or what they are supposed to do. They assume they are to support individual pupils and leave it at that. One TA recently described herself and her colleagues as feeling they were employed as crowd control – what a waste of expertise and human resource! It helps if each teacher who has a TA allotted to them, as in many primary classrooms now, can be involved in drawing up the TA's job description. If this has not happened for you, ask if it could be discussed when your time for review comes.

If you are going to work with a different or new teacher you must find at least a few moments to discuss the following:

- What do you particularly want me to do?

- What are the objectives of the lesson today?

- Which pupils do you wish me to concentrate on?

- What do I do if a pupil in your room asks to go to the toilet?

- Can I write in any pupils' books?

- What contact with parents or carers do you expect of the TA?

- Do you want me to attend consultation evenings?

- Do I take part in SEN reviews?

- Can I do anything at the request of a parent, such as change a child's reading book or search for lost equipment?

- Can I tidy the rooms? Your desks? The resources area?

- Is there anything you do not want me to do?

(adapted from DfES 2003:63)

The classroom process: planning, preparation, performance and review

What goes on in the classroom is the centre of all the school's activities [STL 18, 12 and 24]. It is here that, hopefully, pupils learn. All the other procedures are there to support that process. The teachers, the hierarchy of management, the building, books and equipment should all be directed to this purpose. You are helping this process right 'at the chalkface'. So, you see how everybody's efforts go to make up what actually happens. In any domestic or life process, the better the planning and preparation the better the event goes, and the more often the event takes place the more we learn about how to improve it – provided we review what happened. Learning in the classroom is no different. Sometimes, to a new onlooker it seems to happen effortlessly, but the more time you spend in class, the more you will realise what the background procedures are that have enabled the pupils to learn most effectively. Figure 10.1 develops the Kolb learning cycle to show how it works in a classroom. Now, as an experienced TA, you will be expected not just to appreciate these but to be part of them. It is not possible to do your job fully by just dropping in and out of lessons; you need liaison time with teachers, study time to understand rationales, and preparation time. If you do not have this you must negotiate with your line manager [18.1P1]. You will have ideas, experience and expertise to contribute. You should constantly be reflecting on

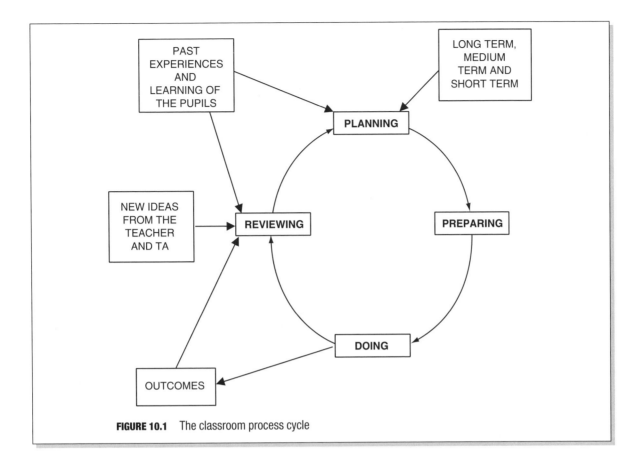

FIGURE 10.1 The classroom process cycle

and reviewing what you are doing while you do it, and you need to feed back these thoughts to someone [23.1P1–5].

Sometimes a newly qualified teacher, having come from college thinking they were now trained to do it all properly and then being faced with the never-ending challenge of a classroom full of pupils, will ask 'When do you get it all sorted out?' Unfortunately, or really fortunately, the answer is 'never'; the process is cyclical and changing. Even in the same room with the same teacher and class and curriculum, the changing nature of human beings means that needs change and so the classroom process will be different. A teacher or TA who is complacent and feels they have got it all 'sussed' is not going to be the best support for the pupils. Where you are still a learner, you are still thinking and are part of a learning organisation.

This chapter concentrates on planning and preparation. Performance and feedback form such a large part of your role that the whole of the next chapter is devoted to them.

Planning

The school will have already decided what their approach is to teaching and learning and many schools have established policies for this area; hopefully you will have a copy. It will cover such things as:

- what kind of teaching methods the schools encourages;
- how the school deals with children of differing ability:
  - whether pupils are to be taught in mixed-ability groups, streamed (in similar-ability classes for most of the time) or setted (pupils of the same age group put together in similar-ability groups for particular lessons);

- how work for individual pupils is to be differentiated;
- how those with learning problems are to be supported;
- whether gifted and able pupils are to have any special treatment;

- how pupils are to be involved in their own learning;

- whether particular active learning strategies or investigative/problem-solving approaches are to be used;

- whether all lessons are to be structured and planned in the same way;

- how oral work is to be conducted – what expectations there are for allowing debate or discussion;

- how written work is to be presented:

  - who marks what and in what way;

- what study skills are to be taught or encouraged;

- how pupils can be rewarded for good work, and what the consequences might be for poor work, or how such pupils are to be supported;

- where staff can seek assistance, resources and ideas.

As you can see from the list, many of the items will affect how you work with pupils. If when you read it you do not understand the jargon – words such as pedagogy – you must ask your mentor or a class teacher to explain. 'Pedagogy' means 'any conscious activity by one person designed to enhance learning in another' (Watkins and Mortimore 1999:3): just what your job is!

There is no substitute for good planning. This does not mean everything you are going to do has to be spelt out in a particular format on a piece of paper; it just means thinking ahead rather than thinking on your feet. Pieces of paper are needed when memory needs a jog, and when others need to know what you are going to do and it is either too complicated or too long to be able to tell them. It is still happening that there may just be no opportunity for verbal communication between a TA and a teacher. It is still common for TAs to be paid only for pupil contact time, and teachers are busy people. Luckily for the pupils, this is changing and the need for TAs to have formal and informal time with the teachers is now seen as vital to underpin good practice in the classroom. The Workforce Remodelling guidance is quite clear and the benefits of such time are being recognised more widely. There are ways of using paper communication to compensate for some of the lack of human contact time but this will not enable creative and positive working partnerships to be built up. They will supplement, not replace, face-to-face communication in quality time.

> Supervision arrangements for all support staff undertaking activities to support teaching and learning should include time for teachers and support staff to discuss planning and pupil progress within the contracted hours of the support staff.
>
> (WAMG 2008:18)

It is important that teachers share their planning with you in some way, so that you know not only what you are doing but how and why [18K4]. All of STL 24 is about contributing to the planning and evaluation of learning activities, and you should read the performance criteria through whatever units you are opting for as they are very relevant, whatever role you take in the classroom. You may know the pupils well but you must know the teacher's intentions, their curriculum objectives for the lesson. You should have your own copy of the NC and be able to relate what the teacher is doing to some of it. Teachers plan for the long term so that pupils do not cover the same material year after year. Together they have developed yearly schemes of work to plan out curriculum coverage over the time the pupils are in the school.

Again you may like to get your own copy of the relevant subject scheme of work. Many primary schools use those available from the internet. You need to have some curriculum understanding in order to fulfil the teacher's objectives, particularly if you are working in a secondary school or employed specifically to support literacy or numeracy or any other subject in the primary school. There is more on the principles of supporting the curriculum in Chapter 12 of this book and specific chapters for literacy (13) and numeracy (14), which are not only important as independent subjects but are used in virtually every other subject and for every pupil [STL 33]. Figure 10.2 gives the school planning process diagrammatically.

Individual teachers, or sometimes year groups of teachers, then plan for the medium term, usually a term ahead. Medium-term plans will consider the sort of resources, events,

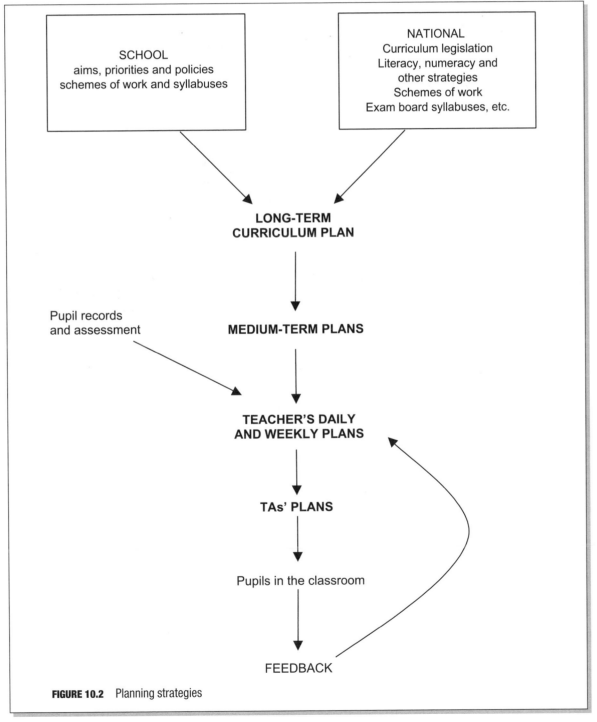

FIGURE 10.2 Planning strategies

activities and ideas which will support the curriculum objectives of the long-term plan and are practical and feasible, given the classroom circumstances. These plans are usually available and you will find them helpful and interesting. Some schools are involving experienced TAs in some of the termly planning sessions for the medium-term plans. By working with them, or even just looking at them, you will know what kinds of thing will be coming up in the term and whether there are any ideas you could contribute.

Teachers then produce short-term plans covering the detail of each week's work, and how they are adapting the curriculum to the needs of the pupils, including those with IEPs and other individual targets, and how the pupils have been dealing with the work up to now. These plans should incorporate your role in supporting the pupils' learning. Within these short-term plans, teachers will produce some individual lesson plans. These should contain the learning objectives and some indication of the teacher's expectations of what the outcomes will be. They may contain some indication of how you can tell whether the objective has been achieved – success criteria – but this is unusual unless the lesson includes a test. This is the kind of thing you can talk about regularly with the teacher you work with or your mentor. The literacy and numeracy strategies have many examples of planning formats which schools have either adopted as their own or adapted. Planning guidance for primary teachers is also available on the teachernet website.

Examples of good practice

A TA in one school came up with the first draft of a planning/recording sheet for the pupils with whom the TAs worked. The teachers saw it as supporting them in their work, and appreciated a mechanism for the TAs to report back to them about the progress of children during a session. Another school allocated a shared planning time on a Thursday. Another recommended that TAs had a copy of the teacher's planning on a Monday morning, and were given time to work on differentiation for their pupils on a Monday afternoon. Another school made the long- and medium-term planning of all teachers available in a folder in the staffroom. In yet another school, the TAs' personal planning was done by them at home at the weekend, after the teachers had given them their plans on a Friday. In this same school the TAs were linked with specific teachers and spent time with them over the summer holidays on the long-term planning. Some schools just encourage the teachers to leave their planning out on their desks and the TAs looked at it as they go into the room to work. One teacher admitted that if the TA was late it could throw her, but nevertheless the preparation and rapport previously established enabled the TA to pick up instantly what was wanted.

Teachers may have separate plans for the TAs, or give them copies in which the TA role is spelt out. Some teachers use an exercise book to write down tasks for the TAs, who then write their comments before leaving the book on the teacher's desk when leaving the room. There are some good examples of systems in use in Balshaw and Farrell 2002 (67–73), and one generic possibility is shown in Figure 10.3.

You then make your own plans – 'shopping lists' of resources or equipment you will need to find or make, books to look out for, or special clothing to take with you. You will also be thinking of varying the strategies to match the requirements of the teachers and the needs of the particular pupils with whom you work. When you know things beforehand, you can think of different ways of presenting the same objectives. This is particularly important with slow learners, who need a lot of repetition to grasp concepts but need to be kept interested and motivated to learn. You will also have your own resources – pictures, books, artefacts, people you know – which can add a different and interesting slant on the teacher's ideas. Do remember: if in doubt, check with the teacher first that they agree to you using your own ideas or equipment.

Date . . . .   Teacher. . . . .   TA . . . .

Lesson . . . .

<u>Learning objective</u>

<u>Activities</u>
Introduction

Group work

Plenary

<u>Resources</u>

Children						
Individual needs						
Feedback comments						

Any general comments:

FIGURE 10.3   A sample planning sheet for teachers and TAs to use

Preparation

It is important that you have time both to prepare things for the teacher and to make your own preparations [18.1P2]. Still too often planning and preparation are done in your own time. Try to negotiate some paid time for this. The section on working with practical subjects should also be read before undertaking any practical work to ensure you have taken all the necessary health and safety precautions and risk assessments.

The learning environment

A 'healthy school', being more than just clean, hygienic and safe, needs the good relationships of those who work there to provide a good working climate. Schools should be providing not only an environment which is safe for exploring and growing bodies but also a learning environment for enquiring minds. The surroundings in which learning takes place influence the quality of the learning. You know yourself that having materials or tools where you know you can find them makes a job easier. Having the right lighting, or a comfortable chair at the correct height makes a difference to how long you can persist at a task. Sharp tools are usually safer than blunt ones. A jigsaw with lost pieces is useless, blunt pencils will not produce good handwriting, paper with curled edges does not encourage good presentation. A welcoming room or building encourages its use.

You are responsible for all the equipment or materials you use, and should provide a role model in your use of them. You will need to find out where items that you will be using are kept and how to use them properly. This will include knowing about storage facilities, what to do if you or pupils you are with break or spill anything, and how to dispose of waste of any kind. This goes for pencils, paper and scissors as well as televisions, whiteboards, audio or computer equipment, scientific equipment or chemicals, tools, toys and books. Check before a lesson that you have correct and sufficient materials for a task; never leave your pupils to go to get something, particularly if they are young and away from their class base.

Music, the company of others or silence, and the freedom from fear or anxiety can all contribute to the creation of a learning atmosphere. The teacher will set the scene of their classroom, providing resource centres, setting out the furniture appropriately and putting up displays to create the atmosphere they feel is most conducive to the tasks to be performed there; the management will decide about the more public places and the budget to be spent on various items. You may have a particular role in maintaining the environment, such as display or plants and animals, and there may be other people doing other things, such as art media and books, or specialist technicians for science or ICT equipment or equipment to support SEN, so you need to know how you fit into the scheme of things. You may even have some curriculum area responsibility yourself.

You also need to be able to adjust the working environment to provide appropriate lighting, heating or ventilation, if this changes while you are in that location. Make sure the pupils you are with are safe and can move about adequately, if they have to, and use the space appropriately. This may mean ensuring they stay with you if you go out into the grounds or do not charge about if suddenly released into a large space, such as a hall. It may be advisable to shut any windows which you have opened, after use, for security reasons; check the procedures for your school. Your example in maintaining a tidy, organised personal work area, with the proper tools decently maintained – from paper and pencils to large expensive equipment – will be a powerful role model for the pupils. If you are asked to get things ready for a lesson, or to spend time supporting the teacher in maintaining the classroom environment, this should be paid time, as you will have to do it when the pupils are not there. You might need to adjust your timetable to enable you to do this, but you should be able to negotiate this with the teacher or your line manager.

Display

Whatever is displayed on school walls, and the manner in which it is displayed, gives messages to pupils and adults about what is valued. If displays become faded and tatty, the message is 'Who cares?' If it is part of your role to renew or create displays for the teacher, there is a standard for display [STL 16] which is also available at Level 2. Some of the following is taken from the Level 2 book (Watkinson 2008a). Have a look at the performance criteria if you are interested. They may provide some prompts for your consideration. Part of the reason for classroom displays – the interactive sort – is to promote enquiry and interest but display has other purposes. It is a really good way to value pupils' work and add a dimension to the curriculum if planned and utilised with thought. Unfortunately, there has been a trend in recent years for more and more of the displays to be merely informative and to utilise professionally produced materials. Commercially produced posters, put up to inform, in the absence of the pupils are merely wallpaper. In this materialistic, fast-moving, large-screen world, where shops outdo each other to attract, children are well used to colourful walls and merely accept them as normal unless involved somehow. Displays should have a function and be renewed at least half-termly; otherwise they can become meaningless and even distracting. They may include:

- health and safety notices, like the fire escape route, washing hands after handling certain things, or use of potentially dangerous tools;
- ideas for using equipment, like books or computers;
- ideas for work to do if set tasks are finished;
- posters giving general information or pictures of relevant interest to topics being studied;
- pupils' work, showing quality presentation, good ideas or just valuing the achievement of class members;
- three-dimensional displays of books or artefacts or models associated with the work of the pupils;
- lists of names, spellings, mathematical tables for reference or learning;
- an opportunity for collaboration and thought by a group of pupils in putting the display together.

The liaison required with teachers throughout the school in order to ascertain purpose and duration is considerable if you are to take responsibility for this area of work. You will need access to ordering and storage facilities, and need to have sufficient understanding and freedom to decide the position of a display and sufficient knowledge to be aware what risks you might be undertaking in putting up and taking down a display and recognise any risks that might be attached to the display itself. The last thing you want is an object falling on someone or a staple going through a caretaker's hand. You need expertise in mounting, safety concerns, appreciation and evaluations.

It may well be part of your role to renew or create displays for the teacher. You need to know what the intention of the display is, but you also need to learn some skills to help you. For instance, choice of backing paper and ways of framing pupils' two-dimensional work can make a difference to whether the display is eye-catching or not. The kind of lettering and its size matters, as well as what is written about the work. Three-dimensional displays can be interactive – allowing pupils to touch and examine objects – or just for visual effect. Care with paper trimmers, scissors and glue shows care of pupils' work. Teachers should give you plenty of advice on what they are hoping to achieve; most of them have become very skilled at it.

PHOTOGRAPH 10.1   A display following work on social and emotional learning

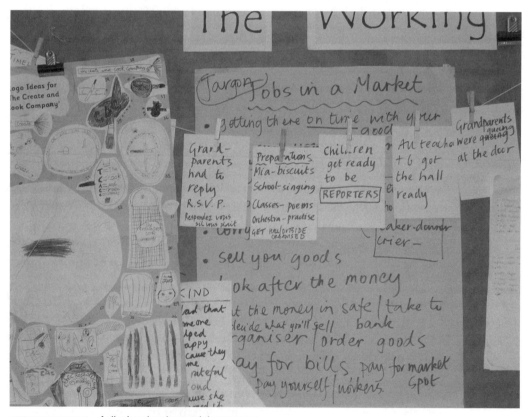

PHOTOGRAPH 10.2   A display showing work in progress

PHOTOGRAPH 10.3   A tactile display using space outside the classroom

Where possible, involve the pupils in ideas of what or how to display their work. Year 2 children are perfectly capable of using a paper trimmer, given guidance, and can have ideas about the look of a display. Older primary children would be able to arrange items on a flat sheet or contribute to 3D displays. Interactive displays can be particularly effective in creating interest and stimulating investigation. They can range from a few questions put among the labels on a flat classroom display to the Science Museum's highly successful Launch Pad. There are ways of simulating design on computers, some of them in 3D. The more children are involved in what goes on walls and surfaces and understand why it is there, the more likely they are to use it.

Sometimes the display can show work in progress of the children. These will not be tidy displays, with a polished finish, but will show process as well as end product and will value the process. Some children, if clumsy, colour blind or just not interested in art and design, can be put off trying to produce anything for display if everything in the classroom is commercially produced or highly finished, so keep a watch out for this and ensure you can see their success in some other venture, as you would with a child who doesn't achieve in PE or any other subject.

PHOTOGRAPH 10.4   A special display in the hall but with interactive 'post-it' notes and a clipboard

Look at at least three different areas in the school, including areas within and outside classrooms:

■   What display is there? What is it for?

■   What condition is it in? How long has it been there?

■   Is it looked at by the pupils?

■   Is it two- or three-dimensional? Why?

■   If you feel it is effective, try to note why.

■   What colours have been used in addition to the items being displayed?

■   What other materials – fabrics, paper, framing – have been used?

■   Is the display cluttered or relatively bare?

■   Are the items in straight lines?

■   Is there any explanatory text added by the displayer?

■   What tools, equipment or materials might be needed to create such a display:

    ■   staple gun, pins, scissors, paper trimmer, framing equipment, paper, fabrics, artefacts, books?

■   Do you know where to find all of these and how to use them?

PHOTOGRAPH 10.5   Small children are quite capable of mounting work

If you want to further this interest, look at displays in shop windows, art galleries, museums, advertisements and libraries to pick up ideas on how the displays are made eye-catching or informative. Practise with your pictures or ornaments at home. If you responsibility is great in this area, it might be an idea to undertake some kind of visual arts training. See if there are courses or evening classes in your local centres.

Making and maintaining equipment, resources and materials [31 and 56]

It may also be part of your role to ensure that things are ready for the pupils' use with the teacher. You should have paid time to do this, especially if, as the WAMG proposals specify, you are to relieve the teacher of some of the tasks that teachers should not routinely be expected to do. You can make specified workcards and worksheets, given a prototype, can make and mend equipment and books, or can sort and organise classroom resources and equipment, according to the wishes of the teachers. There may be specialised equipment used to support particular elements of the curriculum or particular SENs. Check that you know how these are to be used to best effect – they may include counting apparatus, word banks and computer programmes. At NOS Level 3 you should be aware of the rationale behind the design of some of the apparatus, and be able to assess its quality and suitability for the task and report your ideas back to the teacher.

You may become responsible for stock maintenance and reordering. This will entail monitoring the use by other people, inspecting the condition of the resource(s), getting repairs carried out if they are beyond your skill, and ensuring adequate supplies. Follow the school procedures and report any problems you have. STL 56 is about resource maintenance, where you have a particular responsibility in this area. It is particularly for TAs who do not have a specialised area to lead in, such as a technician, a librarian or an ICT coordinator might have. But it means you will have to know the correct procedures for storage and cleaning of any equipment, monitor its use and provide guidance to others on its care and use. The safety aspects of this role were discussed in Chapter 4. Ensure that you understand and follow waste disposal guidance appropriately, especially if there are any hazardous materials, and recycle whatever you can.

Check with the teacher if you have any doubts over what to use, or how much of a particular medium or material you should use – it just could be they were saving that bit of gold paper for a special decoration for a festival, or that was the paint to be used for the forthcoming examination, or someone had ordered that set of disks especially! Pupils of differing ages and stages of development will need different apparatus and you should be able to recognise this. A useful tip, if working with pupils with learning difficulties, is to spend some time in classes of pupils at least two years younger than the ones you work with. Sometimes courses ask you to do this as part of your training. So, if you are in an infant school, ask to spend time in a nursery class or school; in a junior school, go to the infant department or school; and secondary school TAs should spend some time in a primary school. This can be done by arrangement with the managers of each establishment, but do go with a particular agenda in mind; for instance, to see the mathematics apparatus. Going with a focus means you will not be immediately distracted by the wealth of other things going on in a different school, but in any case you will find you come away with many more ideas than those you set out to get. You should be able to maintain resource banks so that the right quantity is available. This could apply to workcards or ICT accessories, depending on the responsibilities which have been delegated to you. You do need time to prepare special resources – find reference books of pictures, locate the games or counting blocks that are shared between classes, and check that the audio-visual equipment or new software programs work. If you have not used equipment before, check how it works, how it is maintained and how to use it safely and effectively.

Remember that the pupils should help with some equipment preparation and maintenance. You must encourage all pupils to use their classroom, school premises, equipment and materials carefully and safely, with the least wastage. You must guide them in the safe use of equipment. They should be able not only to get out but also to clear up and put away equipment and resources, if they are accessible, and leave them safe and ready for others. Paintpot washing is the classic example. It is said, 'If TAs are helping with teaching and learning, who washes the paintpots?' – my answer is 'the pupils!'. If four- and five-year-olds can do this at the end of a session, supervised by a TA, there should not be a problem for most other pupils. This is a matter of time management; you must allow sufficient time at the end of a task for the pupils to clear away books, paper and pencils properly, check the floor and return equipment to its places. You are not their servant. Carry a few sharp pencils, a pencil sharpener and spare pens by all means, but make it clear that it is the responsibility of every pupil to know where to find such materials or to carry them with them. Tell the teacher or line manager if you have any problems with materials or equipment – its allocation, location, quality, availability – or even the space you have to work in; if you do not say, people will presume all is well.

It is your responsibility to ensure that where you work with pupils is safe – you could be asked to take a group in the grounds where there is a pond, for instance – and that any tools you work with are used safely. You should follow all manufacturers' instructions and school health and safety regulations concerning equipment and materials [3.1P1; 3K5]. Pupils using tools, equipment and materials should be taught how to use them and how to put them away appropriately. This goes for cutlery and pencil sharpeners as well as craft knives and complicated apparatus. There may be special rules and regulations, even risk assessments, associated with particular things, especially if you are helping in science, design and technology (DT), ICT or art areas. Part of safety routines will be the proper use of tools and equipment, including care and storage. It will be up to you to ensure there is a minimal risk in using such apparatus. You may need to be trained to use specialist equipment and that may include specialist safety equipment on lathes or other power tools. If in doubt about the use of any tools or equipment, ask and take note. Clearing up afterwards may also include disposing of materials, including recycling some. Do you know where and how to dispose of broken glass, chemicals and other possibly toxic materials? [3.1P4; 3K6]. Be a good role model in the way you use tools and materials, the way in which you organise your own belongings.

Electrical safety and security

You will certainly be using electrical equipment at some time in your school work and it is especially important that you follow the safety precautions and instructions for such equipment. There are a very useful couple of pages in *Be safe* (ASE 2001: 22–3) and a full account of dealing with electrical matters safely in *Safeguards in the school laboratory* (ASE 2006: 57–64), which should be found in every school.

Mains electricity must always be treated with care and you should be constantly alert and regularly check for faulty switches, broken sockets or plugs, frayed flexes and any defects in apparatus which could lead to problems. They should never be used. You should label them as dangerous, take them out of use and report them immediately. Pupils should be trained from the outset how to use apparatus properly and how to deal with sockets, switches and connections according to the policy of the school. Pupils should be taught from an early age that water and electricity are dangerous together, so wet hands or floors are to be avoided when dealing with any of this equipment. Make sure you know where the nearest fire extinguisher for use with electrical equipment is, and where master switches are in cases of accidents. Always switch off the power, if necessary at the mains or the meter, before dealing with any incident or breakdown. If there is an electrical incident, send for help. If you have to act without turning off the power, insulate yourself by standing on a pile of dry paper and use a wooden pole or chair to get the victim away from the source of power.

Batteries need replacing or recharging and may contain toxic materials. Recharging should be done with care, and dud batteries disposed of where indicated by any school procedures. Bulbs are made of fragile glass, a possible hazard in itself. Appropriate storage is important both for the equipment and for things such as batteries, film, tape and bulbs. It needs to be safe and secure, as most electrical items are expensive and sought after.

All these items will have come into school with a handbook for their safe and proper use. Before you work with pupils using any equipment there are several things to do, but particularly when dealing with ICT equipment make sure you have copies of any policies or procedures. Much of the equipment you may already have at home and be familiar with. It is still worth checking that the school equipment is similar. Switches may be in different places or the sequence of operations may be different. Always use the appropriate consumables. Cheap tape, disks, ink or paper can be damaging for some machines. Follow the setting up and operating instructions indicated for the machine you are using; again some actions can damage equipment. For instance, data projectors should not be moved until the bulb cools down, as doing so will certainly shorten the life of the bulb and can even cause it to explode. A certain routine for switching off is essential to prevent damage.

In order to minimise risks, also be alert for things such as the use of correct furniture [3K8, 9]. Using low chairs for computers can cause eye or back strain; trailing flexes through furniture can be hazards. The flexes are often encased in rubber treads where they go across the floor, to prevent people tripping; computers, screens and printers should be near the power source. You may need to talk politely to the teacher in charge of the ICT lesson or the ICT coordinator if you have a concern.

The ICT policy should also have references to the legislation of which users should be aware, and how the school deals with such matters. For instance, software CDs or DVDs are often used under licence; you should never use your own disks from home, unless they are approved by the school. The same copyright procedures used for photocopying may be indicated for scanning and printing materials using a computer. The Data Protection Act covers any use of data for compiling databases, say in a class survey. While most schools will operate a firewall preventing inappropriate incoming data getting to the pupils from the internet, there may be child protection issues when pupils start communicating with each other or with other schools. Ensure you understand the school policies and procedures for dealing with virus control and any kind of internet or e-mail access, use of passwords and other possible sources of problems. With the increased use of digital cameras and video cameras by schools and of phone cameras by many adults and pupils, ensure that you know the school policy on photography. Any photographs of children or young people should only be taken with their and their parents' permission. Most schools now ensure that some kind of coverall permission is obtained from parents, but you must know what this covers and whether any families have opted their children out before using photographic procedures of any kind.

You may need to familiarise yourself with programs used by the school. If you do not have a computer at home, ask if you can borrow one for a limited time or use the school machines for practice. Remember there may be a problem with insurance, as such equipment is valuable and portable; do check. The use of ICT in schools these days, reflecting the widespread use in all our lives, means that it is no longer possible to be a TA and opt out of its use. The planning for many schools is on their intranet, as are the policies. E-mail communication with the teachers you work with may be expected. Electronic performance management information, access to databases, including registration may all be part of the systems in your school. Interactive whiteboards are now common equipment for most classrooms.

Working outside the classroom

TAs are also sometimes made responsible for a physical area outside the classroom, such as the library or entrance hall. You can use your talents for display and organisation here and be a real influence on the climate and culture of the school. Surroundings have messages; tidy, well-organised, attractive entrance halls, corridors and communal facilities indicate a caring and professional staff, and a well-run institution, whether it is a hotel, railway station, hospital or school. Staff rooms that have clean mugs, accessible resources, comfortable chairs and ready refreshments give a real boost to staff morale. 'Just making the tea' is not a job to be undertaken lightly, how it is done can make a real difference.

Outside, all schools have some kind of play area for break-times even if they have no grounds or green space. Early years settings should also have outside play areas and those catering for the under-threes should have day care provision for rest periods. Some schools still have to walk or even bus their pupils to their playing fields and not all of those are in urban areas. Many of you will not only be a classroom TA but also a midday or lunchtime assistant [10K]. The way in which you relate to children in the dining hall is important. Unfortunately, few teachers ever eat with the children to encourage positive social behaviour, and fewer families seem to eat together at tables although more eat out in restaurants together. You, as assistants at this time, can be a very positive influence on how the meal times go. Serving each other, using table manners, clearing up are all procedures which oil the way we relate to each other and respect how people look after us.

The use of the play areas opens up another whole subject for study. There is more about play in Chapter 12. Increasingly, budgets are being set aside to ensure there is additional play provision for these areas, or quiet spaces and activity areas with safety matting or bark beds have been built. Ideally, areas for dens and imaginative play are constructed from hedging or under trees. Special training should be available for supervisors of this outside space. Standard 54 has a lot of detail about helping and enabling self-directed play. You need to know about time-out areas, friendship bus stops, using any facilities painted on the ground (do you know how to play hopscotch properly?), using singing games, skipping ropes and areas for ball games. All the usual things apply about care of apparatus, clearing up and appropriate behaviour management rules for such informal areas. This may sound very much orientated to primary schools, but secondary children also need a break, and stretches of boring tarmac are asking for domination by football and offer opportunities for conflict. Access to quiet areas, reading materials, even study areas should be considered.

Outdoor play for the under-fives should be built into the curriculum but is sometimes seen as an extended version of the primary school playtime – everybody must put coats on, get the bikes out and have a race around. Outdoor play should be available most of the time by choice, and have a changing range of activities which have been designed with as much care as the indoor range. The bikes can become space transport or pizza delivery vehicles, with play houses as space stations or restaurants; the sand and water trays can become places to explore certain containers or build a town. It should all be planned and evaluated for the needs of the children at that time and with a thematic approach, just like the indoor curriculum. Mathematical areas with large shapes to climb on, sensory areas to walk on or listen to or smell can all be built into the outside area. If you are working in an early years setting you will need to make a special study of the outdoor provision.

It is vital that those working in school realise the importance of understanding and using outdoor and growing environments. The pressures of urbanisation all over the world, to produce energy crops for biofuels along with the concreting over of previously fertile land and ever higher standards of living are creating such effects that even land for growing food is coming to be at a premium. There has been a great move towards healthy eating, and converting school menus to support this, and now the move is on to grow that food for the school kitchen, or at least enable children to realise where their food comes from. Some schools are also linking their science and mathematics into monitoring their energy use and changes to having a more sustainable building. The government wants all schools to become sustainable by 2020 (Ofsted 2008:1). Of course, all kinds of energy-saving strategies have to be considered in all new builds. Increasingly, it is recognised that the living environment is not just a source of food. It is known that experience of green spaces has a definite beneficial effect on those with depression or mental illness.

More details of the opportunities such work can offer will be found in the *Outdoor learning manifesto* (DfES 2006). There are many organisations which can help with information, resources and support in developing school grounds such as Learning Through Landscapes or encouraging environmentally friendly activities such as the World Wildlife Fund. Most councils have recycling teams, wildlife trusts have outreach education officers (www.rswt.org.uk), the Royal Horticultural Society has packs on wildlife gardening or growing food in schools (www.rhs.org.uk). Wildlife areas and ponds need management; they do not look after themselves once established. Lack of appropriate and regular management has been a reason for the decrease in use. Areas that have been established have become neglected, untidy and a focus for vandalism. Along with the focus in schools on a formal classroom taught curriculum the outdoor facilities which most schools have are very underused.

This could be an ideal area for any TA to specialise in, as often you are living nearer to the school than the teachers, and may stay at the one school for a longer period of time than staff

PHOTOGRAPH 10.6　A productive and decorative school garden

who need to move to progress in their careers. It has been said that half the NC could be taught out of doors. STL 32.1 lists four areas of learning that can be addressed out of doors: affective, cognitive, physical and team development. STL 32.2 looks at how outdoor learning can be transferable to real lives. The standards as a whole emphasise the importance of reviewing and reflecting on learning. It would be interesting to take any lesson plan and see what activity could take place outside, taking care of all the safety issues that might be involved [3K7, 24]. Even formal planting can serve the curriculum with plants chosen for their colour, smell, shape or use, and a further step would be to have vegetable or orchard areas.

The movement links especially well with the ECM agenda encouraging healthy eating and lifestyles and safe practices. Many children are living highly protected indoor lives, and there is even a concern about some suffering lack of vitamin D because of this. While children are transported from their cocooned, warm, computer dominated lives at home in warm vehicles, to a warm indoor life in school they will lack an understanding of the fundamentals of life in Britain, of seasons, of the wonders of the living world and have no understanding of how to cope with danger when they meet it. The joy of walking in leaves or the beauty of frost patterns, or eating a radish freshly pulled from the ground (and washed!) have passed some by. The Children's Plan has recognised this.

> Children want places to play and parents want their children to enjoy the same freedoms that they had when they were growing up. But they feel there are few attractive places for them to go and they worry about their safety. Supervised and unsupervised outdoor activities are important for children's development and also to reduce obesity, build social and emotional resilience, develop social skills, strengthen friendships, help children learn how to deal with risks – and of course because children enjoy them. However children spend less time in outdoor activities than they want and than their own parents did as children. We will work with communities to create new and safer places to play and safe routes to play areas, and provide structured activities for younger children.
>
> (DCSF 2007a:28)

Outside the school: visits and field trips

Care of living things including wildlife is essential for developing a sense of responsibility as well as looking after our fragile planet. Increasingly, it is recognised that the living environment is not just a source of food. Exploring school grounds, developing wildlife areas, visiting parks and woodlands can enable some children to experience a freedom otherwise denied them. The current initiative known as 'Forest Schools' trains leaders in working with children in such areas (for more information try www.forestschools.com). It is encouraging children to develop a sense of place in a location away from the school grounds where they can be themselves, and play in a safe way in areas like woodland or other green space. It is known that in seaside towns, only half of the children in school will use the facility that many of us travel miles to experience. Provided the safety boundaries are followed and all adults with groups are properly trained in how to behave in such areas, exploring the natural world is a must for all ages. STL 10 at Level 2 has some useful ideas on explorative and creative work. It is known that experience of green spaces has a definite beneficial effect on those with depression or mental illness.

The school will have comprehensive guidance for taking pupils out of school on visits (DfEE 1998c), whether to static displays in museums, for fieldwork or on activity trips. This guidance is supplemented by further notes for those leading adventures, LAs, group leaders and water safety (CCPR and DfES 2002). This latter is relevant for taking walks by the side of a river, pond dipping or visiting a beach. *www.teachernet.gov.uk* has links to all the various documents available for training staff going on visits, using a minibus or going near water. If these guidelines are followed implicitly there should be no fear of litigation or blame. Cost of transport is often blamed for the decrease in trips to nature reserves or other locations and it is a difficult problem to address.

PHOTOGRAPH 10.7 A memorial garden providing sensory and spiritual experiences outside

The kinds of things to consider are first aid, health and hygiene and clothing. It is difficult for children in patent leather shoes to get the most out of a daytrip to a nature reserve if it rains, and parents will complain when light-coloured trousers get spoilt. Some simple guidance before a trip can help with enjoyment as well as prevent accidents or complaints.

School staff of any category who, as a group leader, take pupils away from the school – including a member of support staff who is not being directly supervised – should have demonstrated a knowledge not only of:

■ the educational objectives; and
■ how the learning is to be conducted;

but also of:

■ behaviour and group management;
■ the environment itself;
■ risk management in this context; and
■ the communications system they can use to summon help for the group when misbehaviour or serious injury has occurred.

(DfES 2005b:3)

STL 32 is specifically designed to support those TAs who work outside the classroom with pupils whether in a formal lesson time or on visits or field trips. STL 59 is also relevant for those of you who may be taking special responsibilities in this area. It is mainly about the transfer of learning from an outdoor experience to other areas of life. It is equally important to encourage the transfer of learning in the classroom to working out of doors and to all life experiences. STL 58 particularly focuses on the travel aspect and STL 59 on dealing with the pupils on a visit. You could well have such responsibilities delegated to you, as part of an overall package for which a qualified teacher will be responsible. You may even have a specialist qualification for taking children on trips if you work in the scouting movement, for the Duke of Edinburgh award schemes or for sporting clubs with junior sections. Some of these organisations have specialist training available for volunteers. Where travel is concerned the preparations are similar to taking oneself on holiday – deciding on the mode of transport, checking timetables, costings and seating, thinking of safety, comfort, food and hygiene, of people or pupils with special needs, of adult–pupil ratios and supervision. Risk assessments and contingency planning will be essential. There will be a whole new set of legal, health and safety and behaviour considerations to add to the curricular ones, for instance in adult–pupil ratios [3K11].

One of the helpful things to do is have a meeting of all the adults involved on a journey to brief them properly on what is expected of them. They will enjoy the trip much more if they understand the purpose and their role, just as you can do your job better in the classroom when you understand more and are confident of how and what to do. You could provide a simple plastic zippable bag for each participating adult containing simple instructions about their own role and behaviour, information about the trip, what you hope the pupils will get out of it and how they can help, expectations of the pupils' behaviour, lists of the group they are particularly responsible for, simple guidance on emergency and communication procedures, and maybe a few tissues, pencils and blank paper.

Working outside school hours: extended school activities

The extended school movement also sees increased partnership between providers – the police, health and social services, and partnership between pre-school provision, primary schools and the secondary schools in community clusters, schools being the focal points.

There is no 'one size fits all', and rural areas will have particular problems in making links. Headteachers will have to work more closely together and in some cases federations have been formed with an executive head. Usually, your LA will have appointed someone to coordinate the movement in your area. New schools are being built with libraries, rooms for the elderly or the new mothers to meet, rooms for health inspections or interviews, or community talks to take place. Increasingly TAs are running or are involved with one of the clubs or caring activities outside the classrooms. You need to know how it fits in the scheme of things for your school and ensure you understand all the health, safety and emergency implications of such a responsibility and that you are well trained and up to date in the programming and resourcing of whatever you are involved with. Standard 53 is about leading extra-curricular activities, STL 62 about working with other practitioners and STL 66 about working with volunteers. All of these standards contain useful prompts on things to consider when leading these activities.

While many schools have had clubs or sports after school with volunteer school staff for a long time, there has been a rapid growth in such activities where the leaders are paid and these are often TAs. This now also includes breakfast and after-school kids' clubs, catering for those families who want baby-sitting facilities or where the school has perceived a social need for family support. Many TAs seem to be getting involved with initiating, helping and leading such groups. The government see the 'Extended schools', as they call them, as part of the ECM agenda, where the school works with the local community as much as possible. The aim is to maximise the use of the premises and help communities see the local school as a focus for supporting families. The aim was for all schools to have some kind of extended activities by 2010. However, it is a balancing act and the results will vary with the community. In a rural village with extensive family networks already established, there will be little call for baby-sitting services but possibly some for specific interest clubs, where the initiative may come from the community. On the other hand, schools in areas of urban

PHOTOGRAPH 10.8   Part of a corridor converted to a kitchen for use by a breakfast club and in the curriculum

deprivation may get a great take-up for breakfast clubs. Here there are also spin-off results in terms of the school's learning. Concentration levels go up for the morning's work. In some, the sourcing and cooking of the breakfast has become part of the healthy eating curriculum. Sports, arts and crafts and music clubs add extra time for those who are good in these areas to extend their interests. It can do wonders for self-esteem for those children who do better in subjects which have been squeezed out of the daily timetables.

If you are involved in leading or supporting activities at lunchtime it is most likely that someone in authority will be on the premises, and there will be the normal access to first-aid equipment or an extra pair of hands. Then, normal good practice applies, including proper planning and preparation, clearing up, recording what is necessary and evaluating the activity, taking the proper health and safety precautions, doing risk assessments and so on. There is a useful document called *Extending inclusion* (CDC 2008) about supporting disabled children and young people at these times. But, before and after school is another matter. Teachers do not have to be on the premises usually beyond a quarter of an hour before and after the official pupil time except for the school's directed time (staff meetings and the like). The caretaker will already have certain contractual obligations. If you are going to lead or even support in a before- or after-school activity, you must make especially sure of your legal obligations and the ethical codes which surround such responsibility. What will you do if there is an accident, what if the parent or carer does not collect the

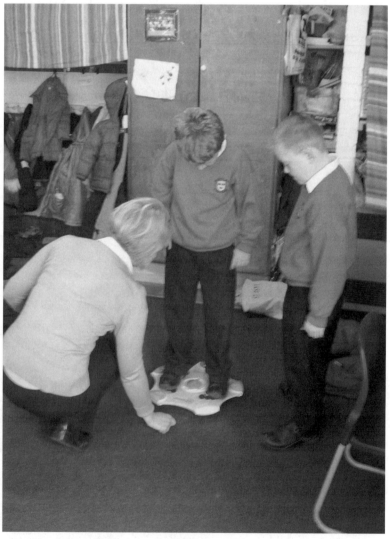

PHOTOGRAPH 10.9   A lunch club activity

child or young person, what if someone gets bored and behaves badly? The buck will stop with you. If you are working with a group like brownies or scouts, the organisation will do its own training of its staff. But, if you are suggesting doing something unattached to a recognised organisation, ensure that you get special training and make all the proper arrangements with the management of the school.

STL 53 also points out that you must clarify the boundaries of behaviour that you will need to observe. Discipline is likely to be more relaxed, but the pupils must still respect the premises, the adults and each other as they would during normal school hours. An activity may even need tighter rules if it has greater elements of risk like sporting activities, for example swimming. The knowledge statements for this standard are very detailed about the kinds of thinking and planning you must do when embarking on such a project. It would be a good idea to help at a session before leading it in order to observe and learn how things work.

Questions to ask yourself

- What did you enjoy most about your lessons when you were at school?

- Which classrooms were most welcoming? Why?

- Which areas of your current school workplace seem inviting? Why?

- Do you leave yourself enough time to think about what you are going to do before you do it? At home? At school?

- Do you present a good role model in the way you organise yourself and the resources you are going to use with the pupils?

- Are you sure of the learning objectives of all the lessons in which you are involved?

- Have you got your own copy of the NC? Have you seen the long-term plans for the curriculum in the subjects with which you are most closely involved? Have you seen the teacher's medium-term planning? Are you part of the short-term planning?

- Have you got copies of all the relevant policies when dealing with specialised equipment or taking children out of the classroom or out of the direct supervision of a qualified teacher?

Essential reading

ASE (2006) *Safeguards in the school laboratory.*

ASE (2001) *Be safe: Health and safety in primary school science and technology.*

DfEE (1999a) *The National Curriculum: Handbook for primary teachers in England; Key Stages 1 and 2.*

DfEE (1999b) *The National Curriculum: Handbook for secondary teachers in England; Key Stages 3 and 4.*

Some further reading

Balshaw, M. and Farrell, P. (2002) *Teaching assistants: Practical strategies for effective classroom support.*

Kyriacou, C. (1998) *Essential teaching skills.*

Kyriacou, C. (1997) *Effective teaching in schools.*

Lee, V. (1990) *Children's learning in school* (especially Parts 2 and 3).

Any subject curriculum handbook for teachers which accompanies any published scheme being used in the school by your class or teachers you work with.

Belair publications on display or creating learning environments for various subjects (Belair Publications Ltd, PO Box 12, Twickenham, TW1 2QL, England).

Useful websites

www.ltl.org.uk: Learning Through Landscapes

www.wwf.org.uk: World Wildlife Fund

www.rswt.org.uk: Royal Society of Wildlife Trusts – for information on you local Wildlife Trust

www.rhs.org.uk: Royal Horticultural Society

www.forestschools.com

www.teachernet.gov.uk

Strategy websites:

www.qca.org.uk

www.nconline.gov.uk

Performance and feedback

THIS CHAPTER continues the classroom process cycle from the previous chapter. Having planned and prepared for a lesson it will take place as per the timetable. So this chapter is about what is sometimes called delivery and what needs to take place afterwards to ensure that what happens can feed into the planning and preparation. Standards 23 and 24 particularly support these activities, but much of STL 18 is relevant of course.

Performance

Most lessons are in three parts – an introduction, beginning or exposition; a middle, often practical or small group session; and a concluding, summarising or plenary part. This was set out in some detail in the literacy and numeracy strategies and its formality seems to have ended any attempts at lengthy periods of work such as could be seen in primary schools in the 1970s and 1980s. Your role in each of the three parts of the lesson needs to be clarified with both your line manager and the teacher, and possibly also with the SENCO. Different schools have differing philosophies or needs for your presence. While it may be valuable for you to sit, apparently doing nothing during the teacher's introduction or exposition, too often it appears that you need that time to understand the purpose of the lesson because of lack of planning and preparation time allocated to you; it may be a more valuable use of your time to be allocated to a specific task elsewhere. You may be needed in that introductory time to keep some pupils in the room, or prevent their attention from wandering or encourage them to respond to questioning. You may need to interpret the teacher's words in sign language or in simpler words, or use the time collecting information for the teacher on particular pupils' responses. Whatever it is, it should not just be an ignored time. You are too valuable.

Your role is usually more obvious during the middle, more active part of the lesson, which is more frequently planned for by the teacher and is often considered the 'meat' of the lesson, when the main learning is done. The end part of the lesson, the recap or plenary, reviewing what has been learned, sometimes gets shortened but is really valuable in reinforcing with pupils what they were in the lesson for. You might be able to use that time for completing any records or writing a few comments for the teacher, or you may be given other tasks to do, such as photocopying or even marking books.

Teaching

TAs definitely teach, but this statement has caused some of the problems with the teaching unions about their status.

Although no one should pretend that teaching assistants are teachers, when they are most successful they show many of the skills characteristic of good teachers: an understanding

PHOTOGRAPH 11.1   Supporting the introduction to the lesson

PHOTOGRAPH 11.2   Prompting responses in a plenary

PHOTOGRAPH 11.3   Encouraging body language in a plenary

of children and their needs and behaviour; an ability to interact effectively with them to promote learning; and the ability to assess where pupils are in their learning and what they need to do to make further progress. Making the most of such abilities should certainly not threaten the professionalism of teachers; rather it should be encouraged and developed to the full.

(Ofsted 2002:18)

The problem seems to be the meaning of words: teach, teaching and teacher. Parents teach their children, brothers and sisters teach each other and our friends teach us. By 'teachers' most people seem to mean adults with QTS. The new proposals attempt to be more specific, but admit

In practice, the difference between the contribution of a qualified teacher and a higher level teaching assistant, or a cover supervisor, will not be defined in terms of simple words but by the quality of what each member of staff can reasonably be expected to demonstrate. It is not reasonable to look to a teaching assistant to demonstrate the full subject expertise and professional judgement of the qualified teacher.

(DfES 2002a:19–20)

You must act under the direction of qualified teachers at all times, and they take responsibility for the teaching and learning of the pupils in their class.

Effective performance strategies

I am sure you have watched teachers with whom you work to see how they approach their teaching. Teaching is a performance, an act. Some teachers still do not like another adult in the room, because they feel they are being watched by a possibly critical audience. Acting needs courage, forethought and practice; so does teaching. You need confidence to show sufficient authority to perform effectively. You must speak clearly, grammatically correctly if possible, and with a confident, but not loud, tone of voice. You will notice that quieter teachers tend to have quieter classes. Watch yourself in a mirror and, if possible, allow yourself to be videoed. Your gestures – non-verbal communication – are very significant. Much behaviour management can be achieved without a word, such as by raising an eyebrow, signalling 'turn it down' and, above all, maintaining eye contact. If you sit looking bored this will signal to pupils that the lesson is boring – it may be, but you must act not bored.

There are many strategies that you can use to support learning, and through experience you will realise which ones work best for which circumstances and which pupils. You can enable the pupils to read instructions, explain, instruct or listen; ensure they take turns or share; and ensure the quietest gets a time to speak and the extrovert gives way to the others at times. You can explain a task to enable the pupils to do it more successfully themselves. You can keep them on task without being aggressive, praise their progress, comment on success, and assist only where necessary – show by example rather than doing it for them. You can make things interesting and relevant to their world. You can use words they will understand, and remind them of what the teacher has said. Your use of language and vocabulary should be a role model for the pupils. If you adapt or modify any of the teacher's instructions because the pupils need something different in order to achieve the teacher's objectives, don't forget to tell the teacher what you have done and why. You might need to go through a piece of work more than once to make sure the pupils have learned what was expected and, instead of doing the same thing twice, you change the order of the words or the colour of the paper or play a game instead of making lists – your ideas are usually only too welcome. At the end of a session, try to leave time to go through with the group of pupils you have been with what they think they have learned or achieved. If things went wrong, or they did not finish, make sure they have worked out why it went wrong and what they can do better next time.

Questioning and challenging

This is a very important way to help children learn, achieve, think and question for themselves. (Education is partly about imparting knowledge, for without it there is no context for understanding, but the process by which we acquire and digest that knowledge is as important. Without questioning either by you or, hopefully, by the pupils, we cannot be sure they understand or make any progress.) Asking questions purely to check knowledge and understanding is a common teaching strategy. It relieves the monotony of the one voice and enables the pupils to feel part of the lesson. The teacher will ask questions of various levels of difficulty (differentiated) to encourage all the children to feel able to answer and be part of the class. Questions can be closed, needing only 'yes' or 'no' answers, or open, sometimes called 'higher order' questions, where the answers can be varied. Open questions are not so often used in a large class situation because there is not enough time for them, but you could use them with a small group. The actual asking of the questions needs the same kind of clarity, eye contact, and structure as an exposition, and practice. One of the things you can do to prepare for a lesson is to make a list of possible open and closed questions.

PHOTOGRAPH 11.4   Questioning

With the agreement of the teacher, note the teacher's questions.

- Can you categorise them into open and closed?

- Who answers which ones?

- Do the same pupils always answer?

Talk this over with the teacher after the lesson.

Intervention and non-intervention

You may be doing this instinctively; it is about enabling the pupils to do as much as possible for themselves. You may need to interpret, scribe, repeat instructions, give an example, or show a skill on a separate piece of material or apparatus. It is no good handing in a piece of work that you have dictated to the pupil; this gives the teacher a false impression of the pupil's capabilities and the pupil has merely learned how to manipulate you. You need to be mobile, so that you do not just sit alongside a particular pupil waiting to wait on them. Praise them, encourage them, comment on their work and assist them, but try to do it at appropriate moments.

A busy teacher may find it easier to give answers to some pupils' questions or do things for them. A TA has that much more flexibility so they can answer questions such as 'How do you spell "elephant"?' or 'Where can I find something about deserts?' or 'Can you cut this out for me, please?' with 'Have a try – sound it out', 'Where did we look for information yesterday?' and 'Have a go on a spare bit of material; look, I'll show you on this scrap piece first, then you try'.

Active listening

Listening to pupils is a very valuable way to spend time. It is not just a matter of hearing what they say but responding, internally taking note of things of importance to their well-being or learning, encouraging them to communicate their needs and ideas and above all encouraging their thinking. It can happen that for 80 per cent of the time in school the teacher or you will be instructing and only 20 per cent of the time the pupils will be actively participating. Pupils have to engage with their learning; it is not a passive exercise.

In the morning, read a short article in the newspaper which contains some statistical information. After a week, try to remember as much detail as you can of what you read. Then repeat the process with a different subject; this time, within an hour of reading the article, tell someone the contents. Then see how much of the second article you remember the next week. Usually the very act of trying to tell someone about a subject fixes it better in the memory. Try explaining a complex idea that you have had to a friend. It could be a way of redesigning your garden or sorting out a domestic problem or an educational project you are involved in. Ask them to comment and then argue or discuss the idea. You may not change you mind or ideas, but you will feel more confident that you understand what you are about to do or how you feel about it.

Sensitivity and response

All the time you are working with pupils you need to keep aware of how they are tackling the task set. While in class your concentration must not slip, so that you know when to intervene or modify what is happening. Sometimes something unusual or unplanned happens. It could be a fire practice, when you have to respond as you have been trained, making sure the pupils you are with understand what to do. It could be a rainbow from a rain shower or even from a sudden shaft of light unexpectedly hitting bevelled glass. This will

PHOTOGRAPH 11.5   Giving time for thinking

distract the pupils, and you can decide whether to use the moment to admire the colours and talk about cause and effect, or try to get the pupils to ignore it. It will all depend on the pupils you are with and the importance of the task they are supposed to be doing. These special moments are unplanned but can be used to appreciate natural phenomena and stimulate interest and curiosity.

An example of good practice

Sheila, a TA, works with Barbara, a Year 1 child who has Down's Syndrome. During a literacy hour, Sheila is sensitive to the needs of Barbara, able to give mild reproach, to comfort or to sit back as appropriate, and so enables Barbara to complete a simple task. Sheila is firm, the boundaries of the situation are clear for both, she repeats phrases such as 'birthday – b'. She challenges, using words such as 'quickly', 'no', 'you do know', 'come on – don't show off' along with 'I'm pleased', 'well done'. She bends to Barbara's level, she concentrates all the time, she is physically close, and her hand and eye movements are particularly significant. She is not static, seated alongside Barbara the whole time, but frequently gets up to help other children when she can, and so lets Barbara have space and time to complete what the teacher has set her. Sheila is sensitive to Barbara when she fidgets, even offering to change chairs with her. She is very persistent and will not let Barbara leave a task of which she feels Barbara is capable. Barbara knows that she has to try on her own. While Sheila works with other children, her body language clearly says 'I am not with you at the moment', although she watches her out of the corner of her eye. She uses a lot of 'what for?' and 'why?' questions with the other children, also Year 1.

Skills teaching

Wherever possible, do not do the activity for the pupil. Do a separate one and show the pupil how you did it. This goes for everything, from cutting out for the youngest pupils to sophisticated science experiments. Practical skills can only develop by the pupil doing it for themselves.

PHOTOGRAPH 11.6   Skills teaching

All the suggestions made for group working – getting pupils organising, planning, talking, questioning, thinking, reviewing and evaluating – hold for practical activities. The booklet *Primary design and technology* (DATA 1996) has some useful tips for showing children how to do something, talking to children while they are working, supporting practical work, supervising a group (including clearing away), organising and maintaining resources and creating a display. The following are some of their tips for helping children in practical work:

- don't do things for them that they can do for themselves, e.g. fetch materials, clear away, use tools;
- encourage them to think about what they are doing and to work carefully;
- remind the children about safe working;
- follow the same rules as the children when using tools or they will soon copy bad habits;
- encourage them to keep their work area tidy, e.g. return tools and equipment which are no longer needed, put unusable scraps in the bin, rearrange equipment and materials on the table so that it is easier to work;
- encourage them to be as accurate as possible, e.g. cutting carefully, measuring food ingredients, marking the position before punching a hole or sticking something down;
- watch how the children are holding tools and how they have positioned themselves and suggest changes if necessary, e.g. 'you might find it easier to stand up to do that', 'try holding it like this', 'use this finger to guide it/keep it still';
- make sure that girls and boys have equal access to tools and equipment – sometimes that is true in theory but not in practice!
- if you need to show a child how to do something, use a spare piece of material rather than their work;
- use the correct names for tools, equipment and materials and help the children to remember them.

(p. 19)

Working with individual pupils, groups or the whole class

Some of your work will necessarily be at an individual level, particularly where the pupils have physical needs, in order that they can take part in class activities. Hopefully these needs will be spelt out in statements or IEPs. This whole area of dealing with the individual needs of those with SEN is dealt with in Chapter 8, and there are many books and sources of information. The SENCO in the school will help you best in this area, as they will also know what particular support you can get locally, such as computer aids or lifting gear. All pupils benefit at some time from having individual attention, but a teacher with a whole class to teach and monitor can rarely spare time for this. You should have time to explore ideas and listen to individual stories, to develop appropriate individual strategies for learning, and to catch the learning moments and boost self-esteem, provided it does not create a dependency culture. Some schools make sure that different TAs are allocated to a pupil at different times of the week. This means, if you are ill or if there is a personality clash, the pupils still receive help.

Sometimes, under the teacher's instruction, you may be asked to monitor the work of the class, while the teacher works with an individual. Do make sure you feel capable of doing what the teacher asks, and that he or she is within call, if not eye contact, if you do this. A common practice was for a TA to take a story-time with younger pupils while the teacher goes over something with one or two other pupils, but unfortunately story-time seems to

PHOTOGRAPH 11.7 Explaining

have slipped from the curriculum in many schools. More often the TA is asked to stand in for the teacher in a cover supervisor capacity where all the pupils are set a task which they should be able to get on with, while the teacher works with one pupil or a group. It just needs someone to walk round the class and check that everyone is occupied on the task set. Unfortunately, the introduction of TAs to many schools was done as a result of earmarked funding for individual pupils, and the funding came in multiples of pupil contact hours associated with particular pupils. Some parents and pupils still think that they have to have so many hours' one-to-one support each week. The Code of Practice clearly states 'that this may not be the most appropriate way of helping the child'(DfES 2001: 53). It should not be the case that the least qualified and trained member of staff always works with the pupils with the most complex needs.

Do talk with the class teacher about the particular needs of individual pupils. You will also be able to fill in some of the detail for the class teacher. This element of exchanging information is essential for you to be able to do the best for individual pupils. Klaus Weddell, who was not only a retired teacher but also a retired educational psychologist, trained in diagnosing and helping pupils with SEN, became an LSA in his retirement. He wrote an account of his experiences in *Untold stories*: 'it can be quite difficult to get specific information about what the teacher finds a child can and cannot do – and under what conditions. It is usually more difficult to obtain information about what a child can do than about where the child is failing. There is a similar problem about discovering the particular situations in which a child performs better than in others, so as to get an idea about teaching approaches' (Weddell 2001 : 92). When a pupil does well it is easier to miss it than when they do something wrong.

One of the points of discussion that occurs frequently is whether pupils should be withdrawn from class for special help. Various research projects have investigated this, and much of the emphasis of the move towards inclusion has been in the direction of increasing group work over individual help, and including pupils in the whole class rather than withdrawing them. Clearly, some support, such as special exercises for a particular condition, may have to be given in special rooms or with particular apparatus, and the same argument could hold for special learning exercises. However, the social context of learning is also important. Learners need language and social interaction to aid them; you can facilitate this, but keep the talk on the subject. Sometimes the argument for withdrawal is not based on equipment location but on the need for a quiet place to enable an easily distracted pupil to have a time away from their peers, and even sometimes to allow the rest of the class or the teacher to have a bit of respite from the interruptions of those who find the subject matter beyond them. It is a matter of balance, and the final decision must be with the class teacher, who themselves will be working within the policies of the school. If you have a problem with the decision, discuss it carefully with the teacher or SENCO.

Make sure, when working with a group, that you are clear as to whether the group is to work together, or whether they are just doing individual work and sitting together. It is tempting, particularly in a primary classroom, to think that because children are sitting in groups they are working in groups. This is not always so. If the pupils are completing individual tasks, social contact needs to be minimal – only asking for help or clarity. The low level of chat which frequently surrounds group work can often be conversation about trivia – football, television programmes, other people. This is the type of gossip found on an assembly line in a factory where routine and boring tasks are being completed. School work should not be like that. Most individual tasks benefit from group discussion beforehand and after completion and at appropriate times in-between – sharing ideas, helping pupils who are 'stuck', giving encouragement, and so on. You should exercise judgement over the helpfulness of communication when pupils are sitting close together, engaged in apparently independent tasks. Concentration usually needs silence.

Alternatively the task may be a collaborative one, or include a combination of collaboration and individual work. The brainstorming sessions at the beginning of a writing task need cooperation; the individual writing task, concentration and preferably silence. Games, sharing equipment in a science experiment, and debates all need the skills of group work, and your job is to act like a facilitator in a conference group or a good chairperson. Set the scene; put in suggestions at appropriate times; try not to influence the thoughts but enable them to be expressed; keep the group focused on the task; ensure that all contribute and that no one person dominates; ensure that thoughts are gathered together, possibly ordered in some way; keep an eye on the time. Dip into the Dunne and Bennett (1994) book if it is on your staffroom shelves; it has many ideas for looking at the way in which pupils work and learn in groups.

You may have to develop group rules, such as when playing a game or even to get pupils to talk in turns. Learning to work cooperatively in a group is part of growing up, and the more you can get the group not only to act responsibly while working together but also to take responsibility for the group, the more you will help the pupils. If you are working with a group or individual in a teacher's class, you should take care over voice levels of your pupil or group: stop talking and stop them talking when the teacher asks for silence or makes any whole-class announcement. It can be very distracting for the teacher who wants to say something to the class, even though it is not meant for your group, if someone is still 'chuntering on' in the background.

Occasionally, TAs have been asked to take a whole class instead of the teacher, as a supply teacher, say. This has occurred much more frequently where managers see you as more effective (and cheaper) than a supply teacher to cover for the teacher's PPA (planning, preparation and assessment) time. You may know the way the class works, the characteristics of the pupils in it and what is planned for the day by the teacher, and be an experienced

TA and quite capable of doing the job better than a stranger. It is the biggest area of dispute in the work of TAs in schools. HLTA status TAs have had their competence recognised in covering. While 'a member of support staff with appropriate training and skills, who knows the pupils' needs and school procedures, may be a more appropriate choice to undertake cover than another qualified teacher or a supply teacher', the crucial phrase is 'with appropriate training and skills'. Do not undertake tasks for which you feel unsuited or ill prepared, it is the pupils who will suffer (DfES 2002b:22). Keeping a large group on task takes a great deal of skill and is a very great responsibility.

Supporting in practical work

Usually pupils enjoy any kind of practical work, whether it means using tools or media or working with their own bodies as in PE or drama. However, some pupils, particularly as they get older, become very self-conscious about expressing themselves, or being slower or less competent than others, things such as dexterity or clumsiness being more obvious in these subjects. It is important, therefore, to maintain the fun element of such activities and to be alert to the possibilities of low self-confidence or poor self-esteem.

You need to know the learning objectives of the activity you are supporting in the same way as for any lesson. The activity should have a shape – introduction, the activity itself and review. You will need to plan and prepare, participate, and ensure completion and clearing up by the pupils in your group. Practical subjects will have elements of skill, knowledge and understanding, just as the more formal activities do. If you are unsure of any of these, do ask. You need to know the degree of accuracy required for measuring purposes, whether preparing materials, measuring with the pupils or recording. You must familiarise yourself with any tools or apparatus to be used before you work with the pupils.

Many of the skills you may use or techniques you may teach will be of value throughout the pupils' lives, serving as leisure activities or outlets for creativity. Unfortunately, many activities such as performances, matches or field trips have been squeezed out by concerns for safety, cost or completing the more formal, testable parts of the curriculum. Without exploration and investigation, children will not gain a sense of ownership of their learning or realise the potential of the materials with which they are working – including the potentials of their own bodies. To accomplish a work of art whether in writing, performance or graphic art you need both skills and freedom to explore the media. Creation or invention takes time, often mistakes, application and appreciation.

Wherever possible, do not do the activity for the pupil. Work alongside the child, and discuss the progress and outcomes. Do a separate activity and show the pupil how you did it, often known as the 'Blue Peter' approach. This goes for encouraging a baby to sit up, and for anything from cutting out for the youngest pupils to sophisticated science experiments. Practical skills can only develop by the child or pupil doing it for themselves. Some of the pupils you support will have physical disabilities which make success in such activities difficult, so your encouragement and praise for small steps of progress are important. Remember the persistence that the paraplegic athletes must have, and the long hours of practice that any successful musician puts in, or your own attempts at learning skills; these kinds of examples will encourage those who easily give up. Pupils with learning problems often achieve success in practical subjects when finding more formal learning daunting.

You can work with a group, organise resources or equipment, use some explaining and tuition, question and observe what is going on in practical work, just as in pencil and paper work. The pupils will be active and mobile and need to be as autonomous as possible. Sometimes, in science tasks, the pupils believe they have to find the answer, when actually the teacher's objective is to give them experience of certain equipment or enable them to find a way to test that can be repeated. In art, the pupil may want an end product, when the teacher's objective has been to explore a variety of media, to find their potential for some other purpose entirely. It is obviously essential that you know the purpose of the task, then you can use appropriate questions to help the pupils think.

If you are working in a secondary school laboratory, studio, gym or workshop you must ensure that you follow the safety guidelines laid down in the school for staff working in such areas. There are likely to be rules regarding clothing and specialist protective garments, for instance using safety goggles in a laboratory or appropriate shoes in a gym. All staff working in these areas should be trained in the use of any hazardous equipment or when new procedures are introduced. You may feel that you should have special training to understand the principles of risk assessment and the safe ways of dealing with Bunsen burners, chemicals, glass, microbes and radioactive substances, all used in school laboratories. Even in primary schools there are right and wrong ways to use measuring equipment and you should know what units to use and what level of accuracy the teacher wants from the exercise.

Good pupil behaviour is essential when doing practical activities, so you should tell the teacher in charge if you have any concerns about any of the pupils you are working with. Usually, pupils are more interested in 'doing' rather than listening, reading or writing and so often behave better in such lessons, but they can get excited when new activities are introduced. There are many rumours about what is safe practice – or not – that are incorrect. Working with paint and other art media like clay and glazes, wire, plaster all bring their own safety precautions but also enable the pupils to be explorative, creative and imaginative. There is a great need for an increase in this kind of activity, so do not be put off by its messiness. Wear protective clothing, have appropriate mops and sponges to hand and enjoy with the children. Keeping areas clear to enable works of art or craft to dry or remain unfinished until another opportunity arises is also important.

You could be working with a group in a cooking activity, or out on the sports field, or using glue guns or craft knives. All of these must be handled safely by you and the pupils you are with. Electrical safety procedures as described in Chapter 10 should always be observed. You may be using chemicals that could be dangerous if eaten, or handling soil or pond water. Precautions for doing these activities should be observed, such as covering open cuts with lightweight gloves and ensuring proper hand washing after use. A list of suitable chemicals for primary schools, as well as those that are dangerous, is included in *Be safe* (ASE 2001 : 19), although it is not comprehensive. The international hazard warning symbols (ASE 2001 : 21) could be displayed and taught to children. It is the duty of all staff to point out to a more senior member of staff any hazards noticed in equipment or procedures.

Some lessons include using ourselves or animal parts, such as bits of skeletons. Here you must be aware of sensitivities about differences between pupils, e.g. shape, colour or size. Tasting and feeling and smelling things should be done hygienically. Examining soft body parts, such as offal, is both permissible and safe provided they are fresh and fit for human consumption; eyes of pigs can be used, but not those of sheep, cows or goats. You may find some pupils dislike this kind of handling, or have cultural or ethical reasons for not taking part. They should never be put under pressure to take part, and the teacher should be told of any problems.

Difficulties

Things do not always go smoothly in class or in the school. Do not worry about this, maybe change what you do the next time. In class you are likely to get into difficulties for several reasons. It may be your fault – you may have forgotten a particular resource, not understood the teacher yourself, arrived late for the lesson or actually not understood the content of the lesson. Do not try to cover up either with the teacher or with the pupils. If you have forgotten something, you can either get it if it is in the room, or improvise or change direction. You cannot leave your group if you are working with them outside the classroom. If you have a good relationship with the teacher and the occurrence is unusual, a quick word with the teacher will probably allow you to solve the problem and go and fetch the missing item. If there is something you do not know or understand then say so, as you should not pass on incorrect information to the pupils. You can either find out together with them by consulting a textbook or just ask the teacher what to do. Make suggestions for improvements, enter into any consultation process. We learn more from mistakes than from doing things correctly.

Problems with the pupils are less worrying personally, but still need attention. If it is a matter of their lack of understanding, feed back to the teacher at the end of the session in one of the ways described below. If it is a safety matter, report the incident to the teacher immediately. The most likely problem is that the pupil or the group gets out of hand because they are seeking trouble or they are bored.

Observation strategies

If you are undertaking a course it is very likely that you will be expected to make some structured observations of pupils learning, or a teacher may ask you to watch a pupil for a particular purpose. Standard 29.1 is about this area of work. You need to understand the purpose of the observation – just interest, or concern over progress, or concern over social interactions within a group. Even if you are not asked to observe, it is always worth spending a little time watching pupils. In this way you will begin to broaden your concept of the normal range of responses and behaviours briefly described in Chapter 5. You should ask the class teacher of the pupils you want to watch first, and find time to discuss the issues and protocols of observation before you start anything formal, as well as spending time with them afterwards discussing your observations.

As with looking at the use of apparatus, you can notice all sorts of things at random, just by being in a class with small children or young people, but it will sharpen your perceptions if you do this with some organisation. You should write down some things in as structured a way as possible, and this means you would be making records on someone else's child, for whom a class teacher is responsible. It means either taking time out of your paid time or doing it voluntarily. It is important that your observing does not become intrusive for the pupil or disrupt any other class activity. You need some agreed ground rules.

Possible protocols to consider for classroom observation

The following need to be discussed between the TA and the class teacher where any observation is to take place:

- the purpose of the exercise is to . . . e.g. understand more about . . .

- the adults involved will be . . .

- the pupils involved will be . . .

- the head teacher/department head/line manager has been told what is happening, and has agreed.

It needs to be checked that:

- anything written is to be shared first with each other, so that comments can be made and points of accuracy checked;

- any comments to be seen by others will be anonymised, or amalgamated with others to preserve confidentiality;

- the main audience of any summary written material will be . . . e.g. the other members of a course, or an outside reader;

- the people observed or interviewed can have a copy of the notes made if they so wish;

- you know what will happen to any written records;

- the intended outcome of the activity is . . .;

- you know what you will do if the observation shows up anything within the classroom or school that someone wishes to address or celebrate;

- if others get involved, they will be covered by the same sort of protocols;

- someone seeks permission of the parents of the children closely involved.

Either side should be able to make comments at any time in the process if there is any discomfort or suggestion about what is taking place or being said.

(Watkinson 2002:39)

There is much more detail about observing in Wragg (1994) although this was written for teachers. Harding and Meldon-Smith (1996) wrote for NVQ students in Child Care and Education and so is a more helpful book for TAs. While it was intended for those working with young children, its principles hold good throughout school phases, and the suggested forms are very useful. These books cover why, what, where and how to observe. They also look at things that can be measured about learning and things that cannot but are equally important.

Observing

You can use a sheet of A4 paper on a clipboard, a spiral-bound memo pad or an exercise book. Focus on one area of interest, one pupil, and observe at regular times, e.g. every 30 seconds or every minute. Decide on a part of their body which is of interest, such as their hands. What they are saying?

Do this for five minutes.

- Did they keep still? Did they touch any resources? Did they touch another pupil? Whom did they speak to? Was it about their work?

- Did this tell you anything more about the pupil, the table or desk they are working on, or the children they are with? Repeat the exercise with a different pupil at the same desk/table, or the same pupil in a different context or classroom.

- Did the same thing happen? How was it different?

OR

Note every five minutes what they are doing, and, if they are talking and you can hear what they say, put that down.

- What have you found out about this pupil?

THEN

- What did the pupil do during that period?

- Was it anything to do with what the teacher intended or not?

- Did the pupil learn anything new during the time you were watching?

- Did they understand anything better?

- Did they practise anything that they had done before?

- Did anyone talk to them or help them? Who? The pupils sitting near them or adults?

- Could you have made things easier for them if you had been sitting there, or if they had been in a different place, or had different resources? In what ways?

Find an opportunity to talk through what you saw with the teacher.

You can develop grids with names and headings of what you are particularly looking for, such as asking or answering questions, or with time markers. If you are going to question the pupils, you can prepare some questions beforehand.

Feedback to pupils and teachers

You need to monitor, even informally, how the pupils are progressing and what achievement they make in a lesson, often to make adjustments to what you are doing as you go along, but also then to feed back to the teacher. Standards 29 and 30 have a lot of detail in their knowledge sections as to the kind of things to consider. Assessment information is best when gathered against the objective for the session, so it is doubly important that you know what this is. It would also be useful for the teacher to know how well pupils are progressing towards their targets, particularly in literacy or in an IEP, as these are likely to be specific and short-term; what their behaviour is like, especially if a behaviour programme is in place; and what unexpected things you noticed.

Feedback to the teacher can be much more informal than the planning process; sometimes just a verbal comment, at the end of a lesson before the TA and teacher separate, in the corridor on the way to the staffroom, or even in the car park on the way home, can help the teacher plan the next step for the pupils with whom the TA has been working. You may have already alerted the teacher if you have had problems during the lesson, but it is better, if you can, not to interrupt him or her and just leave your comments to the end. In one school, the TAs themselves devised a separate written feedback system that would have some consistency for the teachers. Another school had a diary system for noting improvement and problems. TAs also use teachers' assessment forms, after training and guidance, which can be ticked when things are achieved. You could stick a polite post-it note on the teacher's desk when you leave the room, or in the pupil's workbook if the teacher is going to see it – not if it is going home. Make time voluntarily to chat, and gradually your contribution will be recognised, meetings will be convened and paid planning time will be instituted. Feedback can usually be done on the move. This has happened in many schools already.

Feed back informally to pupils, saying 'Well done, you finished today', or 'It looks better than yesterday' or 'You remembered to spell . . . correctly'. Give the pupil something to aim for next time, such as 'Let's see if you can do that without my help tomorrow'. You should have established whether you are to write directly in pupils' books and the approved method of doing this: red or black pen, comments or ticks, correction procedures, etc. You can say 'You tried hard', or 'That is well done for you', particularly if it fulfilled the teacher's targets for those pupils for that lesson. Saying things are marvellous, when clearly they are not, is not helpful. If the work is careless, particularly if you know the pupils well and they can do better, get them to do it again, or if there is not time, at least to recognise that they can do better. Maybe they are having an 'off' day. Try to ensure they finish the task set, giving them a warning as time gets short. If they finish early, they should have some kind of follow-up task to do. You may need to help them complete a homework diary.

Formative and summative assessment: evaluation

All the time teachers work with pupils they inwardly make small judgements. Those with QTS recognise this as informal formative assessment. TAs will also judge, but without training they may not recognise what they are seeing. As you increase in understanding of how learning takes place, and of the needs of pupils and the content of the curriculum, you will be increasingly useful in helping teachers in making more formal formative assessments. You will recognise what is realistic to expect of certain pupils, and what is a fair judgement. There has been considerable emphasis put on assessment for learning in recent times as it had seemed to slip in importance behind planning. The strategies now have support materials for assessment as does the QCA website. The DCSF has produced a special booklet entitled *The assessment for learning strategy* (DCSF 2008). It is all seen as part of the personalised learning thrust.

Eight principles underpin the strategy. Assessment for learning should:

- be part of effective planning of teaching and learning;
- focus on how students learn;
- be recognised as central to classroom practice;

PHOTOGRAPH 11.8 Marking work with the child

- be regarded as a key professional skill for teachers;

- be sensitive and constructive because any assessment has an emotional impact;

- take account of the importance of learner motivation;

- promote commitment to learning goals and a shared understanding of the criteria by which they are assessed;

- recognise the full range of achievements of all learners.

Learners should receive constructive guidance on how to improve.

Assessment for learning develops learners' capacity for self-assessment so that they can become reflective and self-managing (taken from the list on the QCA website, 26 May 2008).

You should spend time with the teacher making sure you agree about what you are looking for, and what lesson or part of the lesson would be best to watch for what the teacher is hoping to see. The feedback from TAs can be as important as the in-class support they are providing to the pupils, and teachers need to make arrangements to obtain this. You can also see there is the potential for disagreement with the teacher as you become more experienced. You may be convinced a pupil has real difficulties where the teacher could have assumed they were just being lazy, or you might consider a pupil was pretending to be slow in order to get your extra help. You must deal with this professionally, be certain you can justify what you are saying and have evidence to support you; and where relationships between you and the teacher are good, and you have pre-agreed the method and criteria to be used, there should not be a problem.

You may be asked to complete more formal assessment sheets as part of your job. If so, ensure you have complete instructions as to what you are to observe and what to write. This may become evidence in a reporting process. Sometimes TAs who have worked closely with pupils with special needs are asked to write their own report of what they are doing, and how their charges have progressed (or not). Again, get full instructions about what is required, ensure you look for strengths as well as weaknesses, and be brief, concise and accurate. If possible, get the document typed, but only by a member of the school staff. Always date any such record and sign it.

It might seem easier to observe and measure what is learned over a period of time than to try to watch it actually happening; but beware, it has its pitfalls. This is called summative assessment. Test results depend very much on how questions are asked, particularly where understanding is needed as well as memory, such as in science. Pictures, or seeing and handling the actual materials about which questions are asked, and being able to enquire about the meaning of the questions, all influence how correct the answers will be. Many of us can remember taking tests or examinations when we did not feel very well or the weather was exceptionally hot. These things can all affect our recall and performance, and hence our test results.

The things that teachers want to assess are the knowledge gained, the understanding that has developed, the skills learned, and the attitudes to learning that are influencing the pupil. Some of these factors are easier to see or measure than others. Tests and examinations tend to test knowledge and understanding; but practical skills have to be observed in action as well as by examination of an end product, and are more usually seen as part of a vocational competence assessment. Attitudes are really only seen in the way pupils cope with learning as it happens. In all of these assessments some kind of standard has to be established and then monitored in order that results from one teacher or class or school are comparable with those from other places. Individual observers will differ – their observations will be subjective. Tests with limited aims can be repeated by different people with similar results; the more people who use them and check them, the more reliable the results.

However, there is always the question of whether a particular test is the valid one to assess a particular area of learning – just as the old IQ tests are now considered invalid because the concept of intelligence has changed. Methods used will also vary with the age of the pupil. Clearly pre-school children will not undergo written examinations, and there is still some concern about the formal testing procedures inflicted upon seven-year-olds with the Standard Assessment Tests or Tasks (SATs). Science is not tested externally until Year 6, and even here there is much debate about how investigative, experimental and explorative work can be tested by written tests. Practical work is not tested until secondary school, and there is still much contention about the use or misuse of project work. Many teachers brought up by a formal academic examination-based route still have problems with the competence observation and portfolio approach of NVQs.

Any kind of assessment procedure needs careful handling by those conducting it, whether it is an informal observation for interest or a formal external examination. If you think back to your own experiences, you may remember a lot of 'hype' among your peers, stern faces from your teachers, the classroom furniture all rearranged so that you would not cheat. The fuss did not make you feel confident and give of your best. You need to minimise the disruption to normal school life, yet ensure quietness and freedom from interruptions. Even simple assessments, such as hearing pupils read in the infant class, can achieve better results in a calm, friendly atmosphere. Most teachers will welcome questions and suggestions you have about procedures to get the best from pupils, provided you offer them in the usual spirit of constructive support. Some families and cultures are particularly keen on examinations and will create tension in the home, and many schools now practise for external tests, sometimes to the detriment of covering the curriculum in other areas. The tension can be counterproductive. Some pupils (and adults) are very sensitive about being observed, hence the need for protocols and care about your presence in the room doing something unusual. In some cases you will be given the examination guides to follow,

PHOTOGRAPH 11.9   Checking and marking practice SATs papers

giving a certain procedure. It is important for validity that you follow these instructions, but you can do this without being officious. Particularly if you are supporting a pupil with SEN, you may be asked to read a test paper to a pupil, or encourage a small child to respond to particular questions. Again, the calm, friendly approach will enable the pupils to give of their best.

As well as ensuring the pupils do their best in any kind of assessment or test, you must always remember that you have to operate within the framework of the school policies and under the guidance of the teachers. Confidentiality about the process and the results is really important.

Recording and reporting

It is particularly important, if you write anything, that it should be accurate, concise, legible and dated and be kept in an appropriately confidential and secure place. Photocopiers can be a particular snare – important documents easily get left under the cover. Be very careful about taking anything home. Most of the points mentioned in the section above about assessment procedures will apply to the keeping of records, as the written outcomes of assessments form the bulk of records kept. Records should be reliable, valid, sufficient and informative. They will vary in nature according to the purpose for which they are kept. Some records will be kept just by the teacher – daily reading records, weekly spelling tests, progress in understanding of certain concepts or comments about attitudes, problems. Most teachers, especially in secondary schools, have mark books which look like registers, with the names of pupils down the margin and a different page for each kind of assessment or test they are conducting. Marks for assignments or completion of tasks, money for trips, and absences can all be entered on this kind of grid. Some teachers will just hand you their mark book and explain how they want it completed; others will want you to keep separate records and enter what they want in their mark books. More and more records are being kept electronically. STL 55 is the unit to look at when wanting to see this area broken down into performance criteria. The Level 2 unit STL 17 is also available at Level 3 for those who invigilate examinations. This one does tend to emphasise the organisational aspects of the job rather than the educational ones. STL 51 is about keeping attendance records.

More formal, end-of-term or end-of-year records will often be kept in a central, secure place and the contents of the files determined by the policies of the school. Parents may request to see the file of their own child or children, giving notice; they cannot see other pupils' records and they do not need to see the day-to-day mark book type of record. Some-times these teacher records are idiosyncratic to the teacher, and sometimes school procedures are in place. The type of record keeping expected, the purpose, organisation, storage and security will all be determined in school policies and there will be specific ones for both assessment procedures and record keeping. All records pertaining to pupils with SEN will be kept or maintained by the SENCO, especially any documentation about School Action, School Action Plus and statements, and all the IEPs and review documentation that go with such action. Other records will be collated by heads of departments or year group leaders to ascertain whether a group of students as a whole are progressing, either in a subject or over a period of time. This monitoring is essential for standards to be kept up. You do not have any right of access to records, except of course your own, unless this is specified as part of your role – you could be responsible for typing data from tests or examinations into a computer, for instance. However, it is often useful for you to see some records, such as the background of a pupil with whom you work who has a difficult or different home background. You must be very careful when handling school records of any kind: confirm your role and responsibility, ask permission if at all in doubt and always return records promptly as agreed.

Increasingly computers are used to store records, both numerical and word data. The school must conform to the Data Protection Act and so computer records are as accessible to parents as paper records; that is, they would not be permitted to see the collection of numerical data, but would be allowed to have a copy of anything written about their children. Schools pass on some aspects of the collated numerical data, such as the percentages of pupils reaching certain levels in SATs or GCSE examinations. Sometimes the sheer volume of data which can be collected seems overwhelming in this age of computers. It has become tempting to collect and manipulate as much as possible, as if the problem is solved once it is recorded. While you must comply with what is asked of you, you can still make suggestions for improvement; you should not just be doing things blindly, without questioning. Report any difficulties and clarify any concerns you have with the teacher with whom you are working. This will include concerns you have about the location of records as well as the actual record-keeping process, particularly if you feel records are being misused.

Increasingly, parents and pupils themselves are being asked to contribute to records as well as see them. Their views on the pupil's progress, attainment, attitudes to learning or interests can be most helpful, in addition to the standard sort of data kept in school records, such as birth date, serious illnesses and schools attended.

Questions to ask yourself

- Which teachers did you relate to well in your own school? Why?
- Are you sure of what you are supposed to be doing for all parts of the lessons in which you are involved?
- Are there any skills that you should practise?
- Have you got all the relevant policies?
- Are you sure about your ability to communicate what you know about other people's children?

Essential reading

ASE (2001) *Be safe: Health and safety in primary school science and technology*.

ASE (2006) *Safeguards in the school laboratory*.

DCSF (2008) *The Assessment for Learning Strategy* (00341–2008DOPM-EN).

DfES (2001) *Special Educational Needs code of practice*.

Some further reading

A series of practical suggestions based on research into teaching effectiveness: the Leverhulme project:

Brown, G. and Wragg, E.C. (1993) *Questioning*.

Dunne, E. and Bennett, N. (1994) *Talking and learning in groups*.

Dunne, R. and Wragg, T. (1994) *Effective teaching*.

Wragg, E.C. and Brown, G. (1993) *Explaining*.

Observation strategies

Harding, J. and Meldon-Smith, L. (1996) *How to make observations and assessments*.

Wragg, E.C. (1994) *An introduction to classroom observation*.

Two really useful practical books on teaching techniques

Kyriacou, C. (1997) *Effective teaching in schools: Theory and practice*.

Kyriacou, C. (1998) *Essential teaching skills*.

Dip into any of the following

Brooks, V. (2004) 'Learning to teach and learning about teaching', in V. Brooks, I. Abbott and L. Bills (eds), *Preparing to teach in secondary schools* (pp. 7–17) and other papers in this book.

Fisher, R. (1995) *Teaching children to learn*.

Hayes, D. (2003) *Planning, teaching and class management in primary schools* or similar books by this author.

O'Brien, T. and Garner, P. (2001) *Untold stories: Learning support assistants and their work*.

Pollard, A. (2002) *Reflective teaching: Effective and evidence-informed professional practice*.

12

Supporting the curriculum

THE CURRICULUM is everything that goes on in school. There is the formal explicit part; the informal part, which covers all the bits everybody knows go on between lessons, in the corridors or the playground, assembly or clubs; and the hidden curriculum, covering the bits about relationships and climate, the way you feel when you work in or visit a place. Much of this chapter is similar to that in the Level 2 book as there are some common themes in the two levels. However, working at Level 3 you must recognise that the expectation of your knowledge and understanding of subject matter by the teachers will be greater. Only you can get that, this book cannot cover all the subjects. One of the standards, STL 28, is specifically about supporting in a subject area other than ICT, literacy, numeracy or early years. There are separate standards at Level 3 for each of these: STL 8, 25, 26 and 27 respectively.

The formal curriculum

This covers what schools hope to teach. If you work in a state funded school, this includes the NC as a legal requirement in English and Welsh schools. Independent schools are free to set their own curriculum, although some follow the NC or parts of it. The NC is dictated by government, and is an entitlement for all children of statutory school age (5–16). Scotland has an advisory NC and Northern Ireland has its own version. Children under 5 years of age do not have to go to school or any other provider. There are no legal requirements on parents or carers to provide any kind of formal curriculum in the home for under fives. For all provision outside the home such as nurseries or child minding there is a statutory framework backed up by inspection. The way this is presented is changing so that by the time the new NOS are in place – September 2008 – the single statutory framework for the under fives will also be operative (DCSF 2007e).

You need to be familiar with the NC for the subjects and ages with which you work, remembering that overall there should be breadth and balance, coherence and consistency, relevance and differentiation. These words are written into the legal descriptions of the NC. The latest revision for the secondary curriculum, published to begin in September 2008, repeats the stated aims of the 2000 NC.

Aim 1: The school curriculum should aim to provide opportunities for all pupils to learn and to achieve.

Aim 2: The school curriculum should aim to promote pupils' spiritual, moral, social and cultural development and prepare all pupils for the opportunities, responsibilities and experiences of life. . . . The four main purposes of the National Curriculum: To establish an entitlement, to establish standards, to promote continuity and coherence and to promote public understanding.

(DfEE 1999a,b:13)

The documents lay out the subjects which have to be studied in England: English, mathematics and science, which were denoted as the core, and the foundation subjects of DT, ICT, art, music, PE, history and geography, and after age 11 a modern foreign language. RE was included in a basic curriculum; Welsh is an additional subject for pupils in Wales. Spiritual, moral, social and cultural education, citizenship and environmental education are now more closely defined. If you are in a secondary school, ask the teacher you work with or your mentor what is being taught in your school, how and why. Get your own copy of the NC for the age group you are working with: it can all be downloaded from the QCA website.

Programmes of Study describe what should be taught, the basis for planning and teaching. Attainment targets provide a framework in a nine-level scale for assessment in eight levels and a level for exceptional performance. They set out the 'knowledge, skills and understanding that pupils of different abilities and maturities are expected to have by the end of each key stage' (Education Act 1996). Level descriptions are defined for each level and describe the types and range of performance that pupils working at that level should show. They provide the basis for making judgements about pupils' performance at the end of Key Stages 1, 2 and 3, and so provide the basis for teachers to make their assessments. SATs are based on level descriptions.

We do not have legislation that insists on the same material being delivered in the same way at the same time on each day of the week, each week, month and year. We do not have standardised, centrally legislated and produced lesson texts from which we all work. Some countries do. Schemes of work, along with the various strategies, are not legally required but recommended, and so have created the impression of a stereotyped curriculum with certain elements having to be 'got through' in a certain time at a certain age. Secondary school curricula with their focus on syllabuses for examinations have always seemed that way. However, the current moves are to free schools to adapt their work more to the needs of their pupils – to personalise their curricula. Schemes of work will be drawn up by each school for each subject. They show in which year particular parts of the NC will be taught in your school, the resources available and probably lots of ideas for activities. QCA has produced model schemes of work for schools, to save them reinventing the wheel. These can be drawn up by schools themselves, based on the NC or on the syllabuses devised by the examination boards for the external examinations.

Ofsted inspects schools and early years' settings using published guidance. This includes specific criteria against which the school is measured, which include the way in which the NC or early years curriculum is planned, delivered by teachers, leaders and support staff, received by pupils and under fives and the learning outcomes.

Curriculum 2000

Curriculum 2000 provided an inclusive framework aiming that the learning across the curriculum should promote:

- spiritual, moral, social and cultural development;
- personal, social and health education and citizenship;
- skills development across the curriculum:

    Key skills
    - communication
    - application of number
    - information technology
    - working with others
    - improving own learning and performance

- problem solving

Thinking skills

- information-processing
- reasoning
- enquiry
- creative thinking
- evaluation
- financial capability, enterprise education and education for sustainable development.

It also said that teachers, when planning, should adapt or modify teaching and/or learning approaches and materials to provide all pupils with opportunities to succeed:

- setting appropriate challenges;
- providing for the diversity of pupils' needs;
- providing for pupils with special educational needs;
- providing support for pupils for whom English is an additional language.

Brighter children reach the levels earlier, and slower learners spend a longer time getting to each level. There were some pilot projects running during 2007/8 where it was possible for the participating schools to test their pupils when they think they are ready, i.e. at that certain level rather than testing all of them at the same age regardless of their progress.

After Curriculum 2000

Curriculum 2000 has been revised for secondary schools (see www.newsecondarycurriculum.org). It will be phased in from September 2008. Year 7 will be using the new programmes of study from September 2008, Year 8 from September 2009 and Year 9 from September 2010. The requirements for Key Stage 4 will come into force as the new GCSE qualifications in the relevant subjects begin. Citizenship and PE begin implementation in 2009 and English, Mathematics and ICT in 2010. Details can be found on the QCA website It will have less prescribed content than Curriculum 2000, enabling schools to be more flexible in determining their own emphases. The purpose is again to help raise standards and help learners 'meet the challenges of our fast changing world'(QCA 2008). The authors suggest their challenge is to create a curriculum that:

- raises achievement in all subjects particularly English and mathematics;
- equips learners with the personal, learning and thinking skills they will need to succeed in education, life and work;
- motivates and engages learners;
- enables a smooth progression from primary through secondary and beyond;
- encourages more young people to go on to further and higher education;
- gives schools flexibility to tailor learning to individual and local needs;
- ensures that assessment supports effective teaching and learning;
- provides more opportunities for focused support and challenge where needed.

(QCA 2008)

The revised programmes of study share a common format:

- *an importance statement* describes why the subject matters and how it can contribute to the aims of the curriculum;

- *key concepts* identify the big ideas that underpin the subject;
- *key processes* identify the essential skills and processes of the subject;
- *range and content* outlines the breadth of subject matter from which teachers should draw to develop knowledge concepts and skills;
- *curriculum opportunities* identify opportunities to enhance and enrich learning, including making links to the wider curriculum.

(QCA 2007:4)

A new set of aims which incorporates the ECM outcomes has been the starting point for the changes.

> The curriculum should enable all young people to become:
>
> - *successful learners* who enjoy learning, make progress and achieve;
> - *confident individuals* who are able to live safe, healthy and fulfilling lives;
> - *responsible citizens* who make a positive contribution to society.

(QCA 2007:6)

The level descriptions have been changed so that they fit with the new programmes of study. The QCA website http://curriculum.qca.org.uk has links to each subject to download the new programmes of study, or hard copy can be ordered from http//orderline.qca.org.uk.

Cross-curriculum dimensions were identified in the early 1990s but were rarely used by schools, but these have been revived in the 2008 secondary curriculum under slightly different titles. It is important for learners to see where what they are learning in school fits into the real world; otherwise it becomes a pointless exercise. The real world is complex and subjects interlink, so the cross-curriculum links are an attempt to make sense of the school subjects. Citizenship features prominently in the government's agenda for schools, hence Standard 47 is included in the NOS set. Standard 48 is also relevant here. The new list of cross-curricular dimensions includes:

- identity and cultural diversity
- healthy lifestyles
- community participation
- enterprise
- global dimension and sustainable development
- technology and the media
- creativity and critical thinking.

(QCA 2008)

The new curriculum also identifies the skills that young people need apart from those that relate to specific subjects. These include the functional skills of English, mathematics and ICT and the personal, learning and thinking skills. These latter are identified as enabling young people to become:

- independent enquirers
- creative thinkers
- reflective learners
- team workers

- self-managers
- effective participators.

(QCA 2008)

Curriculum 2000 will remain relevant for those students not affected by the categories mentioned above and for those in primary schools. There is a slight change to the primary curriculum following the review of reading undertaken by Sir Jim Rose and his team, which identified the importance of synthetic phonics in learning to read (Rose 2006). This is now part of the programme of study for reading in English. Rose has also been identified to lead a team looking at a wholesale review of the primary curriculum under *The Children's Plan* (DCSF 2007a:10). This sets goals for 20:20 and is an attempt to be more responsive to the needs of children, young people and their families and yet another attempt to raise standards. The chapters are partly based on the outcomes of the ECM agenda, being healthy and safe, yet achieving high standards. They hope to produce a curriculum that helps 'children move seamlessly from nurseries to schools, from primary to secondary and then to work or further and higher education' (DCSF 2007a:10). Flexibility and personalised learning are also emphasised in *20:20 vision* (DfES 2006a).

The strategies

Alongside the definitions in the NC of what must be taught came the twin strategies for literacy and numeracy. Many of you may now be employed to work in specially supporting pupils in these areas. English includes literacy – reading and writing – but it also includes speaking and listening. For some of the younger children whom you may be working with, this area is so difficult for them that they will need help with it before they will be able to read and write with any understanding. There is more detail on the implications of using the materials in the following chapters. Some of the catch-up programmes and materials used for booster classes are also available in schools, but you will be given directions for all these materials.

The strategies have resulted in a much more formal teaching approach to the subjects, with suggested structure to lessons, and in the case of the original literacy material even recommended times to be taken over each part of the lesson. However, it is up to the discretion of the school to determine the way in which these strategies are used in other subjects, additional experiences beyond those set out, the style of resources used and the time of day that these subjects take place. You must clarify your role in lessons with the teacher, where possible attend any staff meetings or training associated with the strategies, and get a copy of the handbooks for yourselves. There is also a lot of additional material, some of which is written especially for TAs to use.

A downside of the strategies, which have been very successful in creating consistency in planning and teaching in schools, is that in some schools too much time has been spent on literacy and numeracy, squeezing out the other subjects. Also, the curriculum coherence that came with topic-based teaching in the 1980s was lost. Separate subjects became the norm in primary schools. The idea of a broad and balanced curriculum, accessible to all, enabling all children to experience success, has not yet been realised for some pupils but it is possible (Ofsted 2002b). Partly in response to this, a more flexible Primary Strategy was introduced in 2003 (DfES 2003). It encourages schools to be more innovative and develop a broader and richer curriculum. The withdrawal of groups for specific support can have implications for inclusion, although the children usually enjoy the activities. It is possible that a child receiving specific support in Year 1 may need support throughout their school career, exposing them to a constant diet of being boosted and depriving them of other experiences. Hard decisions have to be made by schools and parents.

The current directives are to return to topic-based curriculum for all the foundation subjects, to ensure that English and mathematical skills are well taught both separately and in the context of the other subjects. In the new secondary curriculum assessment procedures, teachers are encouraged to assess areas like this in other subjects where possible and to link and plan subjects together to prevent overlap as well as make taught matter more interesting and relevant. If you go to the standards site to access the national strategies you can find a page entitled 'What do the new frameworks offer?' There are links from this guidance, planning objectives, subject guidance and support for all secondary pupils in English, mathematics, science and ICT.

Other aspects of the formal curriculum

Schools have to have policies for sex education and behaviour management and can set out anything else they want to teach in their prospectuses. They are also supposed to set out how they intend to teach the formal curriculum. Some books talk about 'delivering' the curriculum, but it is probably clear to you, to use the old saying, 'You can take a horse to water but you cannot make it drink'. Children and young people are not containers to be filled with knowledge. Delivery alone is not enough, the contents have to be understood and used. We must also recognise the importance of individual achievements, and the value of encouraging pupils to want to learn, to value themselves and of stimulating curiosity and creativity. A challenging task! It is also important to realise that behaviour management is not a separate subject. If the formal curriculum is taught with the pupils in mind, in an interesting and engaging way, then behaviour is much less of a problem.

Each school will have its own curriculum policies, laying down how each subject is to be taught, resourced and assessed in that school. If you are regularly helping in particular lessons you need to obtain a copy of the relevant policy and see how your presence fits in with what the school wishes to achieve. If you are in a secondary school, it may well be advisable to consider taking a GCSE in the subject if you do not already have one. This is especially true of science and geography where the technical language is specific to the subject and can be the source of confusion for the student. You need to be sure of your own facts and skills before you can help others. STL 28.1P4 requires you to 'carry out a realistic self evaluation of your subject knowledge and skills'. STL 28.1P6 and 7 require you to identify subject knowledge and skills that would help you improve the support you provide and identify and use opportunities to improve. STL 28.1P8 also points out that you need to be able to apply any knowledge you gain to your own circumstances.

You need to be able not only to read worksheets but to interpret them for students with learning problems, and at Level 3 to compile, evaluate and develop resources and materials. You need to be able to show students how to use apparatus safely and accurately. This goes from using rulers through to complicated specialist equipment. You need to know when accuracy matters, or numbers of results. It is hoped that all TAs have GCSE or its equivalent in mathematics and English or are in the process of obtaining them, in order to be able to help pupils adequately and accurately, as numeracy and literacy underpin recording and communicating information in all other subjects. While these are compulsory only for HLTAs, all TAs are working with pupils using basic literacy and mathematics. It is possible to study for a qualification in English and mathematics and get a Level 2 qualification in them free of charge, paid for by the Learning and Skills Council. Enquire at your local FE or AE college for information or look at the Learning and Skill Council (LSC) website www.caretolearn.lsc.gov.uk.

Supporting pupils in curriculum areas

These strands or aspects of teaching and learning apply whatever the subject but have some subject-specific elements to them. Standard 28 specifically addresses this aspect of TAs' work and Standard 64 is for those TAs who might be leading in a curriculum area. This could happen if the TA was a graduate in, say, music in a secondary school or an ICT whiz in a primary school. These aspects also apply to working with practical subjects such as science and DT, as well as all the other subjects taught in school, although the standards do not make reference to these. For instance, all your work needs to be done within the confines of national legislation and the policies laid down for the school, but there will be subject-specific legislation in the NC and subject-specific policies. All that you do is under the direction of or with the permission of the teacher of the class in which you are working. You need to understand the learning objectives of the teacher and the strategies they wish you to employ in gaining those objectives. There will be differing strategies to support different subjects, and you need the appropriate resources for the subject you are teaching. You need to observe the health, safety and security precautions related to the area you are in, the subject (whether it is a practical one) and materials and equipment you are using. All the classroom procedures should take place with a view to maintaining and developing the pupils' self-confidence and self-esteem, using appropriate praise and things to interest them. If the pupil finds a particular part of a subject difficult, such as spelling or the concept of capacity or working in three dimensions, it is particularly important to deal with such problems in a way to maintain interest and self-esteem. You need to access records and contribute to their maintenance with all the provisos of confidentiality and accuracy. You particularly need to know and understand what special needs the pupils with whom you are working have and how they will best be supported in the subject you are involved with.

The subject-specific detail also comes into understanding the subject for yourself, using the correct vocabulary and procedures for that subject; for instance, how to use special apparatus properly or how to subtract by the currently approved methods. If you had difficulty with a subject at school, this does not mean you will have difficulty helping pupils and supporting teachers in that subject; in fact, it may be the opposite – you may well understand the problem the pupil is having better than someone who is an expert in that subject.

Another aspect of curriculum development, which makes life complicated, is that subject divisions are not as clear cut as the NC sometimes makes them look. Life actually does not work in neat bundles, though it does help to organise thinking in that way and all the things that go with this, such as books, resources, curricula, departments, faculties, personnel; even schools and universities specialise. English and mathematics, particularly, go across the curriculum. Science could not exist without language and number, art needs the scientific information from the study of materials, and so on. Knowledge is holistic. In primary schools, for some years, teachers were encouraged to plan without specific reference to subjects, and used what became known as the 'topic' approach. Most schools kept good subject records and resources but for some children this vagueness in planning meant they did not learn anything properly, hence the legal requirements which came in with the NC. However, computation methods learned without context, the rote learning of things such as tables without any relevance to everyday life is pointless and actually is more difficult. How many of you have helped your pupils or your own children learn their spellings only to find the same words mis-spelt in a letter or an essay? Pupils who cannot communicate their understanding or understand what is being taught clearly are at a great disadvantage. This may be due to having English as an additional language or to learning problems. If this is so, you will need to refer to the EAL and SEN chapters and units as well as the class teachers and SENCO.

Using ICT to support learning

It is not possible to be a TA in a school these days and opt out of using ICT. Standard 8, using ICT to support learners, is available at both Level 2 and Level 3. Using ICT permeates everything the school does. All children leaving school in the twenty-first century should be able to use ICT. Soon, the teaching of ICT as a separate subject will be less dominant as all classrooms will have stand-alone machines, networked to the school system, interactive whiteboards and banks of laptops for general use. Already, most children are more familiar with the possibilities ICT can open up than some staff, and can often troubleshoot problems for them. ICT should be seen as a tool to support learning and it is this aspect of ICT work that the Level 3 STL 8 is aimed at. To gain STL 8 you will be expected to provide functional equipment and the resources required by the teacher. You need to know the sort of equipment and resources that are available and their location; the school procedures that must be followed in its use and maintenance; and the reporting of faults or problems. Helping the pupils means maintaining their interest, independence and self-confidence.

Some TAs have even become ICT coordinators for their school although this should be considered to be working at the level of an HLTA and paid accordingly. There are clearly some specific items relating to ICT that must be considered. First, note that ICT does not just refer to the use of computers and the use of hardware and software, but also, as the scope of the NOS makes clear, to filming and projection equipment, recording and playback equipment such as tape, video and DVD recorders and cameras. All equipment associated with computers and recorders such as disks, tape, paper, networks, whiteboards, printers, mobile phones, programmable equipment digital measuring equipment that are in use in many schools are also included.

ICT is increasingly used to enhance the education of all learners, but for some, the use of digital resources may present barriers because they have special needs or disabilities [8.2P2]. Schools will want ICT resources to be accessible to all their learners – and have a legal duty to make 'reasonable adjustments' to ensure that learners who are disabled are not put at a substantial disadvantage. The ECM agenda highlights this [8K14, 25].

Curriculum for the under-fives

Legally, of course, children do not have to be in any setting outside the home until the term in which they have their fifth birthday. From September 2008 there is a *Statutory framework for the early years foundation stage*, setting the standards for learning, development and care for children from birth to five (DCSF 2007e). This is the result of an amalgamation of three existing documents: *Curriculum guidance for the foundation stage* (DfEE 2000b), *Birth to three matters* (Surestart 2003) and *Arrangements for the childcare of children aged under eight* available from the Surestart website (www.surestart.gov.uk) as a word document (undated). These three documents will be available in the relevant early years settings and may have useful references to resources and reading matter, but their general contents are all subsumed into the one 2007 framework. The ECM agenda underpins the whole new framework. The aim is to set standards, provide for equality of opportunity, create a framework for partnership working, improve quality and consistency, and lay a secure foundation for future learning. It gives both the legal framework and practice guidance. It can be downloaded from www.standards.dfes.gov.uk; www.teachernet.gov.uk/publications or www.everychildmatters.gov.uk.

The four distinct but complementary themes running through the document are:

- *A unique child* recognises that every child is a competent learner from birth who can be resilient, capable, confident and self-assured. The commitments are focused around development; inclusion; safety; and health and well-being.

- *Positive relationships* describes how children learn to be strong and independent from a base of loving and secure relationships with parents and/or a key person. The commitments are focused around respect; partnership with parents; supporting learning; and the role of the key person.

- *Enabling environments* explains that the environment plays a key role in supporting and extending children's development and learning. The commitments are focused around observation, assessment and planning; support for every child; the learning environment; and the wider context – transitions, continuity and multi-agency working.

- *Learning and development* recognises that children develop and learn in different ways and at different rates, and that all areas of learning and development are inter-connected.

You can see from these descriptive words how closely the early curriculum follows the development of the child and talks of meeting their needs. The older the child, the less the developmental stage of the child is taken into account, and actual age and individual subjects become the yardsticks for defining what should be taught. The curriculum match to children's needs seems of less importance than the match to the teacher's planning and assessment as the children get older.

The early learning goals, previously for the three- to five-year-olds, are now set out for the whole age range but cover some similar headings:

- personal, social and emotional development
- communication, language and literacy
- problem solving, reasoning and numeracy
- knowledge and understanding of the world
- physical development
- creative development;

instead of

- personal, social and emotional well-being
- positive attitudes and dispositions towards their learning
- social skills
- attention skills and persistence
- language and communication
- reading and writing
- mathematics
- knowledge and understanding of the world
- physical development
- creative development.

Ongoing formative assessment will take place throughout the child's time in any setting but an end of stage profile will be compiled to sum up the development and achievement on 13 scales derived from the early learning goals. This will have to be completed by the end of the term in which the child reaches five (or 30 June) – which is the statutory starting school age.

The Appendix 2, 'Areas of learning and development', is a most useful and detailed guide to support early years' practitioners. All of you who work in that sector would be well advised to get your own copy for reference. The effective practice section will help you in developing your own skills in supporting more senior members of staff and the children in your care. This is done for six stages of development:

- birth to 11 months
- 8 to 20 months
- 16 to 26 months
- 22 to 36 months
- 30 to 50 months and
- 40 to 60+ months.

You can see how each group overlaps with the two adjacent groups, recognising that children do not all develop at the same rate and norms need to be flexible.

Learning through play

Learning through play in mainstream schools seems largely to have disappeared owing to the demands of the curriculum but there are moves afoot to remedy this. Play is often considered the opposite of work, and parents are worried when children are 'just playing about' in primary school and not sitting learning. Most teachers see 'playtime' as their relief time and not fully part of the formal school. Indeed, some secondary schools now start early and finish at lunchtime so that they do not have to consider either school meals or supervision over the lunch break when not eating meals. Someone has even suggested that there should be different names for constructive, organised, monitored play and the leisure pursuit connotation of the word.

Much of the study of play has been done by early years' practitioners but we all know that when faced with a new situation we have to play about in the widest sense with the materials, try things out for ourselves, experiment, investigate potential and ascertain what that particular subject means for us. This is true whether we are writing poetry, getting a new television or meeting new people. What is sad is that formal school has downgraded this area in the way it has. You cannot tell someone the things they will learn by playing: it is about the doing, not the seeing or listening of the old Chinese proverb. 'I hear, I forget; I see and I remember; I do and I understand' (source unknown). It is how we digest and assimilate our understanding of the world and what it means to live in it. It teaches us how to cope with our emotions; routines provide the training in social customs; experiences with media, toys and the trappings of a rich environment encourage the development of understanding of the physical world but also our own potential in manipulating it and creating new things. Play enables children to develop social relationships, to gain control over themselves and their environment in a safe but challenging way. Play needs to be worked at hard to get the most out of it, just like any other task.

Children can express their ideas, explore and investigate if left to their own devices and it was believed at one point that providing the rich environment was everything. Children need opportunity to choose to do in order to understand properly what happens when they do. Thinking of your own exploring a new piece of equipment you need to be left alone to play with it. But, remember the learning experience suggested at the end of chapter 5 and you realise that an instructor/friend/guide intervention at the right time is just what you needed. The main role of the adult is twofold, to vary the environment to encourage the exploration and stimulate interest, but mainly to watch the 'players' and decide how best to support their learning. This requires an in-depth knowledge of the child and a very acute sense of timing. You can intervene if play becomes too rough or too messy, can join in the game or activity, can allow the play to develop naturally or add extra dimensions to the activity. We all need challenge if we are to progress and achieve our potential.

But even this has to be done with care; too much challenge can undermine self-esteem and self-confidence.

To understand this role you need to go to a well-run nursery and watch the practitioners or play leaders at work. Their observational and record-keeping work is comprehensive, as much of the time the children are left to work/socialise with each other. The time spent on planning and preparation is also lengthy as the quality of the provision will depend on the selection and care of it, and the relevance to each child's needs as identified by the observational work.

In a good early years' setting the curriculum is about the provision of as varied a diet of equipment and experiences as possible but not all at once or the same for all age groups. The adult:pupil ratio will be higher than in schools [3K11]. There should be something to stimulate each of the areas of learning, to support physical, linguistic, intellectual, emotional and social development. In a nursery there are usually geographical areas that can be identified with aspects of learning. You would be able to see quiet areas with books, tables for drawing or writing, creative areas with paints and modelling media, investigative areas, constructive areas and imaginative areas with facilities for role play. Most physical provision is usually put outside, where some open air and some covered areas can be found so that physical play can take place whatever the weather. Some nurseries have sensory areas with different surfaces to walk on, objects to bang and listen to, plants with different smells as well as areas to dig and climb on.

Play is age and developmental stage related. One only has to observe a small child on the beach watching the effect of the tide coming in to see the value of such items as sand and water for play. Sometimes lip service is paid to the provision of play in the early years of the primary school by providing a sand tray or water tray with a few objects in it, but unless the objects are relevant to the topic of the teacher or the interest of the child or group it is a pointless exercise, soon to become tedious and even counterproductive. A sand tray in a class of older primary children introduced as part of a geography topic for a week or two, with access to a source of water would enable the children to explore for themselves the effect of rainfall on sand. Replace the sand with soil, pebbles or clay at different times and a great deal will be learned about erosion and geomorphic change. Put the same tray in secondary school geography, with plants, blocks for buildings, and the learning could be about the effects of man on the environment. I am sure you have also seen or been an adult on the beach with children and enjoyed endless hours trying to keep the water from destroying your carefully constructed castle.

The aim is to provide the facilities in the setting in a safe way, enabling exploration, development (not suppression) of curiosity, challenging without frightening in adult presence to ensure that appropriate boundaries are maintained yet allow freedom of choice. Play provision should be planned and evaluated as for any other area, should be safe, appropriate to age and stage of development, work within a legal framework, be tidied up and progress or changes recorded. The exploration and investigation, the questioning and questing in play is what develops into scientific pursuit given the introduction of a framework in later school life. It also gives a growing child the tools to cope with real life. Adult life is not just a matter of playing with sandcastles but of questioning and challenging politicians and statistics, investigating best buys and trying out 'do it yourself' methods. You can see that things like cooking, gardening and sports activities all stem directly from practical and play activities encouraged in formal settings. The foundations of literacy and numeracy are laid with the speaking, listening and manipulative play of the early years. This rather neglected aspect of the formal curriculum is vital for enriching the curriculum at every stage but also in providing the foundations for adulthood. When safety concerns are properly understood and carried out, the range of such activities is virtually boundless.

Play needs time and develops concentration; it is intrinsically motivated: all children play unless prevented by physical disability or cultural or social constraints. Educationalists see it as crucial for development of the imagination, for problem solving, for a healthy body and mind in the widest sense of the word. Those schools which have extended their provision to include what happens in the playground have seen a decrease in conflict as well as an added dimension to the children's experience. Maybe some teachers and headteachers also need persuading of the value of constructive play?

The informal and hidden curriculum

Because the informal curriculum is not set out in legal requirements, every school will be different in what it expects of this area. Behaviour management systems cover this area as well as the formal teaching. Unless there is a consistency of approach 'this is how you behave when in the school environs' which is dealt with by any adult passing, the pupils soon consider out of classroom areas as 'muck about' areas and show lack of respect for any adult who ignores them out of the classroom. Schools have found it useful to employ male TAs or midday assistants in an otherwise female-staffed school or in a secondary school, in order that the boys' toilets do not become a 'no-go' area. Where children and young people know that once inside the school gates certain rules of courtesy and a lack of tolerance of bad language apply and are enforced, their behaviour can change as they walk in the gates or door.

One of the results of the ECM agenda is the highlighting of the need for extended schools. This is expanded on in Chapter 10. The use of outside places for play or environmental work is also discussed in Chapter 10.

Things that used to be implicit in the way schools worked are becoming more and more explicit, so less is 'hidden'. Matters such as politeness and care of property used to be taken for granted, but now sometimes have to be part of the explicit behaviour policy. Treating everybody with courtesy, whatever their needs, colour, creed or race is spelt out in equal opportunities and anti-discrimination policies. Enjoyment and attitude are all part of a school's culture and climate. Emotional development and behaviour of learners is reported on, as well as the learners' spiritual, moral, social and cultural development and their ability to stay safe and healthy. An Ofsted inspection of a school recognises these less definable areas, and other aspects of personal development. They also look at how well the school ensures pupils' care welfare, health and safety, provides support advice and guidance for pupils, and seeks to involve pupils in its work and development (Ofsted 2007b).

Note how many aspects of the hidden curriculum appear in the following list.

Inspectors will report on:

- description of the school
- overall effectiveness of the school:
    - effectiveness and efficiency of boarding provision
    - what the school should do to improve further
- achievement and standards:
    - personal development and well-being
- quality of provision:
    - teaching and learning
    - curriculum and other activities
    - care, guidance and support

- leadership and management
- the extent to which schools enable learners to be healthy
- the extent to which providers ensure that they stay safe
- how well learners enjoy their education
- the extent to which learners make a positive contribution
- how well learners develop workplace and other skills that will contribute to their future economic well-being.

The following is the description of what is considered good in terms of personal development and well-being:

> Learners' spiritual, moral, social and cultural development is good and no element of it is unsatisfactory. Young children are learning to understand their feelings. All learners enjoy school a good deal, as demonstrated by their considerate behaviour, positive attitudes and regular attendance. They feel safe, are safety conscious without being fearful, and they adopt healthy lifestyles. They develop a commitment to racial equality. They make overall good progress in developing personal qualities that will enable them to contribute effectively to the community and eventually transfer to working roles.
>
> (Ofsted 2007a:14)

You know when visiting schools, maybe on your first visit to the school you are now working in, that schools have a climate. They try to define this in words, describing their 'ethos', but it is hard to legislate for happiness. While 'to be a happy place' cannot be the first aim of a school (we could say that about homes or social clubs), pupils will not learn if they are unhappy and staff will not work with a will if they are miserable. Once you are a member of staff you will also be part of that school and a little responsible for its climate. Respect and support are needed by you, but you will have your part to play to give it to all the other staff as well as the pupils. Your relationships, spelled out in Chapter 3, taking responsibility for your own actions, and the actions of others with pupils as well as staff all contribute to this hidden curriculum.

Freiberg and Stein (1999) said:

> School climate is the heart and soul of a school. It is about that essence of a school that leads a child, a teacher, an administrator, a staff member to love the school and look forward to being there each day. School climate is about that quality of a school that helps each person feel personal worth, dignity and importance while simultaneously helping create a sense of belonging to something beyond ourselves. The climate of a school can foster resilience or become a risk factor in the lives of people who work and learn in a place called school.

Questions to ask yourself

- Have you got your own copies of the NC, any relevant school curriculum policy and the behaviour management policy?
- How much time do you allow the pupils in your care to practise skills for themselves?
- How good are you own skills, knowledge and understanding in English, mathematics and ICT?

- Do you need to do any further study in any other curriculum area or skill tuition in order to support the pupils properly in those lessons? How are you going to do this?
- Who can help you? Have you discussed your curriculum role with the relevant coordinator or head of department?
- Are you aware of how you can contribute to the ethos and climate of the school?

Essential reading

The NC for the subject in which you are supporting

The relevant parts of the school's schemes of work

The school's policy for the relevant subjects

Some further reading

Any books on play or early years by Tina Bruce, Marion Dowling or Janet Moyles, particularly

Bruce, T. (2004) *Developing learning in early childhood.*

Bruce, T. ed. (2006) *Early childhood: A guide for students.*

Drake, J (2004) *Organising play in the early years: Practical ideas and activities for all practitioners.*

Moyles, J. (2005) *The excellence of play.*

Moyles, J. (2007) *Beginning teaching, beginning learning.*

Useful websites

The QCA website http://curriculum.qca.org.uk has links to each subject to download the new programmes of study, or hardcopy can be ordered from http//orderline.qca.org.uk www.caretolearn.lsc.gov.uk: LSC website for those of you who want access to free support at Level 2 in English and mathematics

www.surestart.gov.uk: Surestart website

Subject association websites

for subject magazines, conferences and local branches

www.nasen.org.uk: National Association for SEN

www.nate.org.uk: National Association of Teachers of English

www.m-a.org.uk and atm.org.uk: Mathematics Association and the Association of Teachers of Mathematics

www.ase.org.uk: Association for Science Education

www.data.org.uk: Design and Technology Association

www.subjectassociation.org.uk: a general site

www.becta.org.uk: the ICT support website: British Educational Communications and Technology Agency, a UK agency supporting ICT developments

13

Supporting literacy

MUCH OF THIS CHAPTER and the next repeats the Level 2 book literacy and numeracy chapters with some tweaking for consideration by a Level 3 candidate. Both English and mathematics are fundamental to all that pupils need to do in school and for an adult to function in today's world. They are needed in order to understand and function in most other areas of the curriculum. Even practical and performance areas need them in order to attain the higher levels. Both subjects have been under the spotlight for the last ten years with the publication and dissemination of the strategy materials into schools. The aim has been to raise the standards of literacy and numeracy which were considered very low once national tests became the norm. The NC attainment target levels at Level 4 are considered the basic minimum need, and many children were not attaining that. So, national strategies were launched based on the known evidence for best practice. You need to know how these are interpreted in your school. The strategies have raised standards but there is still work to do. All the materials mentioned in this chapter unless separately referenced are available on the strategies website www.nationalstrategiescpd.org.uk or www.standards.dfes.gov.uk. The Primary Framework is predominantly web-based and both TAs and teachers need to be competent and confident in their use of the computer and the internet and in particular to be able to navigate the Primary Framework site.

Both English and mathematics are areas in which TAs are heavily used to support teachers to raise the adult–pupil ratios in order to give more individualised help. One concern is that TAs themselves may have struggled, particularly with mathematics, when they were at school and may not have the curriculum knowledge or confidence to help as well as they could. If you are in this category and are aiming at a Level 3 qualification you really should study for a GCSE yourself in either or both subjects, or at the very least get a Level 2 equivalent qualification with support from the Learning and Skills Council at a local college. Don't try to hide your insecurity; teachers have had the same problem and will be only too willing to help and support you.

Moreover, all the things mentioned in previous chapters about how children learn, about supporting pupils in lessons and helping the teacher, apply also to English and mathematics: you need to know the teachers' objectives; planning and preparation are crucial; there are appropriate ways to support pupils to preserve their self-esteem and retain their independence, yet challenge them to achieve their best; appropriate praise and good feedback are needed; you may have to simplify the stages in which the pupils undertake a task or the vocabulary you use in order to help them complete it; ask for help when you need it and feed back achievement and concerns to teachers. You need to have read and understood, and perhaps own copies of, the school policies in the subjects, and discuss anything you don't understand with the class teacher, the subject head or the coordinator.

You should be told if there are particular problems with any of the children with whom you are working. When dealing with specific problems you should be able to see the pupil's IEP. This will deal with the specific areas the pupil needs to work on and will give a measure of past targets met. The areas may be general or very specific. One instance of the latter might be that you would work with a pupil with poor spelling skills but for whom other areas of learning present no problem. You may get a chance to discuss the IEP with the SENCO. However, there could be a short-term problem such as an ear infection which could mean that a pupil is not hearing clearly, or a problem after they have been involved in some kind of emotional upheaval. For EAL pupils, refer to Chapter 9 which gives more details about helping them.

English

English is an entitlement for all pupils of primary age and should be taught for a minimum of five hours per week; at secondary, a minimum of three hours. In primary schools, however, it is becoming less common for single lessons to be an hour in length each day. This is due to a shift in culture, meaning that more schools are teaching through cross-curricular methods. Literacy is the ability to communicate and understand language through spoken and written text. English in primary schools is called literacy.

Cross-curricular teaching combines several subject areas in one session. For example, the objective of the lesson may be to write a letter (literacy focus) but in order to do this, pupils need to employ their History and ICT skills as the letter is from Henry VIII to the Pope and will be word-processed. Themed approaches are deemed to enable pupils to have a broad and balanced curriculum and to focus upon the teaching of skills that can be used across all subjects. Therefore in primary schools, practice has changed. The five hours minimum literacy entitlement is often delivered flexibly; some days' sessions are longer than an hour, some shorter. For younger pupils literacy may be taught in short sessions delivered throughout the school day. It is imperative that language skills taught in literacy are practised when talking, reading or writing in all subjects.

The NLS gave teachers a real focus for English teaching. In a drive to raise standards, teachers in all key stages had to teach age-appropriate objectives and have much more rigorous word (vocabulary and spelling) and sentence (grammar and punctuation) level teaching and understanding. The NLS is over ten years old and supplementary documentation has been published to support teachers and pupils further. The strategies are evolving in light of new research and social and technical changes. The strategies for primary schools have been revised and updated and renamed the Primary Framework. This online resource has been developed to assist teachers further in raising standards, providing more opportunities to meet the needs of children in primary classrooms today.

The Primary Framework: Literacy

Teaching objectives for the Primary Framework have been categorised into 12 strands (see Table 13.1). The objectives are no longer confined to a specific term but are end of year age-related expectations. For example, the objectives in Y2 refer to the standard that the pupils need to reach before moving into Y3.

TABLE 13.1 The 12 strands of the Primary Framework for Literacy

1 Speaking	2 Listening and responding	3 Group discussion and interaction	4 Drama
5 Word recognition	6 Word structure and spelling	7 Understand and interpret texts	8 Engage with and respond to texts
9 Creating and shaping texts	10 Text structure and organisation	11 Sentence structure and punctuation	12 Presentation

The objectives are age-related, in line with national averages [6K5]. Age-related expectation at the end of Key Stage 2, for example, is Level 4 so the objectives for Y6 in the Primary Framework are set at this level. Age-related expectations for Y2 pupils are Level 2 by the end of the year, and therefore, the objectives in Y2 are of a Level 2 standard. Standards in learning govern the framework. Age-related outcomes should be achieved by all pupils with the exception of those who have specific cognitive difficulties. Many pupils should exceed these outcomes. The published league tables show this data. Schools with high percentages achieving Level 4 and Level 5 by the end of Key Stage 2 are perceived in the public eye to be 'good' schools. National average for the number of pupils achieving Level 4 is approximately 80 per cent. Schools that have Key Stage 2 results showing a percentage below the floor target (65 per cent) are perceived to be schools requiring support to raise standards. In secondary, published league tables represent the number of pupils achieving five A*–C grades at GCSE. Mathematics and English are core to this and these subject areas must be two of the five. There is a constant push to raise expectations to ensure even more pupils achieve the recommended standards.

Speaking and listening [STL 25.3]

Speaking and listening are skills we all depend on in every aspect of our lives. Development in this area comes before reading and writing in most children without specific disabilities in that area although it is put third in the literacy standard. Chapter 5 referred to the importance of language development as a vehicle for thought. In the early years most children will have mastered a wide vocabulary, be able to use quite complex grammar without realising it and be able to express and understand quite complex ideas. Some talk readily but others are reticent and some, where their background experiences have been limited, may have real problems communicating. This is particularly true with listening skills. The ubiquitous use of television as oral wallpaper, the preoccupation and working practices of some parents and the solitary nature of computer games have all led to an increase in problems in the area of speaking and listening. Sometimes there is a medical problem such as deafness or there may be an emotional one creating delays. Children can sometime just have a quiet nature or be shy. The TA is well placed to get alongside young children and sensitively discover whether there are big problems for which the child will need additional help or whether there are particular things that will help and support a reticent child.

Speech is modelled on what is heard so it is important to be clear, particularly if the child comes from a home where there has been little communication. You will be a role model in this as in other things. You may need to repeat things, change more difficult words to simpler ones to ensure understanding but slowly increase the complexity and variety of vocabulary that you use so that the child will increase theirs. Use a variety of adjectives instead of 'nice', for instance. Use open ended questions and listen yourself to give the pupils as many opportunities to voice their ideas and opinions as you can.

One problem a TA may encounter comes about if their own spoken English is ungrammatical. Some dialects, such as estuarine English, include phrases like 'them things' which are in common usage. TAs should be role models yet need respect for their background just like any other member of the school community. It is a sensitive issue for any manager to deal with, so try to recognise your own foibles and do what you can to speak correct grammatical English but retain your local accent if you suspect a problem. If you know you have this problem, talk to your line manager. Ask them to observe you and listen to you at work, if you are brave enough, and point out where the particular problem lies [25K9]. Sensitivity to pupils' dialects and accents is needed to maintain their self-esteem, just as you need to retain yours.

The child who says 'I taked the apple' is not mimicking adults. They are experimenting with the relationship they have already heard between 'talk' and 'talked', 'walk and 'walked', and applying it, this time incorrectly, to 'take'. Gentle correction from sympathetic adults will soon help the child to sort out 'take' and 'took'. When reading, the child who is struggling to sound out 'swam' will know the word is not 'swim' because the text is in the past tense. Using grammatical strategies or cues is most difficult for children who are learning English as an additional language.

Pupils are assessed in this area to gauge the progression. You need high standards of oracy when supporting in this area. Talk for writing is a key element of Phase 1. Children's ability to communicate and listen effectively to others and to structure and articulate thoughts verbally has a great impact upon the quality of the written outcome. Talk partners are encouraged to enable pupils to have time to prepare answers and discuss ideas. Pupils have the opportunity for focused talk upon a specific objective. Teaching assistants provide the class teacher with another person to model the process with and the TA can initiate discussions with less confident pupils and monitor and re-focus talk.

Separate drama lessons can be very rewarding as children and young people can some-times show other aspects of their personality kept hidden in normal day-to-day school work. They can also find an outlet for their feelings like anger or sadness which can be helpful to them. Any drama leading to production, of course, has the element of public achievement in it but drama lessons do not necessarily have production in mind – just exploring different ways of moving, speaking – acting a part.

The importance of this area has provided a current focus of attention. Speaking and listening are the core skills of literacy. Developing writing through developing speaking and listening skills is nothing new, however: children at all ages and phases of education need strong models to scaffold learning. Talk for writing is key, and oral storytelling is an area which has received recognition for raising standards in writing and developing vocabulary.

Corbett and Rose's (2003) research into oral storytelling identified the development of the following skills:

- improved listening and responding and focused talk;
- speaking in full sentences;
- explaining thought processes orally;
- oral explanations are more ordered;
- the understanding of developments and implications in a story is evident; how to use voice, expressions, intonation and learning to make meaning from this;
- eye contact, non-verbal skills, looking at each other when talking together is evident;
- effective training of auditory memory;
- children tuning in to overall sounds in language is more evident.

Subject knowledge

The NLS underlined the need for pupils and adults supporting them to have secure subject knowledge. Technical vocabulary has become a core part of language teaching.

Phoneme: a single unit of sound e.g. *mood* has 3 phonemes *m-oo-d*
Grapheme: how the sound is represented in letters
Digraph: 2 letters making one sound *–oo*
Trigraph: 3 letters making 1 sound *–igh* in *night*

Noun: subject/object – *car, Devon*
Verb : action – *write, speak*
Adjective : description – *red, small*

Adverb: describes the action – *quickly, softly*

Determiner: focuses upon the noun – *a, the*

Preposition: explains where – *in, at, with, over*

Pronoun: stands in the place of the noun – *he, they, who*

Conjunction: can join clauses together in sentences – *and, because, when, although*

Sentences are made up of clauses.

- *Simple sentences* contain just one clause.

  The pupils ran.

- *Compound sentences* consist of two or more main clauses loosely joined by conjunctions – *and, but, or.*

  The pupils ran and the teachers shouted.

- In *complex sentences*, clauses are linked together in ways which show the interrelationships of ideas. Complex sentences are built up of main clauses and subordinate (minor) clauses. The subordinate clause does not make sense alone.

  When the pupils ran in the corridor, the teachers shouted.

  (subordinate clause)   (main clause)

When supporting pupils, at any age, you need to have a clear understanding of the level of subject knowledge required to assist the pupils accurately and effectively [6K11].

Accuracy in articulating letter sounds and in using grammar, spelling and punctuation is essential for ensuring that pupils have the most appropriate level of support. There is a wealth of documentation to ensure the adult's subject knowledge is always at least one step ahead of the pupils. You need to have access to this information and have a responsibility to ask questions if the required subject knowledge is unfamiliar. The majority of new, recent publications and those in current use are available to read online or download on the *Primary Framework* website www.standards.dfes.gov.uk/primaryframeworks. This site has professional development materials for adults to use to develop their own subject knowledge.

Reading [25.1]

Reading is not only a skill needed for progressing in academic school work but is essential for life. Reading instructions for medicines, on food packets, on how to get benefits and on how to recognise danger are all assumed as universal. But beyond this, the capacity to read for pleasure and extend one's knowledge of any subject opens such a wealth of ideas that it is hard for any of us who read widely to imagine a world without books and libraries. The use of the internet, of course, also needs reading skills, including a critical understanding of how to select what one reads. The reduction of reading to a set of different skills can take away the pleasure of stories, poetry, and the aesthetic appreciation of a well presented and illustrated text if we are not careful. Story time seems to have been lost in many primary classrooms, to the detriment of children's imaginations and enjoyment and the reduction in their desire to discover the joys of reading for themselves. The use of the internet for information seeking has also reduced dependency on a wide range of non-fiction.

The simple view of reading represented in Figure 13.1 shows the two skills we employ to enable us to read: our ability to decode the words and read them and the ability to understand what they mean. Pupils need to work towards having good decoding and comprehension skills. This is why the teaching of reading relies heavily upon good early reading skills employing the use of phonics. The *Independent review* (Rose 2006) has driven many of the changes for teaching early reading.

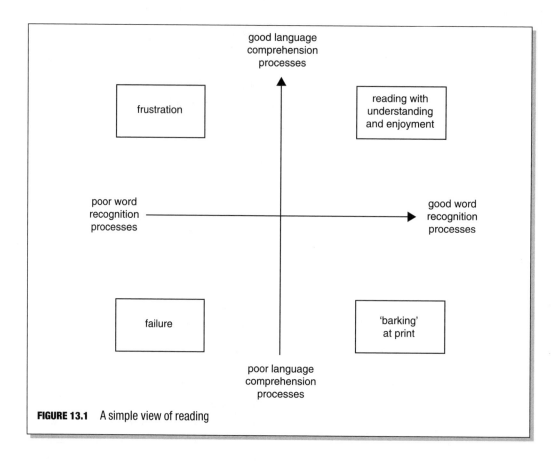

FIGURE 13.1 A simple view of reading

Guided reading

This is a key role for teaching assistants. Guided reading is a planned session for the teaching of reading skills. Teachers in the first instance should lead guided reading sessions and TAs delivering a session do so at the direction of the teacher. Table 13.2 gives the teaching sequence suggested. The aim is to encourage and extend independent reading skills.

TABLE 13.2 Teaching sequence for guided reading

Book introduction	Prepare the pupils. Orientation/discussion drawing on recent experiences, topics of interest, title, author, illustrator, etc, cover illustrations, first impressions, genre. Build confidence – the pupils need to know they can read the book successfully.
Strategy check	Be explicit about the focus of the session – share objectives/targets. Build upon prior knowledge of reading strategies such as what to do when you get stuck on/don't understand the meaning of a word.
Independent reading	Be clear about how much of the text you want the pupils to read and explain/share the questions that will be asked afterwards. For pupils who finish early, remind them of other things they can do, e.g. re-read the best/most difficult part again, carefully prepare an answer to a question you have asked.
Returning to the text	Discussion – check that the pupils have understood the text 'literally'. Time to praise – tackle misconceptions, possibly hear a couple of pupils read aloud a sentence or paragraph to the group/partner/adult.
Response to the text	Discussion, answers to questions valuing contributions from all pupils. Adult to select questions specific to the text – identifying how to use the text to support ideas / feelings.

Key principles

- Pupils grouped according to ability.
- Same group text selected by teacher.
- Text accessible to all pupils in group, less than 1 in 10 miscues.
- Objectives set based upon teaching specific reading strategies.
- Teacher leads session.

Phonics

Phonics is the knowledge of sounds to enable both reading and spelling. In Foundation Stage and Key Stage 1, phonics is taught for a minimum of 15 minutes daily as a supplement to the literacy session. The *DCSF Letters and Sounds* published materials have a structured six-phase programme for teaching phonics. There are many published materials to support the teaching of phonics and all focus heavily upon clear articulation of phonemes. The approach to teaching phonics needs to be multi-sensory to ensure that pupils have the best possible access to learn, practise and apply their skills. Good phonics subject knowledge now has a heightened status with regard to supporting all pupils to read and spell the English language.

Different text types are now used in class. A list is given in Table 13.3.

With the increased use of ICT, visual and multi-modal texts are becoming commonplace. Pupils are engaging with and reading film and responding to and creating texts which combine more than one mode, e.g. pictures, text and sound. Interactive whiteboards linked to the internet or resources on a laptop, along with school ownership of both still and video digital cameras has opened up a wide range of media for self-expression and appreciation.

TABLE 13.3 Different text types

Narrative	Non-fiction	Poetry
Stories/prose	Instructions	Limerick
Myths	Report	Narrative poetry
Legends	Recount	Performance poetry
Traditional tales	Explanation	Haiku
Familiar stories	Discussion/argument	Kenning
Mystery	Letter	Free verse
Adventure	Persuasion/advertisement	Shape poetry
Play-script	Labels, captions and lists	Sonnet

Writing [25.2]

This has been the most difficult area in which to raise standards. Boys seem to have more problems than girls. The best practice is to model the desired outcome and the process for pupils. Modelling in writing consists of writing in front of the pupils and articulating the process. Share how to check for sense, spelling, how to edit and improve. In reading, articulation of re-reading for sense, flow and clarity and how to link ideas together is required. Share, for example, how to refer to own experiences and to question characters' actions to gain a greater comprehension of the text. The second most helpful thing is to scaffold – provide frameworks or ideas or strategies for the pupils – pegs to hang their writing on.

The teaching sequence (see Figure 13.2) been developed to ensure that pupils have a fuller understanding of the text type and the skills required for quality writing. It is expected now that pupils have an extended time preparing to write before writing. In its most basic form, phase 1 is reading, phase 2 is analysis and phase 3 is writing. Each phase should take approximately a week but this is dependent upon the desired outcome for the writing and the age of the pupils.

Advances in technology have led to major changes in the teaching of literacy. Cine-literacy, reading through film, has been developed to engage and motivate learners. Reading in print and on screen are skills required at all stages of education. Teachers are using interactive whiteboards to support teaching and pupils are presenting work electronically. ICT skills are becoming more and more embedded in practice. Pupils use and create electronic images, sounds and texts. Supporting learning in literacy in now more likely to require ICT skills. Keyboard skills enabling use of more than two fingers can be very helpful even at the early stages, but need to be taught in a context. Some schools now have banks of laptops for classroom use by groups of children. Notes made in handwriting for use in word processing are really useful but writing a complete piece by hand, having it corrected and then spending time merely typing this into a computer is not really time well spent.

Guided writing is a small group session, again planned by the teacher to raise standards in writing and to teach skills identified through assessment for learning. Pupils are grouped together by ability or, more specifically, by need to develop writing skills. The key focus is upon developing, extending and refining for quality writing. Clear objectives and success criteria are essential. During the session pupils have the opportunity to see modelled writing, and to discuss, practise and review their own writing in relation to the learning

read → analyse → plan → write → review

read	
1	Writers have a real audience and purpose with an established outcome.
2	Writers immersed in a broad rich and engaging reading curriculum including picture books, graphic novels, ICT and film.
3	Writers engage, experience and empathise through planned drama, speaking and listening opportunities.

analyse	
4	Writers actively unpick the features and characteristics of chosen text/genre.
5	Writers own and understand the success criteria of the agreed outcome.

plan	
6	Writers use the feature of the text and the success criteria to plan their writing.
7	Writers are guided through modelling, demonstrating and supported composition with the teacher and through peer assessment.

write	
8	Writers use their knowledge of reading to help them compose their writing.

review	
9	Writers receive clear feedback linked to the success criteria and understand the next steps in developing their writing.
10	Writers reflect on their outcomes against original audience and purpose and plan for future learning.

continual assessment for learning

FIGURE 13.2   The teaching sequence for writing

PHOTOGRAPH 13.1 Small group work in literacy

objective. TAs supporting pupils during guided writing need to have the appropriate subject knowledge which should be provided by the teacher, but it is the responsibility of the supporting adult to ensure the objective is taught accurately. The DCSF published materials – *Improving writing with a focus on guided writing* – have clear guidance on the content and structure of guided writing.

Assessment for learning

Statutory testing takes place at the end of each Key Stage:

- Foundation Stage: age-related outcome, six points across the six areas of learning
- Key Stage 1: Y2 age-related outcome Level 2
- Key Stage 2: Y6 age-related outcome Level 4
- Key Stage 3: Y9 age-related outcome Levels 5–6
- Key Stage 4: Y11 (GCSE) Levels 7–8 (grade B/C).

The goal, at present, is for all pupils to make two levels of progress across a Key Stage.

Questioning is the first point of assessment. Often, the questions we ask pupils are closed. Closed questions have a pre-determined answer that the adult already knows. Closed questions are used more frequently because of the element of control provided. Open questions have no predetermined answer and therefore higher-level thinking skills need to be employed and the questioner has less control over the answer. During reading there are three tiers of questioning: literal, inferential and deductive, and evaluative.

- Literal questions are closed, e.g. what happened.
- Inferential and deductive questions are higher-order, open questions: the need to 'read between the lines'.

- Evaluative questions are higher-order, open questions, e.g. why the author has used particular words or phrases.

It is recommended that pupils have enough time to think about the question in order to give the best answer. Thinking time lasting 10 seconds sounds short and in practice feels longer but it is essential to allow for it, particularly when asking higher-order questions.

Pupils are assessed against the Foundation Stage profile at the end of their first year in school. English in the Foundation Stage is called CLL (communication, language and literacy). A child achieving six points at the end of the Foundation Stage is 'on track' to achieve age-related outcomes throughout their education. Tracking the progress of pupils in relation to age-related outcomes is of a high status in all schools. Teachers predict where pupils will be at the end of the year and monitor progress towards the end-of-year expectations based upon the previous teacher's assessments. The allocation of support for pupils who are not identified as SEN is often based upon accelerating progress towards achieving or exceeding age-related expectations. Teachers have a greater awareness of the need to differentiate (provide activities appropriate to ability). Often differentiation is in terms of the adult support allocated to the pupils.

The present educational climate has increased the accountability of teachers regarding the progress of pupils in their class. Performance management monitors and challenges teachers' ability to add value to the academic progress of the pupils they teach. When working with groups of pupils the teaching assistant's role is to support the learning, thus assisting the teacher to contribute to the children's academic progress. Increasingly, you need to be familiar with the current academic level of the pupils and the targets they are working towards.

You are crucial to developing the assessing pupil progress model. As the testing culture in schools begins to shift towards an assessment for learning model, teachers are required to assess pupils periodically across a range of text types. The range of evidence collected will provide a truer picture of the pupil. The shift is to 'assess the writer, not the writing; the reader, not the reading'. Ongoing, day-to-day assessment and the evidence of this is to be collected by all adults in the setting. It is thought that the APP (assessing pupil progress) model will eventually replace testing. The Primary and Secondary Strategies have links to APP materials and resources.

Intervention

Assessments inform the next steps pupils need to take. For many pupils interventions have to be planned in order to help them get back 'on track' and 'catch up' with the rest of the class. Primary published interventions are:

- Year 1: Early Literacy Support (ELS)
- Year 3: Literacy Support (Y3LS)
- Year 5: Further Literacy Support (FLS).

These intervention programmes are designed to be delivered by teaching assistants at the delegation of the class teacher. Each programme is aimed not at SEN pupils but at pupils who are at risk of falling behind. The interventions are a supplement to in-class literacy teaching and need to happen outside the literacy whole-class session. Small group intervention such as this is known as Wave 2 intervention.

- Wave 1: whole class, quality first teaching – providing sufficient differentiation;
- Wave 2: small group intervention;
- Wave 3: one-to-one specific catch-up based upon gap analysis.

Wave 3 intervention can be delivered by the TA, again, at the delegation of the class teacher. The sessions will be planned for by the teacher. *Reading catch-up* is a widely used Wave 3 intervention for literacy. The programme is highly structured, with specific guidance for the delivery of the sessions. The principle of Wave 3 intervention is that the pupils make twice the recommended progress while engaged in the programme.

All interventions designed to get pupils 'on track' to achieve age-related outcomes should only be used once per child. For example, a child who did ELS in Year 1 should not do Y3LS in Year 3. The intervention model has not worked if the child is still falling behind. The theory behind this is that the intervention programme would mean that pupils are back working at an age-appropriate level with the rest of the class and quality-first teaching should now meet their needs. There are booster materials available for Year 6 pupils to further support the achievement of age-related expectations.

For secondary pupils, interventions are again at the discretion of the teacher to delegate to the TA. *Intervention tool kits* are available for use to support pupils who are at risk of not meeting age-related expectations. There are *Literacy progress units* for moving pupils from Level 3–4 to be delivered outside the existing English lessons. *Targeting Level 4* reading and writing materials can be built into lessons delivered by the teacher.

Intervention for the more able is to give high-achieving pupils the opportunity to understand ideas and themes more broadly and deeply. The role of intervention for gifted and talented pupils is to enrich their learning.

Questions to ask yourself

- Have you read the school policy on the teaching of English and identified the literacy or English coordinator or head of department?

- How secure are your own skills of language, reading and writing?

- Have you explored the strategy website to see what resources are available?

- Do you know what is already used in your school?

- Are you permitted to attend teacher staff meetings when literacy is discussed? If not, have you enquired why not? If so, are you doing this in paid time or voluntarily? If the latter, have you asked why?

Useful reading

In addition to all the strategy materials:

Corbett, P., *The bumper book of story telling into Writing, Key Stage 1.*

Corbett, P., *The bumper book of story telling into Writing, Key Stage 2.*

Edwards, S. (1999) *Reading for all.*

Frater, G. (2000) *Securing boys' literacy.*

Guppy, P. and Hughes, M. (1999) *On cue: Helping children to read.*

Meek, M. (1982) *Learning to read.*

Palmer, S. (2003) *How to teach writing across the curriculum, KS1.*

Palmer, S. (2003) *How to teach writing across the curriculum, KS2.*

Palmer, S. (2004) *Speaking frames Y3,4,5,6.*

Useful websites

www.standards/dfes.gov.uk/primary_frameworks

Innovation Unit: The Story Making Project: http:www.innovation-unit.co.uk/education-experience/project-archive/the-story-making-project.html

Developing numerate pupils

IF YOU HAVE NOT READ Chapter 13 please turn back to it and read the first few paragraphs as they are an introduction to both literacy and numeracy. Both are areas essential for both school work and life and both have had considerable attention in the last few years. All that applies in general to English also applies to mathematics. You need copies of the school policy, you need to talk to the coordinator or head of department about your work, you need to be able to attend the staff meetings in the subject and be paid to do so. You need access to a computer connected to the internet as many of the resources are now accessible only through the web. You need to be sure of your own skills knowledge and understanding in the area. Mathematics is a subject many of us ducked at school: we found it hard, often unintelligible and usually irrelevant to what we wanted to do or be. However, there is now a tremendous effort to make it understandable and relevant. We need to be numerate to understand cooking recipes, healthy food data, green issues and the associated statistics, be able to use bank accounts, even understand our payslips. Consider undertaking some kind of Level 2 course in mathematics if you are feeling at all inadequate in this area. Also, do not be frightened of asking if you do not understand: you will not be alone – if you do not understand it is quite likely that the pupils won't understand either!

There are some children who seem to have a good grasp of the mathematics involved in any given situation. This is often called having a good 'feel for numbers'. They seem to know automatically if they have done a calculation wrong or to grasp which strategy is suitable for calculations. For example, in KS1 if a child who is asked what 93 – 89 is equal to realises that the numbers are very close together they will approach the calculation in a very different way from the child who just sees two numbers that bear no relation to each other.

The aim of the National Numeracy Strategy (NNS) is for all children to have a 'feel for numbers' and to be numerate. To be numerate a person needs to know more than just the four rules. A key point would be being able to apply their knowledge. Being numerate includes knowing algebra, shape and space, measures and data handling. Mathematics is essentially a social, practical activity and as such should involve pupils in using practical apparatus and enjoying problem-solving activities. These types of activity can present more difficulties than the more straightforward practice of calculations. This dual understanding is reflected in there being two elements to Standard 26 – supporting pupils in numeracy skills [26.1] and supporting them to be able to use and apply mathematics [26.2]. The glossary talks of confidence as well as competence, something with which you might empathise.

The daily mathematics lesson

This is now firmly established within both primary and secondary schools.

PHOTOGRAPH 14.1   A practical mathematics lesson

Oral and mental starters (OMS)

Within the OMS, you should work primarily with those pupils needing greatest support. Model with these pupils the activity being run by the teacher. You should have any resources needed readily to hand, such as:

- whiteboards and marker pens
- number cards
- hundred squares
- calculators
- counters
- number lines.

Your involvement greatly assists the teacher in maintaining pace and in providing a brisk, interactive and meaningful start to the lesson; the interaction between the teacher and TA is seamless. The TA usually sits at the back of the class with a cohort of less able pupils. Other pupils who are not always very confident tend to gravitate towards the TA, dipping in and out of the support as and when necessary. This prevents the distinctive 'labelling' of pupils. All the class see you as a resource to be used. It is important that the support is confidence-building or strategy-giving, not doing the work for the pupils by giving the answers. In secondary classrooms you are most likely to be working with a targeted student or a small group, depending on how the class furniture is arranged.

The main part of the lesson

It is here that there is most variance in practice at all key stages. In lessons with a substantial teaching element, that is where a new topic is being introduced, you can sit with and assist the less able group of pupils or targeted student, modelling for them the teaching being delivered. Once the direct teaching part of this type of lesson is complete and the pupils are engaged upon some other activity (written or other) you will probably remain as direct support for the less able pupils. In this way there is a significant support structure in place for those very pupils who need most support when learning new concepts or skills, this being the case in secondary classrooms too.

If the lesson is a follow-up lesson or a consolidation lesson, with minimal input from the teacher at the start of the second phase, you should not be restricted to working with the less able pupils; even if your brief/contract is for a specific child you should give support to others if and when needed or directed. There is a requirement that the class teacher works with all pupils within a class and this means that the teacher has to spend at least one of the week's mathematics lessons working more closely with the least able pupils. On such occasions you should operate with other groups, including the most able. Sometimes you could even hold a watching brief over two groups, thus providing less intensive support but monitoring and intervening as and when appropriate.

You need to pay particular attention to:

- ensuring children are using the appropriate mental strategies and formal written methods for calculation;

- ensuring that the children fully understand the mathematical reasoning. For example, when multiplying by ten many children will say 'add a nought' but this will not work with decimals;

- extending children's knowledge by effective use of open questions and allowing children to spot patterns and rules;

- ensuring that calculators are being used appropriately (schools should have a policy on the use of calculators, but it is often under-use rather than over-use that is the problem);

- enabling children to estimate the answer and use appropriate strategies for checking the results of calculations.

During each week all pupils need time to work unaided, as they need to develop as independent learners. One of the most recent changes in education policy has been the change to the national key stage tests (SATs). From 2003 more using and applying questions have been used. You need to allow children to explain their answers verbally and in writing – usually in that order. Make sure that you have seen exemplar questions from the national tests in order to familiarise yourself with the expectations.

The plenary

One of the main purposes of the plenary is that it provides the teacher with an opportunity to assess the learning that has taken place during the lesson, and you can assist the teacher in this objective. You need to use the plenary to obtain and use information about a pupil's ability to understand and use numbers. You can also, by use of questions and prompts, help these children to cement the learning of the lesson, to firm up their ideas and to help cancel out any misconceptions which have arisen during the work part of the main teaching activity.

Good use of language, questions and vocabulary is clearly vital and you may need the same sort of resources as in the OMS, plus blank paper for jottings and vocabulary cards to assist the children with formulating answers using the correct words.

Assessing understanding in mathematics

One method of obtaining information about a child's ability is observing and taking notes during the oral and mental starter or the plenary. Another is to analyse children's SATs. These tests cover the range of work that children are expected to do in a year. The tests are statutory in Years 2, 6 and 9 and optional in Years 3, 4 and 5. There are also SATs papers for Year 7 and currently a pilot project is under way to look at the use of single level test papers in both Key Stages 2 and 3. The results of this pilot project could be that SATs papers become a thing of the past and teacher assessment is used to determine children's levels of progress. This has future implications for the further development of your role and may make it necessary for you to have an even greater working understanding of mathematics. The drawback is that these tests only give information about what a child does or does not know.

What you really need to be aware of is why a child is getting something wrong. You should be aware of how teachers use the two days' 'assess and review' lessons at the end of each half term to carry out assessments. The NNS materials include a useful book called *Using assess and review lessons*. As the lessons are activity based rather than pencil and paper tests, they enable the teacher or assistant to ask the children questions which help gauge their understanding.

Central to all the activities is the role of discussion and the importance of children's explanations. Valuable insights are provided by children explaining how they arrived at the correct answer (or the incorrect answer). On many occasions, what seems like a completely wrong answer is hiding a misconception, which, when corrected, will enable the children to get the right answer. For example, when calculating 48×16, the child might give the answer 336. It is only by asking the child how they did it that you would ascertain that the child was multiplying 48 by 1 rather than 10 (then adding it to 48×6).

A point you need to be aware of is that children's ability in numbers can vary widely from their ability in shape, space and measures. It is not uncommon to find an able child who finds it difficult to look at a shape and, for example, work out whether it has a right angle, particularly if the shape is orientated differently from usual.

Mathematics resources

Most primary schools have a maths area where large resources are kept; for example, different types of scales, trundle wheels, metre sticks, weights and capacity jugs. Class teachers often have smaller resources either in their year group or their classroom. You should have your own box of resources, including devices to develop understanding of shape and space. Particularly useful would be geoboards or pegboards for children to make 2D shapes. Secondary maths departments often have an office in which is kept some equipment and each teacher may have their own supply of resources. It will be different in each school, so you should enquire as to what is available and where it can be accessed.

An excellent resource is the *Springboard* materials (KS1 and 2) available on the framework website and in paper form within schools. These are intervention programmes that are used to support children who are falling slightly behind their peers but are not on the SEN register. These materials only support number work and complement the daily lesson. Most schools are using these intervention strategies and you will find the materials useful to look at, particularly as they include video demonstration of lessons. At Key Stage 3 equivalent materials are provided through the national strategy.

Strategies for supporting mathematical development [6K5]

Possibly the most crucial strategy is enabling children to experience practical activities (this need does not diminish as the child ages and practical experiences are important at all key stages). This starts off in Reception classes when using cubes for addition and subtraction. However, there can be a danger that children will rely on the physical object for too long. For example, rather than committing to memory the number bonds to ten, children often continue to use their fingers.

Practical activities are also vital when working on shape and space. Children need to have experience of making shapes on geoboards and then drawing them. You must be very clear about the properties of shapes as this is an area of common confusion. For example, a square is a special rectangle. Purchasing a mathematical dictionary or *Mathematics explained for primary teachers* (Haylock 2006) would be a good investment.

Do be aware of how powerful the use of the empty number line is to model and explain various mental strategies, for example when working out 93 – 19. See Figure 14.1.

The number line is also used to show repeated addition and subtraction with its links to multiplication and division. In terms of mathematical development, the most important aspect of primary and early secondary teaching is children's understanding of the number system. For this, children need to be able to see, and you need to help them see, the connections between various areas of mathematics. For example, children need to see and use the relationship between $3/4$, 75% and 0.75.

Estimation is a key developmental point. There are problems in estimation. Children are often conditioned to get the correct answer and can see estimation as the teacher wanting them to get the answer deliberately wrong. Using measures is an excellent way to teach estimation and it is crucial that children have plenty of experience of practical measuring activities. Once estimating skills are established they can be extended to areas of numbers. For example, a child estimating 43×56 could work out that the answer would be somewhere between 2000 (40×50) and 3000 (50×60) and then hone it down to estimate that the answer would be about halfway between the two numbers.

The most difficult but potentially the most rewarding lessons for you are those involving the solving of problems. With the classroom teacher, think very carefully both about the questions you will ask children and about the type of recording children will use to solve the problem. The intervention questions need to be carefully graded in order that the answer is not virtually given to the child. They should give the child who is stuck a clue which enables them independently to access the task. This is particularly appropriate for children with different learning needs.

Problems in mathematical development

Some of the difficulties that occur as children develop mathematically are ironed out as they get older but there are some key areas that hinder their progress [6K10].

The first of these is the issue of place value. Children need a thorough and regular grounding in place value work. Part of the original intention of the oral and mental starter in the NNS was to include regular counting activities. While these are still regular occurrences in classrooms, TAs need to be aware of the purpose of counting. Just as in any other part of mathematics, areas of misconception should be targeted. For example, most children

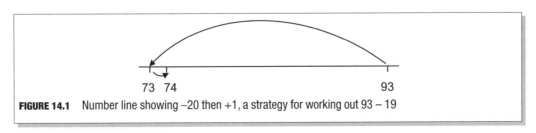

FIGURE 14.1   Number line showing –20 then +1, a strategy for working out 93 – 19

by Year 2 can count in twos and tens (starting from zero) up to quite large numbers, but the area of misconception would be counting in tens, starting from a non-multiple of ten, and crossing the hundreds' boundary, e.g. 171, 181, 191, 201, 211, etc. It is often counting in tens that confuses children and you need to deliberately target this in your support.

Another area of common confusion, and possibly the most important, is how children learn mental strategies and how they move to written calculations. There is a difference between rapid recall of facts and mental strategies. Rapid recall is the calculations that children are expected to just 'know', whereas mental strategies are calculations that need to be specifically taught and applied according to the situation. For example, double 35 = 70 is a fact that should be known by Year 4 whereas knowing that a quick way to calculate 35 + 36 is to double 35 and add 1 would be a strategy that needs to be applied. The booklet *Teaching mental calculations strategies* (QCA 1999a) is an excellent resource and explains all the strategies and age expectations.

Parents (and some teachers) often comment that children are expected to learn too many strategies. You should understand why there is this expectation. If one was presented with the following calculations: $£8 - £2.99, 45 + 46, 16 \times 7, 55 + 37, 135.4/10, 428 \times 2, 900 - 500, 36 - 18, 78 - 32$, one would reasonably expect that they could be answered mentally, but the strategies used would all be different. Children need to be taught different strategies and then, crucially, when it is appropriate to apply them. For example, if you were supporting pupils in a lesson that was concentrating on using near doubles, you would give the children practice examples that were appropriate for this strategy, e.g. 30 + 31, 24 + 25, but at some point in the lesson you could ask the child what 55 + 37 is. Using near doubles would obviously not be a good strategy to work this out. What you are doing is leading the child to look at the numbers first and see if there is any connection between them before attempting the calculation.

It is a clear intention of the NNS that by the end of Key Stage 1 children should be able to mentally answer any two-digit addition or subtraction question. When children move into Key Stage 2, the focus switches to written calculations. The intention of the NNS is that by the end of Key Stage 2 children should have a standard written method for all four rules of numbers. This means one standard written method for each operation. A small but significant number of children have not mastered these techniques by the time they enter Key Stage 3 and the TA within the secondary school needs to be able to call upon the methods used in KS2 to assist these children with their mathematical development.

The difficulty that children experience is how they move from mental to written calculations, particularly in Years 3 and 4. *Teaching written calculations* (QCA 1999b) explains this in detail. You can support this movement from mental to written by ensuring that the children think about what method they are going to use. For example, if a child was given 2001 – 1999 to calculate, it would be inappropriate and inefficient to set it out as a written calculation when the child could easily count up 2. The first question to ask when supporting a child with a calculation is 'Can you do it in your head?' If the calculation is inappropriate to work out mentally, the child should use a standard written method at Key Stages 2 and 3.

Another problem that could arise is recognising when it is appropriate to use a calculator. Guidance is given on the role of the calculator in the NNS framework.

Links between mathematics and other subjects

In the Foundation Stage it is commonplace for links to be made between mathematics and other subjects. This becomes less commonplace in Key Stage 1 and certainly by Key Stages 2 and 3. Excellent guidance is given in the introduction to the NNS framework, page 16.

Several secondary schools are in the process of revisiting maths across the curriculum and a policy should be in place within the school. Many schools have produced materials to develop the links between maths and science, art, music, geography etc.

Questions to ask yourself

- How did you feel about learning mathematics at school?
- Are you confident in supporting pupils in mathematics?
- Do you need to further your own knowledge and skills outside the school scene?
- Are you able to participate in the school INSET programme for the numeracy strategy?
    - If not, why not?
    - If your circumstances are the problem, can you reorganise some regular events in your life in order to be able to understand the school mathematics practices better?

Essential reading

The school mathematics policy

Any relevant parts of the mathematical strategy

Some further reading

Haylock (2006) *Mathematics explained for primary teachers.*

Any materials from the strategy website.

Useful website

www.standards.dfes.gov.uk/primaryframework/mathematics/

15

Thinking ahead

Your values

CHAPTER 2 ASKED YOU to consider your values. Level 3 is about no longer being just adequate but contributing, being consistent, having effective communication and working relationships with your colleagues; being part of the team building, the ethos and climate development; and showing initiative and undertaking responsibility, while recognising the constraints of being a TA and the responsibilities of the teachers and the school.

While TAs do not yet have a professional association or a code of ethics, some of those already published come near to one. Barber (1996: 237) talks of a code of ethics for teachers:

- a commitment to the development of children and young people who become increasingly independent;

- a commitment to foster learning and understanding of learning among parents and other adults;

- a commitment to refine and develop professional skills as an individual and to assist that process among other members of the profession;

- a commitment to the promotion of learning and education in the development of healthy communities and democratic society;

- and finally, a commitment to the notion that learning has a part to play in the growth of global understanding and the sustenance of the planet.

Have a look at the following from *The statement of professional values and practice for teachers* and consider how far you can uphold the professional values and practice required of qualified teachers. Clearly the sections dealing with teachers' standards are not relevant but in taking a Level 3 qualification you will be qualifying to a national standard for TAs.

The high standards of the teaching profession

First and foremost, teachers are skilled practitioners.

They have insight into the learning needs of children and young people. They use professional judgment to meet these needs and to choose the best ways of motivating pupils to achieve success. They use assessment to inform and guide their work. They are highly skilled at dealing with the rigours and realities of teaching.

Teachers inspire and lead children and young people to learn, in and beyond the classroom. They enable them to get the most out of life and develop the knowledge, skills and attributes for adulthood – so that they can achieve their potential as fulfilled individuals and make a positive contribution to society – while staying safe and healthy.

Teaching is a vital, unique and far-reaching role requiring high levels of individual knowledge, skill and judgment, commitment, energy and enthusiasm. It is one of the most demanding and rewarding of professions.

Teachers work within a framework of legislation, statutory guidance and school policies, with different lines of accountability. Within this framework they place particular importance on promoting equality of opportunity – challenging stereotypes, opposing prejudice, and respecting individuals regardless of age, gender, disability, colour, race, ethnicity, class, religion, marital status or sexual orientation.

Teachers recognise the value and place of the school in the community and the importance of their own professional status. They understand that this requires judgment about appropriate standards of personal behaviour.

(GTC 2006:2)

The statement also deals with the professionalism of teachers in practice in dealing with:

Children and young people: Teachers place the learning and well-being of young people at the centre of their professional practice. . . .

Parents and carers: Teachers respond sensitively to the differences in the home backgrounds and circumstances of young people, recognising the key role that parents and carers play in children's education. . . .

Professional colleagues: Teachers see themselves as part of a team, in which fellow teachers, other professional colleagues and governors are partners in securing the learning and well-being of young people. . . .

Learning and development: Teachers entering the teaching profession in England have met a common professional standard. . . .

(GTC 2006:3,4)

Take the sets of values set out above, your thoughts on your own values which you considered at the beginning of the book, and your copy of the NOS.

- Look for overlap.
- Identify where you can see they interrelate.
- Try to draw up a set of TA values.
- Suggest your colleagues try the same.
- Discuss your set with those of your colleagues.
- Have you found any conflicts between the various sets of values?
- Can you agree a code of practice for TAs, remembering that teachers take the final responsibility for teaching and learning of pupils and TAs are always working under their direction and supervision?
- Does it vary depending on the level of competence?

Sometimes you may find a conflict between your own values and those of the school or your considered TA values. You also need to consider what you might do in such circumstances [22K7].

Developing as a professional TA

Teaching is a professional activity, where teachers are considered professionals alongside lawyers and clergy. It is high time that teaching assistance was considered in the same light, a profession in the world of education, drawing a parallel with the nursing profession in the world of medicine.

Teaching assistance as teaching is a reflective activity, a feature that this book has encouraged in you from the start (Calderhead 1994). By studying at Level 3 you now also have acquired a body of specialised knowledge about pupils and their learning methods and needs, teaching methods and curriculum content which you will rely on in your everyday work. You know about learning development and what affects it. You are also 'goal orientated'; that is, you aim to fulfil the learning objectives of the teachers for the pupils with whom you work, to enhance their learning and to support the ethos and aims of your school. You are accountable to these pupils and to your colleagues for the quality of your 'performance'. Your context, like that of teachers, is often complex and you have to use your personal judgement to analyse what is going on and what to do about it, with the interests of the pupils uppermost in your mind. You also have a body of developed skills, based on your experience and learning, which you adapt to the context in which you find yourself. It is only a matter of time before this knowledge, understanding and skills base is defined as a pedagogy similar to but different from that of the teaching profession.

It remains for you to have your own professional association, recognising those characteristics and supporting their development, and possibly registration as a recognised member of the profession. There may well come a time in the next few years when you will be required to be registered, as teachers and nurses are, with entry requirements or qualifications for each level. As things are, anyone can be appointed to any TA job, provided they are CRB cleared. A pay negotiating body with nationally determined pay scales is promised, but schools will still be free to determine where on the scale a TA sits.

The DCSF aims to have an independent chair and framework in place by September 2008. The Support Staff Working Group (SSWG) is made up of people representing support staff trade unions, local government employers, self-governing schools and government. A draft constitution is in place. The list of organisations represented can be found with their websites at the end of the chapter.

Management and parents still have no clear idea of who is suitable for what jobs. WAMG have issued joint guidance notes to stimulate schools into appropriate deployment strategies especially following the contractual changes for teachers but TAs are still exploited and used inappropriately. You should be interested in following these developments, and taking charge of your own destiny.

Reflective practice [22K1-11 especially K4]

You can be a real part of the future:

- with children and young people:
  - provide stable relationships and a role model
  - explain, question, challenge
  - enable independent learning
- have critical friendships with colleagues and teacher
- assist in the provision of a safe yet stimulating learning environment.

Accepting responsibility for what happens

The future is in your hands:

- For yourself
    - always remain a learner
    - try out new ideas within the school boundaries
    - take CPD opportunities – reading, reflection, courses.
- Get a voice
    - networking – here today and back in your clusters
    - union membership for pay and conditions
    - professional associations need forming
    - lobby authority – local and national.

Taking charge of your own development

Part of the process of professional development is about being a life-long learner. Learning is like the scientific process, the plan–do–review cycle; it never stops. Each time you do something and reflect upon it, you refine how you do that particular thing the next time. A critical, questioning approach is not about being negative. If something does not work for you or mean a lot, then find something that does. We can learn more from our mistakes than from getting things right. Be prepared to change. As you become a reflective practitioner, taking responsibility for your own development, building on the contributions of others to both the reflection and the development, you will provide better support for other learners and greater job satisfaction for yourself. You should take part in government consultations on practice or content. For example, at the time of writing there is a big consultation on the primary curriculum. Go into www.primaryreview.org.uk for more information and have your say. Also as part of that review, there are a lot of commissioned reviews of aspects of primary practice, available from that website, which you can read. There are also a series of government commissioned reports on the deployment and impact of support staff including TAs, not all of which are published yet. They can be rather technical but if you access them, just try reading the summaries (Blatchford *et al.* 2006, 2007 and 2008).

Being a professional also includes a sense of responsibility. One of the reasons people say they like being TAs is the lack of responsibility. But even if you do not have the ultimate responsibility for pupils' learning, you do have a responsibility to do your best for them, a responsibility of care, a responsibility to your colleagues and to the school, a responsibility to reflect on your practice and challenge beliefs [22K6]. By retaining the power to be an active learner yourself, you will empathise more with those you help and work with. Plan your own pathways, set yourself realistic goals or targets with a realistic timeline, and recognise milestones of achievement as you progress.

Development does not all depend on available courses, nor will any course provide all the answers. A lot of your development will depend on your own initiative, making the most of any opportunities. Also, it is salutary to remember that your efforts may not 'pay off' in terms of increased pay or opportunities for advancement, but they will definitely increase your job satisfaction, your value to the school and the pupils with whom you work, and should provide you with transferable skills for other roles you may undertake in your life. Young people training to be nursery nurses, when later having their family, have found that their knowledge and understanding of child development is invaluable. Honing your team skills can spin off into a club activity. Any course of study sharpens your mind and gets the brain working.

Teachers are asked to:

reflect on their own practice, develop their skills, knowledge and expertise, and adapt their teaching appropriately to take account of evidence about effective practice and new technology; they understand that all of these are vital if young people are to receive the best and most relevant education.

Teachers make use of opportunities to take part in mentoring and coaching, to evaluate and adapt their own and institutional practice, and to learn with and from colleagues in the wider children's and school workforce.

(GTC 2006 : 4)

Keeping up to date or going further up the career ladder

You do not have to decide immediately what lies in the future for you – your personal circumstances may change anyway – but do keep your learning up to date. Read magazines, trawl the websites with topics you are interested in. TAs are now a recognised profession with at least 200,000 of you being employed. There is a bimonthly journal for primary TAs called *Learning Support* which has many useful articles to support your work and editorial to bring the latest news. The weekly newspaper for teachers, the *Times Educational Supplement*, found in many staffrooms, has a regular resources section as well as news and teachers' jobs. The government publication *Teachers* goes to each school and has useful sources of resources as well as articles exploring examples of good practice. You can order your own copy to be delivered to your home. The monthly magazines for special education, *Child Education* (Key Stage 1) and *Junior Education* (Key Stage 2) are purchased by some schools. All the subject associations have their journals; the Association for Science Education, for instance, has several: one general, one for primary teachers and one for technicians, among others, along with many of their own publications and their own website. Apparently more TAs than teachers watch *Teachers TV*. Look out for programme listings.

Some LAs send out newsletters to TAs but some authorities, with long-established delegated management strategies, do not even know how many TAs there are in their schools. Perhaps, if there is ever a national TA association, they will publish their own materials to support TAs. Just a word of warning: the National Association for Professional Teaching Assistants (NAPTA) does exist but it is a sales arm of Pearson Publishing to distribute their assessment tool for TAs' self-assessment.

The TDA website has all the information regarding career progression for TAs, about the HLTA status, work place or college ways in to teaching if that is for you. With the ECM agenda and the Children's plan there is more recognition of having transferable skills across the children's workforce. Table 15.1 gives you the picture as it was seen by the NJC (National Joint Council for Local Government Services) in 2003. You may decide you like the social work aspects of working with children better than the teaching, curriculum based ones. Follow the links on the TDA website, or try www.childrensworkforce.org.uk or www.cwdcouncil.org.uk for more information. The *Common core of skills and knowledge* (DfES 2005a) and *Building brighter futures: Next steps for the Children's Workforce* are both useful reading in this respect (DCSF 2008e).

One way of keeping up to date and exchanging interesting ideas and sharing problems is to attend local meetings of TAs. If you have not got a group like this, one of your development points could be to start one. Some LAs and cluster groups of schools already have these. Maybe one day they will join up with representation and hence a national voice.

TABLE 15.1 Support staff job profile summary (NJC 2003 : 5)

Expected skill level/equivalent	Induction/basic skills	NVQ 2	NVQ3 specialist knowledge/skills	NVQ4 specialism/higher level TA management responsibilities
Teaching Assistant supporting and delivering learning	**working under direction/instruction supporting access to learning** ■ welfare/personal care ■ small groups/one to one ■ general clerical/organisational support for teacher	**working under instruction/guidance enabling access to learning** ■ welfare/personal support – SEN ■ delivery of pre-determined learning/care/support programmes ■ implement literacy/numeracy programmes ■ assist with planning cycle ■ clerical/admin support for teacher/department	**working under guidance delivering learning** ■ involved in whole planning cycle ■ implement work programmes ■ evaluation and record keeping ■ cover supervisor ■ specialist SEN/subject/other support	**working under an agreed system of supervision/management delivering learning specialist knowledge resource** ■ lead planning cycle under supervision ■ delivering lessons to groups/whole class ■ management of other staff
Teaching Assistant behaviour/guidance/ support			**working under guidance delivering learning** ■ pastoral support ■ learning mentors ■ behaviour support ■ exclusions, attendance	**working under an agreed system of supervision management systems/ procedures/policy:** ■ pastoral support ■ mentoring/counselling ■ behaviour ■ exclusions/attendance
Curriculum resource support	**working under direction/instruction** ■ preparation/routine maintenance/operation of materials/equipment ■ organisational support for teaching staff ■ support/supervision of pupils in lessons ■ general clerical/admin/technical support	**working under instructions/guidance** ■ preparation and maintenance of resources ■ support for pupils and staff ■ specialist equipment/resources ■ routine invigilation/marking ■ general admin/technical support where some technical/specialist knowledge required	**working under guidance** ■ specific support in technical/specialist area ■ preparation/maintenance of resources/equipment ■ implementing specific work programmes including assessment ■ demonstrations/operation of specialist equipment	**working under supervision/ management specialist knowledge resource** ■ management team ■ management of budget/resources ■ staff management ■ lead specialist ■ delivering lessons in subject specialism under supervision ■ support special projects ■ advise teaching staff on specialist area/equip/resources
Administration and organisation	**working under direction/instruction** ■ general clerical/admin procedures ■ typing, photocopying etc. ■ maintenance records/data ■ collect/record finance ■ organisational support for staff/schools	**working under instruction/guidance** ■ some skilled work e.g. WP/secretarial ■ routine financial administration ■ regular interface with public ■ specific curriculum/dept support ■ record keeping/production data/information	**working under guidance** ■ complex finance ■ operate complex tasks/systems ■ management/analysis of resources/data/information ■ advice/information/training/supervision of other staff ■ skilled PA/WP etc.	**level 4 manage:** ■ budget, resource/systems, people, business, premises **level 4+ responsibility for:** budget, resource/systems, people, business, premises

Starting a local group

Get your headteacher to agree to you meeting in your school, probably in the evening (you may have to pay a hire charge). Contact your cluster schools, or the half-dozen geographically nearest to you. Invite their TAs to come. Try to get (free of charge) a speaker to come to start you off – maybe:

- one of the SENCOs
- an EP
- a local tutor
- a local adviser
- a therapist.

Lay on tea and coffee and biscuits. Charge the minimum to cover your costs. Get a representative from each school to be on a steering committee. Arrange to meet in one of the other schools next term – you have a local association in formation! From these little acorns, the national tree could grow.

You may be considering specialising but staying as an experienced TA. Look around for local courses in the area you are interested in. Look for websites belonging to associations in the area you want – an SEN area or curriculum area, say – and see what is on offer. Look at the titles of standards in both Level 2 and Level 3 and you will see the diverse range already developed. Try to visit other schools and talk to local advisers in the area you like.

An example of specialisation

One TA decided to specialise in speech and language development. Her school had several children with poor skills in this area, so the SENCO timetabled her to support all those with this particular need. She contacted the speech therapist and found resources and associations to help. The speech therapist has since left the area and so this TA is a vital part of the school's provision. The school has purchased books for the TA to study and use, and is encouraging her to visit specialist speech and language units in the authority. The recent Ofsted report singled out this provision for special praise and commended the practice to others.

You could consider moving schools, just taking a different job which may or may not be on a different pay scale. This would broaden your experience, particularly if was a different phase of education or served a different catchment area. All schools are different, whatever the apparent background, and you could easily be helping a different age range or taking groups instead of supporting one particular pupil. Try talking about the differences with colleagues from other schools, if you have a network meeting or go on a course. The next step up the ladder is to consider a foundation degree (two-thirds of an honours degree) in teaching assistance or the HLTA status. Note, however, that the status is not a qualification and the basic three-day 'training' merely trains you to fill in the assessment paperwork and prepares you for some in-school assessment interviews. If you have completed a full Level 3 NVQ or similar award it will not seem to be a comparable award, although it does recognise experience. The foundation degree is really the next full step after Level 3.

You may be considering teaching, but whatever way you approach this you will still have to get a degree, and in it must be included an element of curriculum understanding and knowledge. If you are considering this route, you should look on the TDA website for what is available and what the entry requirements are. Contact your local higher education provider to see what they can do (not all have Initial Teacher training departments) and your LA – some areas have School-based Initial Teacher Training (SCITT) schemes. Talk to your headteacher as well, as your school may be willing to support you through training in order to 'grow their own' teacher. There are both registered teacher and graduate teacher routes available where support is given for the school to put you through the final stages of teacher training.

Check out the following:

What people can help you?

- In school:
    - mentor
    - line manager
    - the headteacher; other senior managers, especially the SENCO or subject leaders.
- Outside school:
    - networks
    - advisers.

What books do you have or have access to?

- texts like this one, published by Routledge
- copies of the NOS
- DCFS, Ofsted, QCA and TDA publications relating to TAs
- guidance from the LA regarding TAs
- school textbooks which accompany any schemes used in school, including the strategy materials
- school guidance and policies
- your local library or college collections.

What training is available?

In-house training:

- training days, staff meetings, team meetings
- informal meetings.

Off-site training:

- provided by the LA
- at a local college or university
- distance learning – Open College or Open University opportunities.

What websites have you checked out? (some are listed at the end of the chapter)

- DCFS, Ofsted, QCA and TDA
- publishers and magazines
- awarding bodies
- unions.

Opportunities for informal and formal observation of good practice in others and opportunities to participate in any school-based research initiative.

And now finally . . .

Much of the last chapter can be summed up in a little rhyme from Rudyard Kipling's *Just So Stories*:

> I keep six honest serving-men
>   (They taught me all I knew);
> Their names are What and Why and When
>   and How and Where and Who.

Continue learning and planning for the future! Enjoy being an experienced TA!

Questions to ask yourself as you think ahead

- How did you feel when you first picked up this book or went to your first course session?

- Have things changed at home or in your school since then?

- How do you feel now?

- What was the most interesting?

- What was the most challenging?

- What changes have you made to your practice?

- What else do you want to:

  - learn more about?

  - think about?

  - tell somebody?

  - read?

  - explore further?

- Why?

- Do you need anyone or anything else to do these things?

- When can you do them?

Some further reading

Barber, M. (1996) *The learning game: Arguments for an education revolution.*

Calderhead, J. (1994) 'Teaching as a professional activity', in A. Pollard and J. Bourne (eds) *Teaching and learning in the primary school.*

Eaude, T. (2004) *Values education: Developing positive attitudes.*

Useful websites

www.ukstandards.org.uk for the standards themselves

www.tda.gov.uk for the official guidance to the standards and most material relevant to TA qualifications and information

www.dcfs.gov.uk for official educational information

www.curriculumonline.gov.uk for curriculum support materials www.fultonpublishers.co.uk or www.routledge.com for useful books for TAs, teaching and learning and SEN specialisms

www.lsc.gov.uk for help with English and mathematics qualification training

www.nc.uk.net for curriculum information and support materials for inclusion, SEN and G&T

www.ngfl.gov.uk for general gateway to educational resource

www.qca.org.uk for support materials, especially schemes of work and assessment information

www.standards.dfes.gov.uk for statistics and strategy materials

www.teach.gov.uk for information on training to be a teacher

www.teachernet.gov.uk for support materials and documents in general

www.teachernet.gov.uk/teaching assistants for general information for TAs

www.tta.gov.uk/hlta for general information about and for HLTAs

www.nationalstrategiescpd.org.uk for information and publications about the strategies.

Professional associations or unions being used by TAs

www.unison.org.uk: a union for support staff

www.gmb.org.uk: a union for support staff

www.amicusthe union.org/: now known as Unite

www.pat.org.uk: Professionals Allied to Teaching (PAtT): accessible via the Professional Association of Teachers (PAT)

www.napta.org.uk: an association formed by Pearson Publishing to provide services to TAs

Other organisations in SSWG

www.cofe.anglican.org/: Church of England

www.cesew.org.uk: Catholic Education Service

www.fasna.org.uk: Foundation and Aided Schools National Association

The main teachers' associations

www.teachers.org.uk: National Association of Teachers (NUT)

www.teacherxpress.com: Association of Teachers and Lecturers (ATL)

www.nasuwt.org.uk: National Association of Schoolmasters and Union of Women Teachers (NASUWT)

The main awarding bodies

www.cache.org.uk: CACHE

www.city-and-guilds.co.uk: City and Guilds

www.edexcel.org.uk: Edexcel

www.ocr.org.uk: Oxford and Cambridge and RSA examinations (OCR)

www.open.ac.uk: The Open University

Magazines

www.learningsupport.co.uk: Learning support for primary TAs

www.tes.co.uk: *Times Educational Supplement*

www.scholastic.co.uk: Child Education and Junior Education

www.nurseryworld.co.uk: Nursery World

www.teachersmagazine.co.uk: the government-produced magazine associated with www.teachernet.gov.uk

References

Abbott, J. (1996) 'The critical relationship: Education reform and learning'. *Education 2000 News*, March, 1–3.

Abbott, J. (1997) '*To be intelligent*'. Educational Leadership, Association for Supervision and Curriculum Development, Alexandria Virginia. (Available on the website of the 21st Century Learning Initiative: www.21learn.org/publ/edleadership1997.html)

Adey, P. and Shayer, M. (1994) *Really raising standards: Cognitive intervention and academic achievement*. London and New York: Routledge.

ASE (2001) *Be Safe: Health and safety in primary school science and technology*, 3rd edn. Hatfield: Association for Science Education.

ASE (2006) *Safeguards in the school laboratory* (11th ed.). Hatfield: Association for Science Education.

Baginski, M. (2000) *Child protection and education*. London: National Society for the prevention of cruelty to children.

Balshaw, M. (1999) *Help in the classroom* (2nd ed.). London: David Fulton Publishers.

Balshaw, M. and Farrell, P. (2002) *Teaching assistants: practical strategies for effective classroom support*. London: David Fulton Publishers.

Barber, M. (1996) *The learning game: Arguments for an education revolution*. London: Victor Gollancz.

Blatchford, P. and Sharp, S. (1994) *Breaktime and the school: Understanding and changing playground behaviour*. London and New York: Routledge.

Blatchford, P., Bassett, P., Brown, P., Martin, C., Russell, A., Webster, R., and Haywood, N. (2006) *The deployment and impact of support staff in schools* (Research report RR 776). London: Institute of Education, University of London and Department for Education and Skills.

Blatchford, P., Bassett, P., Brown, P., Martin, C., Russell, A. and Webster, R. (2007) *Deployment and impact of support staff in schools: Report on findings from the second national questionnaire survey of schools, support staff and teachers* (Strand 1, Wave 2 – 2006) (DCSF-RR005). London: Institute of Education, University of London and Department for Children, Schools and Families.

Blatchford, P., Bassett, P., Brown, P., Martin, C., Russell, A. and Webster, R. (2008) *Deployment and impact of support staff in schools and the impact of the national agreement* (Results from Strand 2, Wave 1 – 2005/6) (DSCF-RB027). London: Institute of Education, University of London and Department for Children, Schools and Families.

Bloom, B.S., Krathwohl, D.R. and Masia, B.B. (1956) *Taxonomy of educational objectives: Cognitive domain*. New York: McKay.

Booth, T. (2002) *Index for inclusion: Developing learning and participation in schools*. Bristol: Centre for Studies on Inclusive Education.

Brooks, V. (2004) 'Learning to teach and learning about teaching'. In Brooks, V., Abbott, I. and Bills, L. (eds) *Preparing to teach in secondary schools* (pp. 7–17). Maidenhead and New York: Open University Press and McGraw-Hill Education.

Brown, G. and Wragg, E.C. (1993) *Questioning*. London and New York: Routledge.

Bruce, T. (2004) *Developing learning in early childhood*. London: Paul Chapman Publishers.

Bruce, T. (ed.) (2006) *Early childhood: A guide for students*. London: Sage.

Bruner, J. S. (1966) *Towards a theory of instruction*. Cambridge, Mass. and London: The Belknap Press of Harvard University Press.

Calderhead, J. (1994) 'Teaching as a professional activity' In Pollard, A. and Bourne, J. (eds.) *Teaching and learning in the primary school*. London and New York: Routledge with the Open University.

CCPR and DfES (2002) *Group safety at water margins*. London: Central Council for Physical Recreation and the Department for Education and Skills.

CDC (2008) *Extending inclusion: Access for disabled children and young people to extended school and children's centres*. London: Council for Disabled Children, National Children's Bureau, Department for Children, Schools and Families, and Surestart.

Collarbone, P. and Billingham, M. (1998) *Leadership and our schools* (Bulletin). London: Institute of Education.

Corbett, P. *The bumper book of story telling into Writing, Key Stage 1.*

Corbett, P. *The bumper book of story telling into Writing, Key Stage 2.*

DATA (1996) *Primary design and technology: A guide for teacher assistants.* Wellesbourne: The Design and Technology Association.

DCSF (2007a) *The Children's Plan: building brighter futures: summary.* London: Department for Children, Schools and Families.

DCSF (2007b) *New arrivals excellence programme guidance* (00650–2007 BKT-EN). London Department for Children, Schools and Families.

DCSF (2007c) *The use of force to control or restrain pupils (Non-statutory guidance).* London: Department for Children, Schools and Families.

DCSF (2007d) *Supporting children learning English as an additional language: Guidance for practitioners in the Early Years Foundation Stage:* London: Department for Children, Schools and Families

DCSF (2007e) *Statutory framework for the early years foundation stage: Setting the standards for learning, development and care for children form birth to five.* London: Department for Children, Schools and Families.

DCSF (2008a) *The inclusion of gypsy, Roma and traveller children and young people.* London: Department for Children, Schools and Families.

DCSF (2008b) *Working together: Listening to the voices of children and young people* (00410–2008). London: Department for Children, Schools and Families.

DCSF (2008c) *The education of children and young people with behavioural, emotional and social difficulties as a special educational need.* London: Department for Children, Schools and Families.

DCSF (2008d) *The assessment for learning strategy* (00341–2008 DOPM-EN). London: Department for Children, Schools and Families.

DCSF (2008e) *Building brighter futures: Next steps for the Children's Workforce.* London: Department for Children, Schools and Families.

DES (1978) *The Warnock report* London: Department of Education and Science.

Dessent, T. (1987) *Making the ordinary school special.* London: The Falmer Press.

DfEE (1998a) *Excellence for all children: Meeting Special Educational Needs* (Green paper). London: Department for Education and Employment.

DfEE (1998b) *Meeting Special Educational Needs: A programme for action* (MSENPAS). London: Department for Education and Employment.

DfEE (1998c) *Health and safety of pupils on educational visits* (HSPV2). London: Department for Education and Employment.

DfEE (1999a) *The National Curriculum: Handbook for primary teachers in England; Key stages 1 and 2.* London: Department for Education and Skills and the Qualifications and Assessment Authority.

DfEE (1999b) *The National Curriculum: Handbook for secondary teachers in England; Key Stages 3 and 4.* London: DfEE and QCA.

DfEE (2000) *Curriulum guidance for the foundation stage* (QCA/00/587 edn). London: Department for Education and Employment.

DfES (2000) *Working with teaching assistants: A good practice guide* (DfES 0148/2000 edn). London: Department for Education and Skills.

DfES (2001) *Special Educational Needs code of practice.* London: Department for Education and Skills.

DfES (2002a) Consultation DfES/0751/2002. London: Department for Education and Skills.

DfES (2002b) *Time for standards: Reforming the school workforce* (Proposals DfES/0751/2002). London: Department for Education and Skills.

DfES (2003a) *Excellence and enjoyment: A strategy for primary schools* (Advice DfES/0377/2003). London: Department for Education and Skills.

DfES (2003b) *Raising standards and tackling workload.* London: Department for Education and Skills with Workforce Agreement Monitoring Group (WAMG).

DfES (2003c) *The education (Specified work and registration) (England) regulations 2003.* London: Department for Education and Skills.

DfES (2004a) *Every Child Matters: The next steps.* London: Department for Education and Skills.

DfES (2004b) 'Intuitive and deliberate learning' in *Learning and teaching in the primary years* from Excellence and enjoyment: Primary National Strategy CD-ROM materials. London: Department for Education and Skills and Surestart.

DfES (2004c) *Role and context module: Induction training for teaching assistants in primary schools.* London: Department for Education and Skills.

DfES (2005a) *Common core of skills and knowledge for the Children's Workforce*. London: Department for Education and Skills.

DfES (2005b) *School staff and their roles beyond the classroom*. London: Department for Education and Skills.

DfES (2006a) *20:20 vision: Report of the teaching and learning in 2020 review group* (Review group report PPOAK/D16/1206/53). London: Department for Education and Skills.

DFES (2006b) *Supporting looked after learners: A practical guide for school governors*. London: Department for Education and Skills.

DfES (2006c) *Safeguarding children and safer recruitment in education* (04217–2006BKT-EN). London: Department for Education and Skills.

DfES (2006d) *Learning outside the classroom*. London: Department for Education and Skills.

Donaldson, M. (1984) *Children's minds*. London: Fontana Paperbacks.

Drake, J. (2004) *Organising play in the early years: Practical ideas and activities for all practitioners*. London: David Fulton Publishers.

Dryden, G. and Vos, J. (1994) *The learning revolution*. Aylesbury: Accelerated Learning Systems.

Dunne, E. and Bennett, N. (1994) *Talking and learning in groups*. London and New York: Routledge.

Dunne, R. and Wragg, T. (1994) *Effective teaching*. London and New York: Routledge.

East, V. and Evans, L. (2006) *At a glance: A quick guide to children's special needs,* 2nd edn. London: Continuum.

Eaude, T. (2004) *Values education: Developing positive attitudes*. Birmingham: National Primary Trust with Oxfordshire County Council.

Edwards, S. (1999) *Reading for all*. London: David Fulton Publishers.

Fisher, R. (1995) *Teaching children to learn*. Cheltenham: Stanley Thornes (Publishers).

Fox, G. (2001) *Supporting children with behaviour difficulties*. London: David Fulton Publishers.

Frater, G. (2000) *Securing boys' literacy*. London: The Basic Skills Agency.

Freiberg, H.J. and Stein, T.A. (1999) 'Measuring, improving and sustaining healthy learning environments', in Freiberg, H.J. (ed.) *School climate* (pp. 11–29). London and Philadelphia: Falmer Press.

Gardner, H.K.M.L. and Wake, W.K. (1996) *Intelligence: Multiple perspectives*. Florida: Holt Rinehart and Wilson.

Gibbons, P. (1991) *Learning to learn in a second language*. Primary English Teaching Association (Australia).

Goleman, D. (1996) *Emotional intelligence*. London: Bloomsbury Publishing.

GTC (2006) *The GTC statement: The statement of professional values and practice for teachers*. London and Birmingham: General Teaching Council for England.

Guppy, P. and Hughes, M. (1999) *On cue: Helping children to read: for parents at home and supporters in school*. Tamworth: National Association for Special Educational Needs.

Hall, D. (2002) *Assessing the needs of bilingual learners: Living in two languages*. London: David Fulton Publishers.

Harding, J. and Meldon-Smith, L. (1996) *How to make observations and assessments*. London: Hodder and Stoughton.

Hargreaves, D.H. and Hopkins, D. (1991) *The empowered school*. London: Cassell Education.

Hastings, S. (2004) 'Emotional intelligence'. *Times Educational Supplement*, 15 October, pp. 11–14.

Hayes, D. (2003) *Planning, teaching and class management in primary schools*. London: David Fulton Publishers.

Haylock, D. (2001) *Mathematics explained for primary teachers*, 3rd edn. London: Sage.

Higgins, S., Baumfield, V. and Hall, E. (2007) 'Learning skills and the development of learning capabilities' (*Research Evidence in Education Library*). London: EPPI-Centre, Social Science Research Unit, Institute of Education, University of London.

Holt, J. (1964) *How children fail*. London: Penguin Books.

Holt, J. (1967) *How children learn*. London: Penguin Books.

Hook, P. and Vass, A. (2000a) *Confident classroom leadership*. London: David Fulton Publishers.

Hook, P. and Vass, A. (2000b) *Creating winning classrooms*. London: David Fulton Publishers.

Hounslow (2007a) *EAL at KS1: Framework for Early Years*. Available from Hounslow Language Service.

Hounslow (2007b) *KS2 Beginners scheme of work*. Available from Hounslow Language Service.

Innovation Unit, *The Story making project*: http:www.innovation-unit.co.uk/education-experience/project-archive/the-story-making-project.html

Kerry, T. (2001) *Working with support staff: Their roles and effective management in schools*. Harlow: Pearson Education.

Kyriacou, C. (1997) *Effective teaching in schools: Theory and practice*, 2nd edn. Cheltenham: Stanley Thornes (Publishers).

Kyriacou, C. (1998) *Essential teaching skills*, 2nd edn. Cheltenham: Nelson Thornes.

Lacey, P. (1999) *On a wing and a prayer*. London: MENCAP.

Lacey, P. (2001) *Support partnerships*. London: David Fulton Publishers.

Lambeth (2004) *Admissions and induction good practice for mid-term or non-routine admissions*. Available from Lambeth EMTAS.

Lazear, D. (1994) *Seven pathways of learning: Teaching students and parents about multiple intelligences*. Arizona: Zephyr Press.

Lee, V. (1990) *Children's learning in school*. London: Hodder and Stoughton for the Open University.

LGNTO (2001) *Teaching/classroom assistants National Occupational Standards*. London: Local Government National Training Organisation.

Lovey, J. (2002) *Supporting Special Educational Needs in secondary school classrooms*, 2nd edn. London: David Fulton Publishers.

MacBeath, J., Boyd, B.J.R. and Bell, S. (1996) *Schools speak for themselves*. National Union of Teachers for the University of Strathclyde.

Maslow, A. (1970) *Motivation and personality*, 2nd edn. New York: Harper & Row.

Maynard, T. and Furlong, J. (1995) 'Learning to teach and models of mentoring', in Kerry, T. and Mayes, A.S. (eds.) *Issues in mentoring*. London and New York: Routledge with the Open University, Milton Keynes.

McGregor, D. (2007) *Developing thinking, developing learning: A guide to thinking skills in education*. Maidenhead and New York: McGraw Hill and Open University Press.

Meek, M. (1982) *Learning to read*. London: The Bodley Head.

Mosley, J. (1993) *Turn your school round*. Wisbech: LDA.

Moyles, J. (2005) *The excellence of play*, 2nd edn. Maidenhead: Open University Press.

Moyles, J. (2007) *Beginning teaching, beginning learning*, 3rd edn. Maidenhead: Open University Press.

NJC (2003) *Support staff: The way forward!* London: Employers Organisation for the National Joint Council for Local Government Services.

O'Brien, T. and Garner, P. (2001) *Untold stories: Learning Support Assistants and their work*. Stoke on Trent and Sterling: Trentham Books.

Ofsted (1993) *Handbook for the inspection of schools*. London: Her Majesty's Stationery Office.

Ofsted (2002a) *Teaching assistants in primary schools: An evaluation of the quality and impact of their work* (HMI 434). London: Ofsted.

Ofsted (2002b) *The curriculum in successful primary schools* (HMI 553). London: Office for Standards in Education.

Ofsted (2007a) *Using the evaluation schedule: Guidance for the inspection of schools* (September 2007 edn.). London: Office for Standards in Education.

Ofsted (2007b) *Every Child Matters: Framework for the inspection of schools in England from September 2005* (September 2007 edn.). London: Office for Standards in Education.

Palmer, S. (2003) *How to teach writing across the curriculum, KS1*. London: David Fulton Publishers.

Palmer, S. (2003) *How to teach writing across the curriculum, KS2*. London: David Fulton Publishers.

Palmer, S. (2004) *Speaking frames Y3,4,5,6*. London: David Fulton Publishers.

Pollard, A. (2002) *Reflective teaching: Effective and evidence-informed professional practice*. London and New York: Continuum.

PricewaterhouseCoopers (2007) *Independent study into school leadership: Main report* (Research Report RR818A). London: Department for Education and Skills.

QCA (1999a) *Teaching mental calculations strategies*. London: Qualifications and Curriculum Authority.

QCA (1999b) *Teaching written calculations strategies*. London: Qualifications and Curriculum Authority.

QCA (2007) *The new secondary curriculum: What has changed and why*. London: Qualifications and Curriculum Authority.

QCA (2008) *The secondary curriculum: A curriculum for the future*. Qualifications and Curriculum Authority [from www.qca.org.uk 2008, 6 January 2008].

Richmond-upon-Thames (2008) *Don't panic: Meeting the needs of new arrivals*. Available from Richmond-upon-Thames EMTAS.

Ritchie, C. and Thomas, P. (2004) *Successful study-skills for teaching assistants*. London: David Fulton Publishers.

Rogers, B. (1991) *You know the fair rule*. Harlow: Longman.

Rogers, B. (1994) *Behaviour recovery*. Harlow: Longman.

Rogers, B. (2006a) *I get by with a little help*. London: Paul Chapman Publishing.

Rogers, B. (2006b) *Classroom behaviour: A practical guide to effective behaviour management and colleague support*, 2nd edn. London: Paul Chapman Publishing.

Rose, J. (2006) *Independent review of the teaching of early reading* (0201–2006 DOC-EN). London: Department for Education and Skills.

SCAA (1996) *Education for adult life: The spiritual and moral development of young people* (Discussion papers: No. 6). London: School Curriculum and Assessment Authority.

Senge, P.M. (1990) *The fifth discipline*. London, Sydney, Auckland and Parktown, SA: Century Business.

Senge, P.M., Cambron-McCabe, N., Lucas, T., Smith, B., Dutton, J. and Kleiner, A. (2000) *How schools learn*. London and Yarmouth, USA: Nicholas Brealey Publishing.

Smith, A. (1996) *Accelerated learning in the classroom*. Stafford: Network Educational Press.

Spooner, W. (2006) *The SEN Handbook for trainee teachers, NQTs and teaching assistants*. London: David Fulton Publishers with NASEN.

Surestart (2003) *Birth to three matters: an introduction to the framework*. London: Surestart and Department for Children, Schools and Families.

TDA (2006a) *Teaching assistant file: Primary induction*. London: Training and Development Agency.

TDA (2006b) *Teaching assistant file: Secondary induction*. London: Training and Development Agency.

TDA (2007) *National Occupational Standards in Supporting teaching and learning in schools: Levels 2 and 3*, [website] ukstandards.org.uk.

TDA (2008) *Guidance on the National Occupational Standards for Supporting teaching and learning in schools*. London: Training and Development Agency. www.tda.gov.org

Thomas, G., Walker, D. and Webb, J. (1998) *The making of the inclusive school*. London and New York: Routledge.

Vincett, K., Cremin, H. and Thomas, G. (2005) *Teachers and assistants working together*. Maidenhead: Open University Press.

WAMG (2008) *Regulations and guidance under S133 of the Education Act 2002*. London: Department for Children, Families and Schools for the Workforce Agreement Monitoring Group.

Watkins, C. and Mortimore, P. (1999) 'Pedagogy: what do we know?', in Mortimore, P. (ed.) *Understanding pedagogy and its impact on learning*. Thousand Oaks, CA, London and New Delhi: Paul Chapman Publishing/Sage Publications.

Watkinson, A. (2002) *Assisting learning and supporting teaching*. London: David Fulton Publishers.

Watkinson, A. (2008a) *The essential guide for competent teaching assistants: Meeting the National Occupational Standards at Level 2*, 2nd edn. London: David Fulton Publishers (Routledge).

Watkinson, A. (2008b) *Leading and managing teaching assistants*. London: David Fulton Publishers (Routledge).

Weddell, K. (1983) 'Some developments in the concepts and practice of special educational education'. *New Horizons Journal of Education*, 24: 99–108.

Weddell, K. (2001) 'Klaus' story: The experience of a retired professor of special needs education', in O'Brien, T. and Garner, P. (eds.) *Untold stories: Learning Support Assistants and their work*. Stoke on Trent and Stirling: Trentham Books.

West-Burnham, J. (2004) *Building leadership capacity: Helping leaders learn*. (PDF) National College for School Leadership. www.ncsi.org.uk

Whetton, N. and Cansell, P. (1993) *Feeling good: Raising self-esteem in the primary school classroom*. London: Forbes Publications.

Williams, T., Whetton, N. and Moon, A. (1989) *Health for life: Health education in the primary school*; the Health Education Authority's primary school project. Walton-on-Thames, Hong Kong, South Melbourne, Ontario: Nelson.

Wood, D. (1998) *How children think and learn*, 2nd edn. Oxford: Blackwell.

Wragg, E.C. (1994) *An introduction to classroom observation*. London and New York: Routledge.

Wragg, E.C. and Brown, G. (1993) *Explaining*. London and New York: Routledge.

Index